The Cost of Being Poor

SUNY series, The New Inequalities
A. Gary Dworkin, editor

The Cost of Being Poor

*A Comparative Study of Life in Poor
Urban Neighborhoods in Gary, Indiana*

Sandra L. Barnes

State University of New York Press

Published by
State University of New York Press, Albany

For information, address State University of New York Press,
194 Washington Avenue, Suite 305, Albany, NY 12210-2365

Production by Diane Ganeles
Marketing by Michael Campochiaro

Library of Congress Cataloging-in-Publication Data

Barnes, Sandra L.
   The cost of being poor : a comparative study of life in poor urban
neighborhoods in Gary, Indiana / Sandra L. Barnes.
       p. cm. — (SUNY series, the new inequalities)
   Includes bibliographical references and index.
   ISBN 0-7914-6467-9 (hardcover : alk. paper) — ISBN 0-7914-6468-7
(pbk. : alk. paper)
   1. Poor—Indiana—Gary. 2. Minorities—Indiana—Gary—Economic
conditions. 3. Minorities—Indiana—Gary—Social conditions. 4. Gary
(Ind.)—Economic conditions. 5. Gary (Ind.)—Social conditions.
6. Poverty—Psychological aspects. I. Title. II. Series.

HV4046.G37B37 2005
362.5'09772'99—dc22
                                                          2004015670

10 9 8 7 6 5 4 3 2 1

Dedicated to my parents,
Henry and Clara Brown

Contents

List of Illustrations

Figures

Map

List of Tables

Acknowledgments

Several persons and groups made significant contributions to this book. I wish to thank the Purdue University School of Liberal Arts Development Fund, the Purdue University Research Fund, and the Department of Sociology & Anthropology at Purdue University for providing research grants for these efforts. I especially appreciate the African American Studies and Research Center for their support and encouragement. Thanks also to Drs. Ken Ferraro, Carolyn Perrucci, and Robert Perrucci at Purdue University, as well as Drs. Charles Jaret, Dawn Baunach, and Charles Gallagher at Georgia State University for their support, advice, and instruction. Special thanks to David Hess, Indiana Room Librarian, for his thorough research skills and support. I am thankful to the residents in and around Gary, IN, who graciously opened their homes and lives to me. This book would not have been possible without their involvement. I am also grateful to my editor at SUNY Press, Nancy Ellegate, and her assistant, Allison Lee, for direction in organizing the book.

My extended family and friends have been critical in helping me reach this point. I would like to give the greatest amount of credit and thanks to my parents, Henry and Clara Brown, to whom I dedicate this book, for their lifelong sacrifices that have enabled me to achieve my goals. I have yet to meet another person who possesses their character, intestinal fortitude, capacity for unconditional support, and ability to find value in all of humanity.

Introduction:
Structure vs. Agency
and the Poor Urban Experience

Urban poverty and its deleterious effects are well documented. In studies, urban poverty is associated with economic, social, and in some instances, cultural challenges that undermine upward mobility, engender angst and crime, and ravage neighborhoods. In other literature urban poverty is characterized as an albatross around the neck of society that, despite social policy to arrest it, drains economic resources and threatens to invade the apparent tranquility and stability of suburbia. Scholarship suggests that urban conditions are worsening. However, the everyday experiences and problems of urban residents are often an absent or secondary query in research.

The goal of this book is to examine a specific set of challenges or "costs" incurred by residents in a poor urban center. The structure vs. agency discourse represents the backdrop for studying costs associated with urban poverty as a structural force and the subsequent choices residents make.[1] Current urban studies seem to focus on macro-level dynamics correlated with unemployment, residential segregation, and social disorganization. And while these issues are justifiable given their far-reaching effects, other costs that residents incur daily that result in long-term negative economic and sociopsychological effects are also important. Through the use of quantitative and qualitative data, this book examines noneconomic as well as often-overlooked economic costs associated with life in poor urban neighborhoods to illustrate ways in which structural forces impact the day-to-day lives and choices of residents. I argue that many residents in poor urban centers incur costs resulting from the "dual dilemma" of being poor or near-poor and residing in a poor urban area. I report on over three years of research in Gary, Indiana, an impoverished city, to provide a comparative examination of the costs of being poor based on the type of neighborhood in which one resides and exposure to poverty. As such, I am able to examine some of the manifestations and implications of neighborhood-concentrated poverty.[2]

This book adds to the literature and compliments macro-level studies on the effects and implications of urban poverty in several ways. First, I focus on ways residents incur tangible/intangible and economic/noneconomic costs due to poverty. The concept *cost* is broadly used here to refer to actual expenses persons incur to meet basic needs, such as providing food, shelter, and clothing for their families, as well as important, indirect expenses related to logistics, timing, and differential treatment. The comparative nature of the research design allows for tests regarding how factors such as race/ethnicity, neighborhood type, and location influence the costs under study, as well as possible joint effects. Finally, the book chronicles the cyclic nature of certain costs and sociopsychological tolls that can result, as well as coping mechanisms, strategies, and non-traditional approaches used by residents to counter the costs of being poor or near poor, as they attempt to effectively and expeditiously complete the *daily round* in the face of various structural constraints. Using terminology from Logan and Molotch (1987), the daily round is considered "the wider routine in which one's concrete daily needs are satisfied" (p. 103). Activities are broad and vary, but include shopping for food and other essentials, clothing, and other family needs.

Structural Constraints and the Urban Experience

Urban scholars have presented the shift from manufacturing to service occupations, out-migration of working-class and middle-class families and businesses, increased social isolation, and current and historical discrimination as primary factors that stymie the economic and social successes of many urbanites.[3] Studies associate these structural dynamics with increased welfare dependency, unemployment, community demise, sociopsychological malaise, increased female-headed households, and ultimately, concentrated poverty. Macro-level forces provide the context for an understanding of urban conditions, but certain authors also acknowledge specific consequences for the lives of residents.

For example, when economic restructuring and residential and social isolation are considered, Squires (1994) hypothesizes that a conservative policy agenda has contributed to community decline, racial inequality, and uneven development in urban cities due to the deindustrialization of the urban core and the flight of capital to suburbs, the Sunbelt, and abroad. He contends that such structural development is not due to naturally existing market forces, but rather to politics, power struggles, and conflicting interests based on race and class. Squires notes, "when corporations seek out greener pastures they tend to seek out whiter ones as well" (p. 3). According to Squires, structural changes in cities have subsequently destroyed jobs, reduced education and public service revenues, and increased the chasm between African American inner cities and White suburbs.

Similarly, Jargowsky (1996) asserts that economic segregation—the spatial segregation of households by income or social class—has increased for Hispanics, Whites, and African Americans since the 1970s and 1980s, and that marked increases have been noted between Hispanics and African Americans in the 1980s. As high-status, better-educated minorities experience upward mobility to greater degrees than their low-status, less-educated counterparts, economic segregation within a minority group increases, causing increased social distance, especially in urban areas. Global as well as local economic restructuring have resulted in decreased demand for blue-collar workers—employment arenas that have historically been heavily occupied by urban residents. The resulting unemployment has been especially acute for less educated African American young males. These shifts in cities from "centers of production and distribution of goods to centers of administration, finance, and information exchange" (Kasarda 1989, p. 28) have taken their toll on African American employment potential not only in the form of shifts from blue-collar to more technical occupations, but also from employment opportunities in central cities to suburban areas.

The term "hyperghettoization" has been coined to characterize chronic joblessness, and economic and social isolation in inner cities. This process begs that we question the existence of a "welfare ethos" among the inner-city poor and instead points to social-structural constraints as exemplars of ghetto poverty—inner city areas where economically and socially marginalized persons tend to be concentrated. A closed opportunity structure, spatial and industrial changes, and migratory forces that seem to beckon poor and near-poor racial/ethnic minorities to already impoverished inner cities and simultaneously encourage the exodus of more economically stable families are all precipitating factors of urban poverty.[4] And in what is tantamount to, at best, gatekeeping, and at worst, racial discrimination, some urban employers use network hiring methods that impede employment opportunities of African Americans in favor of voluntary immigrant groups. For example, employers at Latino job sites that tend to hire immigrants and less-skilled individuals, often rely on information from current immigrant *model* employees when openings arise.[5] The cumulative effects of these implications and other job-related inequities on employment opportunities for inner-city residents are clear, as presented in the important work on racial occupational inequality by Fossett, Galle, and Kelly (1986). By examining occupational trends from 1940 to 1980, the authors note national and regional variation in employment opportunity based on race. In addition, strides made by African Americans are attributed, to a large degree, to systemic changes, such as civil rights legislation and social interventions specifically put in place to bring about racial equality and check institutionalized discrimination. In an attempt to move the discourse beyond its focus on African Americans, scholars such as Tienda (1989) attribute economic disparity between Puerto Ricans, Mexicans, and Cubans to structural factors and inequalities in the labor market. Subsequent studies suggest that, over their life course, many poor Hispanics accumulate disadvantage in the form of lower levels of education and work experience, and greater periods between employment spells.[6]

Although not exhaustive, this summary of studies illustrates some of the most commonly studied macro-level factors shown to influence urban conditions and the experiences of residents. Results show that the structural constraints typically associated with urban ills are: 1) globalization coupled with deindustrialization that results in shifts from manufacturing to service positions; 2) residential inmigration and out-migration patterns; 3) social isolation; 4) employment demand shifts toward the more technology trained; 5) racial, residential, and housing discrimination and segregation; and 6) business out-migration from urban areas to the suburbs. The cumulative effects of these social forces contribute to the existence and prevalence of concentrated urban poverty.

Agency and the Urban Experience

Agency-based studies acknowledge urban plight, but focus on choices made by residents and, in many instances, their efforts toward self-sufficiency. An adaptive, resilient model characterizes residents in poor urban neighborhoods who, despite a myriad of continual challenges, manage to maintain families and combat negative social forces.[7] Their problems and challenges stand at the forefront of research that points to residents who embrace more mainstream[8] dictates but who may not experience them largely due to structural forces.[9] Within this context, segments of urban America are believed to make difficult choices in difficult circumstances.

Urban ethnographies since the early 1900s focus on the experiences of middle-class, working-class, and poor residents who embraced achievement ideology and delayed gratification, and held disdain for their neighbors who did not.[10] More recent accounts chronicle the increasingly negative effects of urban poverty and "street families" who embrace a counterculture and "decent families" who embrace a Protestant ethic that belies the economic problems they face.[11] In his singular study, *Climbing Jacob's Ladder: The Enduring Legacy of the Black Family*, Andrew Billingsley (1992) illustrates the adaptive, resilient nature of African American families from preslavery to postindustrial periods within the backdrop of a myriad of social problems, such as slavery, segregation, discrimination, racism, and increasing poverty, especially among families headed by single-parent females. A similar premise of proactivity in the face of poverty is suggested by Newman (1999), as she presents the varied employment obstacles poor urbanites face. Her study of the great lengths some persons travel to work at the fictional *Burger Barn* illustrates ways the poor face difficult odds daily to meet economic challenges. Newman's work is complemented by other ethnographic studies that counter claims of limited self-efficacy on the part of residents in poor urban settings, attribute more positive characteristics to them, and consider class- as well as race-based models for understanding urban conditions.[12]

And just as studies on agency examine the experiences of persons who choose to remain employed in low-waged occupations and employ various strategies to survive, it is important to recognize the complexities of such decision making. For example, some African Americans opt out of certain low-level positions readily accepted by many Latinos and other immigrants due to rising personal expectations. Thus they purposely choose to remain unemployed rather than be underpaid, but in doing so, indirectly undermine their ability to establish some degree of economic stability.[13] Similarly, some poor mothers forgo employment in order to receive public-funded healthcare for their children and subsidized housing. These mothers often employ various strategies—from providing in-kind assistance within a primarily female network and coercing their children's fathers to secure child support to working in the underground economy.[14]

The "agency" camp also includes a cadre of more conservative academics and political pundits who suggest that some persons who experience poverty make inappropriate choices that undermine economic and social stability. These authors often contend that continual exposure to poverty, on one hand, and liberal social policy, on another, result in an absence of positive traits, such as personal and family sacrifice, frugality, a strong work ethic, and delayed gratification.[15] Oscar Lewis's (1966) "culture of poverty" thesis, Mead's assertion of a poor work ethic and defeatism among the chronically unemployed, Ogbu's "oppositional culture" among involuntary minorities that undermines achievement, Massey and Denton's "culture of segregation" that manifests due to extreme spatial segregation and social isoaltion[16]—all paint a sobering portrait of stymied upward mobility and leveled aspirations. Despite findings to the contrary,[17] the experiences of such persons are often suggested to reflect some variant of a deficiency model, where their choices and the rationale for choices further exacerbate already negative conditions and engender continued reliance on social programs supported by the larger society. However, caution is important among opponents of this latter group of writers due to the potentially dangerous tendency of suggesting that certain segments of impoverished America are "doing a better job" of negotiating poverty than are others.

In the structure vs. agency discourse, it is reductionist to assume two diametrically opposed factions, but rather divergent frames of reference that lie on a continuum. At best, they may inform each other and stimulate further research and discussion, and at worst, they provide fodder for continued debate. A comprehensive investigation on the relationship between structure and agency means acknowledging: 1) problems and less prudent choices residents make; 2) that mainstream beliefs remain common among historically impoverished groups; 3) optimism and cynicism among urban dwellers with similar economic experiences; 4) possible fluid identities in the face of harsh reality; 5) productive, proactive attitudes and behavior that are supported in theory and exhibited as neighborhood conditions improve, and; 6) correlates between urban problems and political and economic decisions made outside urban spaces.[18]

As the discourse on urban poverty continues, whether research focuses on negative effects, macro-level forces, aberrant attitudes and behavior, or resilience in the face of negative circumstances, it is clear that poverty is an ever-present, rapidly growing nemesis of the urban dweller and the larger society. The roles of structural forces, as well as personal and collective choice, are central to a more complete understanding of the poor urban experience. As such, it is important to continue to investigate how residents in poor urban neighborhoods are affected by poverty, how they feel, and how they cope. In this book, I explore the degree to which poverty constraints result in various economic and noneconomic costs for urban residents in Gary, Indiana, and their daily challenges and choices.

Book Format

Chapter 1 provides an overview of current research with an emphasis on disproportionately affected and underrecognized groups. In the chapter I also present the thesis of "neighborhood poverty concentration effects" as the foundational research framework for this study and summarize its relationship to broader historic, economic, and social processes that affect poor urban areas, in general, and Gary, Indiana, in particular. Chapter 2 details the major structural changes that occurred in Gary, Indiana, from the 1970s to the present. Census, regional, and local data provide the analysis context to illustrate the relationship between macro-level economic and residential restructuring, changes in the local economy, and the resulting poverty and to examine the relationship between residents' sociospatial positions and the costs they incur. The chapter also compares and contrasts the availability of basic resources in Gary, Indiana, and surrounding areas and how the presence (or absence) of venues such as large grocery stores and other service providers are related to economic and noneconomic costs.

In chapter 3, considerable detail is given to the examination of economic and noneconomic costs to feed one's family. The chapter specifically examines availability, quality, and direct costs for basic goods and services and customer service during the shopping process. The chapter includes results from several comparative analyses of costs for goods and services in urban and suburban areas in and around Gary, Indiana, to examine differences in prices and services. Cost assessments include specific prices as well as amenities. Of special interest are possible differences in the costs that are incurred in urban areas with similar levels of poverty, but dramatically different racial/ethnic composition. Next, chapter 4 focuses on economic and noneconomic costs to clothe one's family. The chapter follows the retail transitions that have occurred in downtown Gary and other sites in the city and surrounding suburban areas. Of particular interest are in- and out-migration patterns and the macro-level decisions behind them, as well as respondent shopping patterns and strategies used to augment their incomes to secure purchases that are typically more expensive than groceries. To further explore the experiences of residents, chapters 3 and 4 include results from 25 in-depth interviews with persons who live in and around the city, as well as participant observation results regarding goods and service providers.

Through the use of case studies, chapter 5 presents the experiences of three poor or near-poor families—an African American, White, and Hispanic—from different poor or near-poor areas around Gary, Indiana, and the costs they incur to provide for their families. The chapter considers often overlooked challenges families encounter, as they take part in seemingly routine chores and activities that may be taken for granted by the nonpoor or those outside poor urban settings. The implications of these "impracticality costs" are discussed. The chapter is also unique in that each respondent who previously lived either in Gary or in an urban center like Gary, has since relocated, and is thus in a unique position to provide commentary on life inside and outside an urban locale.

Chapter 6 focuses on some of the sociopsychological aspects of life in poor neighborhoods, the coping strategies some residents employ to combat their economic problems, and how respondents make sense of their experiences. The chapter also illustrates certain dimensions of the cyclic effects of poverty and how residents attempt to negotiate the uncertainty associated with being poor or near poor or residing in poor areas. The concluding chapter 7 summarizes and integrates the overall study findings within the framework of neighborhood poverty concentration effects and provides suggestions and implications for urban residents, policymakers, social service agencies, and organizations and individuals who provide services to the poor. In the final section, I forward a thesis that I postulate can be applied to better understand the experiences of some residents in poor urban neighborhoods.

This book relies heavily on census data to illustrate trends in Gary as well as results from existing research. Quotes and summaries from 25 in-depth interviews, three case studies, and direct observations, all performed from August 2000 through April 2003 are used to correlate the societal level changes that occurred in Gary with the experiences of residents. These findings are not presented to suggest generalizability across all impoverished urban settings. Although I avoided the use of snowball sampling techniques, the purposive nature of this sample (as detailed in the Appendix, respondents had to be 18 years old or older, have at least one dependent child, or receive SSI or unemployment compensation) precludes randomness as generally defined. However, a comparison of the sample demographics to those found among Gary residents and similarly impoverished "rust-belt" cities, such as Detroit and Flint, Michigan, suggests that these findings may provide insight into the everyday experiences in urban spaces beyond those of the focal site.[19] Just as Detroit, Flint, and parts of Chicago have witnessed the negative effects of deindustrialization in a manner similar to Gary, segments of these cities can also be expected to incur the types of economic and noneconomic costs under study here. To this end, I believe these results are important for better understanding some of the circumstances currently experienced in poor urban America.

Costs under Study

Structural changes inside and outside Gary, Indiana, correlated with space, race/ethnicity, and class have influenced the city's present-day course and provide the contextual backdrop for this study. Rather than perform a cursory examination of a myriad of factors, I chose to focus attention on a specific set of costs and provide detail. The analysis centers on economic as well as noneconomic costs including tangible and intangible factors associated with economic and social change in the city. This means economic costs of basic food and staples, clothes, and household goods as well as local services, such as banks and transportation. Noneconomic costs center on access, availability, quality, affordability, and treatment, as residents from Gary and surrounding areas take part in their daily round. And although noneconomic, intangible costs are somewhat more challenging to capture, they are part and parcel of the sociopsychological dimensions of life in poor urban areas that are not examined with frequency. From these issues arise coping mechanisms and strategies used to negotiate poor and near-poor conditions.

The study is purposely framed to consider many "everyday" costs incurred by residents to situate persons in a context that is both familiar *and* comparable to persons who live inside and outside urban locales. Similar concerns and responsibilities—feeding and clothing one's

family, paying bills, developing strategies to make ends meet—are part
of the daily round for most Americans. Thus the goals and objectives of
residents in poor urban settings become quite common ones—although
their experiences may sometimes be uncommon. And whether and how
these issues are considered, negotiated, and resolved are important in
better understanding "quality of life" dynamics.

Studying the Familiar

Having spent my formative years in Gary, Indiana, my initial interest in examining changes in the city came about as I, upon relocating nearby, noticed the visible differences in the place where I
grew up. Although I knew the importance of the steel mills in the
city as a youth—it was not unusual for males to graduate from high
school one week and begin working at a local mill the next—I was
not fully aware of the industry's far-reaching influence on the survival of the city. When I decided to proceed with the project, it was
important to develop a methodological plan to insure validity and reliability of the data and subsequent analyses. And although my past
in Gary expedited certain portions of the data collection process
(such as, knowing where to locate certain types of information), it
was my graduate school stint and the large literature on urban
dynamics that best prepared me for the endeavor.

I relied on previous urban studies, experts in the field, and long-
standing empirical measures and methods. For example, the research was informed by the types of questions posed in the Urban
Poverty and Family Life Survey (1987) and economic and social indices used in studies by William J. Wilson and other urban scholars.
The commentary and research methods section provided in the introduction and appendix of Mary Pattillo-McCoy's (1999) *Black
Picket Fences* reinforced the required structure needed to objectively
explore familiar terrain.

CHAPTER ONE

The *Economics*
of the Poor Urban Experience

The topic of neighborhood poverty concentration effects can best be characterized as an overarching research framework in the study of urban poverty rather than a sociological theory in the strictest sense. Much of the research on national and local structural changes and their related urban consequences have been supplanted by more recent work that considers global competition and the implications of economic restructuring in Internet driven markets. And while this book is informed by the implications of internationalization, it is more in the spirit of earlier analyses by scholars such as Drake and Cayton [1945](1962), Hannerz (1969), and Williams (1981), as well as more recent studies by Duneier (1992) and William Julius Wilson (1996), and focuses on the relationship between societal changes and outcomes at the local level to explore the experiences of urban residents most affected by neighborhood concentrated poverty.

Neighborhood Poverty Concentration Effects

Neighborhood poverty concentration effects suggest a direct relationship between urban poverty and negative economic and social conditions. In the broadest sense, this framework assumes increasingly dire conditions, as the proportion of impoverished residents within a given area increases. Neighborhood can be used to represent social and cultural connectedness (although the term "community" may be most appropriate, see Craven and Wellman [1973] and Wellman and Leighton [1979]), however within this context, neighborhood is usually synonymous with census tract. The latter definition provides a more concrete approach to examine and compare historic and current socioeconomic trends using census data. Similarly,

11

poverty is defined based on the official poverty line used by the U.S. Census to reflect a set of rock-bottom food expenditures for families based on composition and area of residence.[1] And although the inadequacies and limitations of this poverty threshold have been illustrated, given its wide use and appeal as a statistical baseline, it serves as an adequate point of reference here.[2] Based on these criteria, *poor neighborhoods* are defined as census tracts, where more than 20 percent of residents live below the official poverty threshold; using terminology made popular by Wilson (1987), Jargowsky (1994, 1996), Massey and Denton (1993) and other scholars, over 40 percent of impoverished residents in a given census tract constitute a "ghetto-poverty neighborhood." Although these definitions allow us to empirically associate physical locales with socioeconomic indices, their implications are more far-reaching.

Earlier scholars from Drake and Cayton [1945](1962) to their contemporaries suggest that, prior to the 1970s, dramatic increases in urban poverty were kept at bay due largely to the influences and lifestyles of middle- and working-class families who lived in segregated, socioeconomically heterogeneous, but manufacturing-dependent cities. More recently, urban centers that are densely populated with impoverished persons have been unable to effectively counteract the deleterious effects of neighborhood poverty. As neighborhood poverty increases, the following types of outcomes are expected to result: social disorganization, high unemployment,[3] female-headed households, welfare dependency, lack of marriageable men, increased crime, constrained social networks, inadequate housing, malaise, segregation, and isolation. Other possible manifestations include aberrant social behavior and countercultures.[4]

The neighborhood poverty concentration effects framework may seem somewhat deterministic in that it presupposes economic barriers preclude other mechanisms for social control, local solidarity, and community. To imply agency on the part of residents, some scholars emphasize prevailing "mainstream sentiments" in inner cities, caution against generalizing the effects of concentrated poverty to all urban dwellers, and suggest that, for those residents who do not succumb to the effects of poverty, changing opportunity structures can result in changes in attitudes and behavior.[5] The terms *census tract* and *neighborhood* are used interchangeably in this study when referring to empirical data, with the understanding that the latter term may also inculcate a broader meaning that reflects social and economic interactions in a given locale.

The two-pronged question to be addressed here is how structural changes associated with class and race/ethnicity influence the experiences, choices, and responses of urban residents, in particular, those in Gary, Indiana. And although it is generally believed that some residents in urban settings possess a certain degree of self-efficacy and wherewithal to combat social forces, the longevity, pervasiveness, and history of structural forces imply that their effects are more formidable than individual initiative alone can arrest. The neighborhood poverty concentration framework guides this inquiry because of its ability to correlate issues of structure and agency in ways that are important in academic, applied, and policy-making settings.

Economic Effects of Deindustrialization and Disinvestment

Industrial occupations provided an opportunity for many hard working, less formally educated men to earn a family wage. In the late nineteenth century, small towns and subsequent cities began to emerge as sites for industrial workers and their families. At certain periods, particularly during World War I, the demand for unskilled labor became so great, recruitment efforts reached the southern and western regions of the United States. For example, in 1950, the country produced 50 percent of the world's steel;[6] related industries in textiles, meat packing, automobile, and railroads located in central cities also produced the bulk of these resources.[7] It has been suggested that the United States failed to recognize the inevitable decline in demand for manufactured products internationally, increased competition and production efficiency of competitors such as Japan and China, and the effects of the burgeoning technological age. In addition, many industrial workers did not predict the dramatic economic changes that were about to occur in the late 1900s and the implications for their livelihood. Without foresight, younger men often opted for steel mill positions rather than college, and many heads of household were not prepared for the "rainy day" that was postindustrialization.

In response to increased competition globally and from nonunion shops, industries often found it cheaper to relocate abroad, to the suburbs, or in some instances, to southern locales, where they could benefit from higher profits due to lower operating costs and enjoy both lower land prices and taxes. Although generally implemented later than its foreign competitors, U.S. technological improvements also made it possible to produce more efficiently and, in some cases, increase production, with fewer workers.[8] This efficiency resulted in considerable downsizing of the labor force. By the late 1900s, most persons previously gainfully employed in northern industrial cites found themselves either unemployed, underemployed, or working in service occupations for substantially lower pay and reduced benefits.[9] Urban centers, where most manufacturing plants were located, were hurt the most.[10] Flanagan (1999) notes:

> From 1963 to 1977 the total number of manufacturing jobs in the central cities of the 25 largest metropolitan areas dropped by 700,000, while their suburbs added about 1.1 million. What was more serious for the populations of the older industrial regions was that such employment opportunities were moving out of their metropolitan areas altogether. From 1958 to 1972, the more established industrial cities of the North lost between 14 to 18 percent of their manufacturing jobs, while the cities of the Sunbelt increased theirs between 60 and 100 percent. (p. 211)

Cities such as Chicago, New York, Detroit, and Philadelphia lost over half their manufacturing jobs during the 20-year period following 1967. This translated into 500,000 jobs in New York, 326,000 in Chicago, 160,000 in Philadelphia, and 108,000 in Detroit.[11] Economic-driven changes that severely limited or closed opportunity structures, coupled with factors such as poor infrastructure and housing to accommodate urban masses, group conflict and competition over jobs and space, redlining, discrimination, racism, and public/private sector tensions ultimately resulted in today's poor urban cities.

Related and secondary economic enterprise in manufacturing-dependent cities also suffered as a result of deindustrialization. The negative implications were evident in Chicago: "During the 1960s, Chicago lost 500,000 white residents, 211,000 jobs, and 140,000 private housing units. As the West Side of Chicago was enveloped in an expanding core of poverty . . . 75 percent of its businesses disappeared" (Grogan and Proscio 2000, pp. 40–41). Recent data show a 50 percent decline in local businesses in some poor urban settings, where the "local commercial environment [is] dominated by liquor stores, bars, small groceries, and the illegal drug trade" (Chin 2001, p. 96). Many small, local businesses are often owned by immigrants with limited ties to the community and tenuous relationships with residents.[12] And although the negative economic effects of deindustrialization on cities are evident, a myriad of correlated factors have irrevocably altered the quality of life of urban residents. Yet Wilson (1996) provides an important observation regarding diversity within even the most impoverished areas:

> Three quarters of all the ghetto poor in metropolitan areas reside in one hundred of the nation's largest central cities; however, it is important to remember that the ghetto areas in these central cities also include a good many families and individuals who are not poor. (p. 12)

Social Implications and Neighborhood Organization

Neighborhood poverty has long been considered a key influence on the social milieu of many urban areas. Wilson (1996) suggests that the life chances of the poor are further reduced, if they also reside in impoverished neighborhoods. The social environment found in more economically stable neighborhoods is said to reinforce appropriate (often referred to as "mainstream") norms and values, aid in the proper socialization of youth, and help cultivate important informal networks. It has been suggested that some of the social implications of neighborhood poverty concentration effects manifest in the form of low self-efficacy, involvement in the illegal workforce, and poor personal choices that perpetuate poverty. Acute social isolation has been shown to result in oppositional identity and aberrant attitudes and lifestyles as compared to individuals in the larger society.[13] In its milder form, oppositional identity may manifest in clothing, speech forms, and attitudes considered counterculture. At its most negative, oppositional lifestyles have been correlated with criminal behavior and violence. However, it has been documented that the vast majority of urban residents, even some who experience abject poverty, often embrace norms and values typically associated with the larger society.[14]

The size and density of cities have been linked to the prevalence of crime. Logic dictates that the larger the population, the greater the likelihood of offenses and victimization. Further examination of urban literature illustrates that large, densely populated areas of poor and near-poor persons tend to exacerbate such conditions. Research suggests a direct relationship between poverty, unemployment, and urban crime. Conservative authors associate urban criminal activity with lower class culture.[15] Others concede the existence of urban countercultures, but conclude that the majority of urban residents are law-abiding citizens who must contend with a numeric-minority criminal element and consequences of proximity to various illegal economies.[16] And still other scholars suggest urbanites adapt to varying situations that, in some instances, require a law-abiding persona, and in others, require them to take on "street" mannerisms and behavior to survive.[17] However, the most telling depictions of the gradual effects of poverty on social control and neighborhood organization illustrate how residents who have been socialized to accept and work toward the "American Dream" and the benefits of following societal dictates become critical and bitter over time and ultimately reject prevailing norms and values as counterintuitive based on their daily problems.[18]

Social disorganization has also been associated with constrained interaction, both formal and informal, with the larger society. In this context, many residents in poor areas are said to have limited exposure to persons in the main and few "weak ties" needed to procure job, resources, and information.[19] And although social and physical segregation, the out-migration of gainful jobs, and young mothers with limited parenting skills among other factors have been associated with social disorganization in urban areas, it is important to also consider the possible implications for those persons whose preoccupation with basic daily survival issues may overshadow other concerns, such as neighborhood involvement and social control. The topic of social disorganization also considers leveled aspirations and failure to adhere to prevailing societal guidelines due to economic conditions that ultimately give rise to crime, an inability to maintain control over youth, particularly young African American males, and a loss of residential solidarity and camaraderie. This study expands the notion of social disorganization by focusing on the implications of citywide economic demise as a result of precarious public/private sector ties that failed to stimulate business, the resulting low tax base, limited real and perceived residential clout to effect change, and the relationship between racial/ethnic and economic homogeneity and limited enterprise. In this context, I examine how residents in Gary, Indiana, contend with the social and economic disorganization that comes about as a result of deindustrialization and disinvestment in their city and neighborhoods.

Disproportionately Affected and Underrecognized Groups

Racial / Ethnic Groups

In spite of the various groups that experienced downward mobility as a result of deindustrialization, the "face of poverty" is often depicted as African American, female, and urban. Media sources earn rating share and profits by reinforcing prevailing beliefs,[20] despite facts that more Whites are poor than are African Americans and rural residents rather than urbanites are more likely to be impoverished. Given the potential disconnect between scholarship and public sentiment, in order to investigate various costs associated with life in Gary, Indiana, it is important to identify key persons, groups, and organizations, their histories, inter- and intragroup relations, and how the nexus between race/ethnicity, class, and place influence contemporary conditions in the city. Such a query will shed light on those groups most affected by poverty.

Although census data show that about 75 percent of all impoverished person are White, poverty among Whites appears to be less expected, less recognized, less stigmatized, and less often the focus of research and social commentary. Poverty among Whites disproportionately affects women, especially those who are single-parents or divorced with children. Based on 2000 census data, 8.1 percent of non-Hispanic/Latino Whites live below the poverty level; about 5 percent of White persons 18–64 years old are poor. Of those Whites living below the official poverty threshold, about 8.9 percent are 5 years old or younger, and 59.6 percent are 18–64 years old. And of White families that are poor, about 29.4 percent are married couples with dependent children under the age of 18, and 36.4 percent are female-headed households with such children. Flanagan (1999) summarizes the prevalence and profile of poverty in U.S. cities:

> The higher overall concentration of poverty in central cities is in large part the result of the concentration of poor *whites* [emphasis is his] in these areas: At the time of the last general census poverty rate for African Americans and Latinos who live in nonmetropolitan areas is actually higher than the rate in the central cities. These distinctions are important to note, because they inform us that the assumption that most of the central city poor are minorities is false; most are white. (p. 264)

Although more Whites experience poverty, people of color, women, and children are at greater risk. Aspirations of gainful employment in industrial factories and economic security, coupled with the desire to escape oppressive conditions in the South, resulted in an exodus by African Americans to places such as New York, Indiana, Illinois, Pennsylvania, and Michigan. In 1920 the urban African American population increased by almost 50 percent. The benefits of the industrial era were short-lived, and the technological age brought many challenges for African American urbanites, especially the working class, who tended to be employed in the manufacturing arena. Deindustrialization meant downward economic mobility for the less educated, blue-collar workers—a disproportionate number of whom were urban African Americans. And African Americans continue to be one of the groups most affected by urban poverty. According to 2000 census figures, 22.1 percent of African Americans are poor (down from 23.6 percent in 1999), and over 40 percent of African American children are growing up impoverished. The majority of impoverished African Americans reside in urban centers.

Dreams of economic and political betterment also precipitated migration of persons of Hispanic descent. One writer notes, "of the 22.3 million people in the United States in 1991 with ties of identity (however distant) to New World Spanish colonial territories, 52 percent lived in central cities and 93 percent in metropolitan areas."[21] Most were originally from Mexico, Puerto Rico, Cuba, and Central and South America. Just as African Americans are concentrated in northern cities and "rust-belt" locales, Hispanic urbanites tend to reside in large cities such as Chicago, New York, and Miami and in the Southwest. Like many African Americans, segments of the Hispanic population experienced discrimination, racism, and social isolation in inner cities. However, factors such as mobility patterns, human capital, place of origin, and assimilation rates have contributed to the upward mobility of certain Hispanic subgroups (example, Cubans) as compared to African Americans, Mexicans, and Puerto Ricans.

In 2000 approximately 21.2 percent of Hispanics lived in poverty; the comparable figure in 1999 was 22.8 percent.[22] When areas in New York and Los Angeles are considered, patterns similar to those of impoverished African Americans emerge—female headed households, chronic unemployment, segregation and isolation in barrios, and persons with limited education and training. And negative conditions are particularly acute for many Puerto Ricans, who have been characterized as the "other underclass"

(Lemann 1991, p. 96). Flanagan's (1999) general observation is germane to this analysis, "Once we have absorbed these subtleties of classification we are left with the most important fact: many poor African Americans, Latino, and white people live in cities" (p. 264). The importance of comparing and contrasting racial/ ethnic experiences with poverty is not to illustrate that certain groups are *better at* negotiating poverty than others, but rather to illustrate inter- and intragroup patterns, as well as possible distinctive features for groups who experience similar social and economic challenges.

Women and Children

When identifying groups most affected by urban poverty, some overlap is evident between poverty found among racial/ethnic groups and poverty among both women and children. Factors such as employment restructuring resulting in pink color jobs with low wages and limited or no health care, lack of affordable housing and child-care, absentee fathers, difficulty enforcing alimony and child support edicts,[23] divorce, limited "marriageable males," and changing values about marriage and childrearing[24] have all been correlated with the feminization and juvenilization of poverty. Furthermore, these dynamics have contributed to the disproportionate percentage of poor urban women and their children. Female-headed homes are common in urban settings and indicative of overall trends in marital relations in the United States. But with this change has also come increased risk of socioeconomic instability, especially for African American and Puerto Rican women.[25]

According to 2000 census data, about 34.3 and 46.4 percent of female-headed households with children under 18 and 5 years old, respectively, are poor; substantially greater representation occurs for households headed by females from racial/ethnic groups. The importance of marriage in staving off poverty is further illustrated by 2002 census data. While about 9.6 percent of families in general live below poverty, slightly over 5.3 percent of married couples are poor. Comparable census measures for African Americans and Hispanics are substantially higher. Thus the economically stabilizing character found in many nuclear families stands in stark contrast to the precarious economic status of many households that deviate from this structure.[26] Studies on facets of the experiences of poor and near-poor women parallel census data. Wilson and Wacquant (1989) note that substantially more women comprise the ranks of the ghetto poor, while McLanahan and Garfinkel (1989) contend that female-headed households may represent the "crystallization of an urban under-class" (p. 93). Similarly, Pearce (1983) suggests that "the 'double' disadvantage experienced by African American women is actually, in quantitative terms, a geometrically increasing 'quadruple' disadvantage," (p. 72) because such women contend with micro-level disadvantage at the hands of African American men, as well as macro-level effects in the form of racial and gender discrimination.

Women's poverty has also been attributed to weak labor force attachment and limited human capital for currently demanded jobs. Lower labor force participation has been found for African American single mothers as compared to their White single parent and African-American and White married counterparts. In summary, research suggests that: 1) female-headed households have increased, and women of color are more likely to live in such households;[27] 2) poor and near-poor women of color are more likely to reside in cities; 3) unmarried women with children are more likely to bear the brunt of economic and noneconomic support for their children;[28] 4) women tend to earn $0.70–$0.77 to every dollar earned by men; and, 5) some inner-city women will continue to have relationships with men who are not "marriageable" from whom children may result.[29] The combined effects of these trends for Whites, racial/ethnic groups, and women and children inform our understanding of the current levels of concentrated poverty in urban centers, in general, and in Gary, Indiana, in particular.

Structural Changes and Neighborhood Concentrated Poverty in Gary, Indiana

History in Economic Context

Macro-level structural changes associated with economic shifts and racial and spatial arrangements have transformed many once relatively stable urban centers into blighted shells of their former selves. Early cities were confronted with poverty, but residents still had buffers in the form of access to jobs, class heterogeneity among households within neighborhoods, and local businesses, organizations, and service providers.[30] However, in the 1970s, urban cities like Chicago, Detroit, and Gary, Indiana, that were dependent on manufacturing industries experienced increased poverty. Although recognized, but not often the focus of studies, is the fact that structural changes, such as business relocations, out-migration of many economically stable families, and concentrated poverty, have also resulted in an absence of basic service providers, such as grocery, drug, and clothing stores, banks, and gas stations in affected areas. Such establishments are often replaced by check cashing facilities, corner and liquor stores, and pawnshops.[31] Gary, Indiana is one such case in point; current conditions in the city belie its former state.

Gary, Indiana was founded in 1903 as a center for the U.S. Steel Corporation's manufacturing operations and a place of residence for steel workers and their families. The city was named after Judge Elbert Gary, U.S. Steel's chairman of the board. To some, Gary and other neighboring cities such as Waukegan, Aurora, and Joliet represented manufacturing satellites of the bourgeoning transportation industries in Chicago.[32] The early twentieth century witnessed the migration of African Americans to Gary in large numbers from the South to take advantage of manufacturing jobs. According to Hurley's (1995) historical account:

> Between 1920 and 1930, more than 15,000 migrants, most of them from Mississippi, Alabama, Tennessee, Arkansas, and Georgia arrived in Gary to work in the mammoth lakefront factories . . . the following decade, another 20,000 African Americans came to the Steel City to fill industrial positions created by the wartime boom. (pp. 112–113)

By the 1940s, U.S. Steel, in addition to two other steel mills, Bethlehem and Inland, provided the city with as much as half of its labor force. And by 1950, about 75 percent of African American men in Gary worked in the industrial sector. The benefits of industrialization were great for African Americans:

> The continued availability of manufacturing jobs through the 1950s and 1960s made Gary somewhat of a mecca for blacks. In 1956 *Ebony* magazine ranked Gary as the best place in the country for African Americans; by 1969, Gary's blacks had a higher median income than their counterparts in any other U.S. city. (Hurley 1995, p. 113)

Less than four decades later, the postindustrial city would be referred to as the murder capital of the country.[33]

Gary remained a steel-producing leader until national out-migration of steel manufacturing in the late 1970s resulted in high unemployment rates, especially among African American men and the replacement of many manufacturing jobs with lower-paying service-oriented occupations over the subsequent 25 year period. In his political and historical analysis on the city, Catlin (1993) notes that the Gary metropolitan region saw a decline in steel mill jobs from 70,000 in 1979 to 40,000 in 1982. Such jobs in the *city* of Gary fell from 30,000 in 1974 to under 6,000 by 1987. This employment change also led to the exodus of other businesses and residents, infrastructure decline, a reduced tax base, and other economic and social ills that occur when work disappears. Businesses that out-migrated were not replaced in kind and, in 1986, the 20 percent unemployment rate found in Gary was almost three times the national average and seven percentage points higher than in neighboring counties.[34] The gradual out-migration of Whites to nearby areas like Merrillville and Portage, Indiana, occurred simultaneously.

Gary's population declined from 175,415 in 1970 to 151,953 in 1980, and to 116,646 in 1990. According to 2001 U.S. Census figures, the city spans approximately 57.24 square miles, is currently populated by about 102,746 predominantly African American residents, and has a population per square mile of about 2,046. Although Gary is predominately African American, predominately White districts such as Black Oak remain in the city. Although Gary is in close proximity to the town of Merrillville and the city of Portage, both are predominately White, smaller, and less densely populated than Gary (areas of 33.32 and 27.43 square miles, 30,560 and 33,496 population counts, and 918 and 1,316 persons per square mile, respectively). The gradual postindustrial economic decline in Gary contrasts starkly with increased economic stability in Merrillville and Portage. Both are economically linked to Gary, especially Merrillville, due to its shopping mall district frequented by Gary residents for goods, services, and jobs. In addition, both places provide affordable housing options and employment prospects for some Gary residents. However, certain segments of Merrillville and Portage also experience high levels of poverty. In many respects, Gary's history parallels that of other manufacturing-dependent cities such as Milwaukee, Detroit, and certain parts of Chicago that experienced globalization and deindustrialization, coupled with current and historical racism, discrimination, segregation, political disempowerment on the statewide landscape, and the resulting out-migration of businesses and more economically stable residents.

Changes in Gary and surrounding cities and towns illustrate important demographic and economic factors needed to undergird a strong economy. Table 1.1 includes economic and social indices for Gary and neighboring Merrillville and Portage. The latter two areas are central to Gary's transition, because they were often beneficiaries of businesses, middle-class residents, and other establishments that vacated the city. For example, Gary experienced an 11.9 percent population decline from 1990–2000, while Merrillville's population increased by 12.1 percent during the same period.[35] An inverse relationship exists between the percentages of White and African American residents that occupied the city each period. And just as Gary saw a decrease in Whites between 1970 and 2000, the number of Whites in Portage also grew. It should be noted that, just as more economically stable White and African American families exited Gary, the lack of jobs meant that fewer emigrants moved there, and continued economic problems made the city less attractive to others who might have considered relocating there. Just as the proportion of women, primarily single mothers, grew in the city over the 40-year period, similar increases were not apparent in Merrillville and Portage.

Trends show a significant decline in manufacturing positions in the 40-year period from the late 1960s. By 2000 less than 20 percent of employed residents worked in the manufacturing industry, while about 24 percent were employed in service occupations. Given that the estimated average yearly earnings for the two occupational categories for Gary residents were $57,368 and $26,891,[36] respectively in 2000, the city experienced a substantial change in both the types of gainful employment available and the earning power of those who remained employed. The decline in manufacturing jobs as the mainstay source of revenue, both for the city and its residents, was accompanied by increases in poverty and unemployment. Although Gary experienced a drop in poverty since the 1990s, in 2000, Gary's poverty rate was almost six times the rate in Merrillville and three times that in Portage.

Rural and Urban Differences

Although Gary and Portage are, by census definition, cities, and Merrillville, a town, both Portage and Merrillville have certain characteristics that may benefit the poor that are often absent from resources in the inner city. When rural immigrants began to enter the United States in large numbers, most followed family members to large cities. For example, Klebanow, Jonas, and Leonard (1977) note that by 1870, although only 15 percent of the total U.S. population

Table 1.1
Demographic Changes in Gary and Surrounding Areas
in Indiana, 1970–2000

| | Gary | | | |
	2000	1990	1980	1970
Total Population	102,746	116,646	151,953	175,415
% African American	84.0	81.6	73.6	53.3[+]
% White	11.9	16.3	26.4	46.7
% Hispanic[‡]	4.9	5.7	7.5	—
% Female	54.2	54.0	52.8	57.4
% Manufacturing industry	19.0	21.7	38.9	48.8
% Service occupations	24.0	16.0	14.7	13.2
Unemployment rate	8.3	16.7	14.5	8.8
Poverty rate	25.8	29.4	20.4	15.1

| | Merrillville | | | |
	2000	1990	1980	1970
Total Population	30,560	27,257	27,677	15,918[±]
% African American	22.9	5.0	0.001	0.001[+]
% White	69.7	91.7	99.9	99.9
% Hispanic[‡]	9.7	6.9	0.1	—
% Female	52.3	52.1	51.7	67.1
% Manufacturing industry	19.4	23.5	31.8	38.3
% Service occupations	14.3	9.1	11.0	6.9
Unemployment rate	2.9	4.2	5.9	3.3
Poverty rate	4.3	3.6	3.2	2.6

| | Portage | | | |
	2000	1990	1980	1970
Total Population	33,496	29,060	27,409	19,127
% African American	1.4	0.4	0.001	0.3[+]
% White	92.5	97.1	99.9	99.7
% Hispanic[‡]	9.9	6.4	0.1	—
% Female	51.5	51.3	50.8	73.2
% Manufacturing industry	26.4	30.5	39.3	46.5
% Service occupations	16.8	11.7	11.8	9.5
Unemployment rate	3.2	6.2	8.9	5.8
Poverty rate	7.5	7.9	5.1	3.8

Sources: Profile of General Demographic Characteristics: Census 2000 Summary File (SF 1), Race and Hispanic or Latino: Census 2000 Summary File, Profile of Selected Economic Characteristics: Census 2000 Summary File 3 (SF 3), Income and Poverty Status: Census 1990 Summary Tape File 3 (STF 3), General Population and Housing Characteristics: Census 1990 Summary Tape File 1 (STF 1), 1980 and 1970 General Social and Economic Characteristics: Census of Population Part 16 Indiana Section 2. Note: Poverty rate represents values for individuals: + 1970 figures included Negro and other non-White races combined: ‡ Hispanic ethnicity may be part of White or Black race: ± Includes Merrillville, Lottaville, and Rexville.

consisted of immigrants, 34 percent of residents in the 50 largest cities were foreign-born. Residents in Portage and Merrillville may benefit due to their proximity to farms, where produce can be purchased less expensively. In some cases, poor rural families tend plots of lands to grow food to augment their constrained budgets.[37] And although the density in a large city may give inner-city poor greater access to certain organized social services and churches that provide assistance, the rural poor often live with or in close proximity to family members who provide economic and instrumental support.[38] In addition, places like Merrillville and Portage exhibit "city and town" features (example, access to farming and social services) that may benefit residents. And although rural residents aren't exempt from poverty, the highest levels of *concentrated* poverty continue to be found in central cities.[39] However, because of the influence of media representations and stereotypes that associate poverty with urban residents, rural poverty, like White poverty, tends to be less visible, less acknowledged, and less stigmatized.

Race Relations in Gary, Indiana

If economic restructuring is considered the central catalyst behind contemporary urban poverty, race relations can be considered a mitigating factor in the process. Just as an analysis that is uni-causal in its emphasis on racism as the reason for urban poverty should be questioned, suspicions should arise when scholarship that explores societal inequities fails to consider the implications of racism or other discriminatory practices. The cumulative effects of historic institutional racism in political, economic, and social arenas continue to manifest and impact life chances of many residents in poor urban areas. The history of Gary and cities like it shows that tenuous race relations, discrimination, and institutionalized racism had an indelible impact on the city's development and current impoverished conditions.

Migratory groups to Chicago, Cleveland, Detroit, St. Louis, Toledo, and Gary were initially small as compared to indigenous and immigrant Whites who lived in cities.[40] Thus African Americans (and Mexicans) were not initially considered a threat for jobs, space, or power. In some cities, minorities were actively recruited to fill lower-level, mostly manual-labor positions made available during periods of restricted European immigration in the 1920s and during World Wars I and II. The majority of minorities were employed in manufacturing or transportation-related industry. According to Mohl and Betten

(1986), by 1920, 14 percent of the U.S. Steel labor force was African
American. But in 1928, only 4.7 percent of African American steel-
workers were skilled laborers. The majority were considered unskilled
workers. Thus African American and Hispanics were concentrated in
the lowest job levels. According to the same authors:

> Gary had only a few hundred blacks in 1920, but . . . during the
> next two decades . . . the city's black population rose to 5,299 in
> 1920 and 17,922 in 1930. During both decades, Gary led every
> other American city in the percentage of black population in-
> crease—1,283.6 percent during the teens, and 238.2 percent
> during the twenties. By 1930, blacks in Gary constituted 17.8
> percent of the city's total population—a proportion higher than
> that of any other industrial city in the North. (p. 49)

However, as suggested by Blumer (1958), White anxiety over perceived group threat and potential power shifts due to significant increased minority presence meant racial backlash in Gary after 1920.
And because most minorities were prevented from working in all but
the most menial, lowest-paid positions, discrimination also served to
create a two-tiered economic system within most industries. Up until
the late 1950s, African American and Mexican steel workers in Gary
were usually barred from competing with Whites for better positions
and active union involvement, and were typically the first groups to
be downsized during periods of economic problems. Mohl and Betten
(1986) describe the scope of race relations in the city:

> Like Gary's white immigrants, the black newcomer arrived in
> the steel city hoping to fulfill economic aspirations and to
> achieve a new and better life for themselves and their children
> . . . But because they were black, they faced persistent prob-
> lems of discrimination and segregation with which white im-
> migrants did not have to contend . . . The segregation of Gary's
> population did not develop accidentally out of housing pat-
> terns. Rather, discrimination and segregation in education,
> housing, employment, public services, and recreation was
> established and carried out by the city's white elite—business-
> men, bankers, realtors, educators, steel company officials, and
> local government leaders. Indeed, the history of Gary provides
> an illuminating case study for analyzing the evolution of
> racism against a background of working-class ethnic and racial
> conflict. (pp. 49–51)

The segregation of minorities in every arena of society was also readily enforced by the legal system and law enforcement. Economic disenfranchisement was driven by the private sector and political officials in local and state government and was reinforced in the public sector. Ironically, most European immigrants who *initially* arrived in the city lived near and interacted with minority groups; little conflict between African Americans and working-class White immigrants was recorded. However, most White immigrants were quickly socialized regarding the hierarchy of segregation, and they too began to reap benefits of a separate and unequal city. The experiences of Gary's racial/ethnic minorities support the following observation by Myrdal in *American Dilemma* (1962):

> Even the poor classes of whites in the North come to mistrust and despise the Negroes. The European immigrant groups are the ones thrown into most direct contact and competition with Negroes: they live near each other, often send their children to the same schools, and have to struggle for the same jobs. Recent immigrants apparently sometimes feel an interesting solidarity with Negroes or, at any rate, lack the intense superiority feeling of the native Americans educated in race prejudice. But the development of prejudice against Negroes is usually one of their first lessons in Americanization. (p. 293)

Similar observations were confirmed in the *Gary American* (1945), the city's African American newspaper: "When they [European immigrants] find that native white Americans make a practice of disadvantaging the Negro, . . . the foreigners were ready, willing, and even eager to follow" (p. 4). In addition, new White *employees* were said to be socialized to discriminate against minorities, further entrenching institutionalized racism in the local steel industry. "Anti-Negro" campaigns were frequent, promoted in local papers, enforced by the police force, and condoned by White residents. Mexican immigrants did not fare much better.

Hispanic immigrants, primarily Mexicans, also migrated to Gary and other northern cities in the early 1900s to fill industrial positions. For example, Mexican workers were recruited to offset the 1919 steel mill strike. By 1920 over 2,500 Mexicans were employed in the steel and railroad industries. By 1928 Mexicans comprised about 11 percent of employees in 15 of the area's meat packing, steel, and other plants and approximately 43 percent of the track and maintenance workers on 16 major railroads in the Chicago-Gary region.[41] The following series of quotes, all taken from Mohl and Betten (1986), inform an understanding of the racism and sanctioned discrimination that occurred in employment settings in Gary. One employer in 1923 noted: "What we need is 'Hunkies' and lots of 'em . . . the Mex doesn't come under the quota law and he's willing to work long and cheap, so we'll keep on importing him" (p. 92). Several other employment managers echoed similar discriminatory comments: "When I hire Mexicans at the gate, I pick out the lightest among them. No, it isn't that the lighter-colored ones are any better workers, but the darker ones are like the niggers . . . when employment slackens the Mexicans are the first ones off. They are not Americans" (p. 98).

Like many of their African American counterparts, Mexicans were housed in crowded, dilapidated shacks on the city's south side, often in conditions more deplorable than those of the former group. Although such acts were commonly meted out on them, minorities of color were often associated with crime and violence. Stereotypes were reinforced by politicians and local newspapers, such as the *Gary Post-Tribune*, "Next to the bad negroes, the bad Mexicans were declared to be the worst offenders."[42] However, unlike African Americans, who were U.S. citizens, Mexicans in Gary experienced a series of initially voluntary and later coercive repatriation campaigns during the 1920s Depression Era. In 1932 about 1,500 Gary Mexicans and 1,800 from surrounding areas in Lake County were repatriated, and by mid-1932 voluntary repatriation evolved into forced expulsion. Harassment and discrimination against remaining Mexicans intensified. By the 1960s, the city reflected an entrenched, three-tired hierarchy of economic, political, and social power, where native Whites were located at the top of the pyramid followed by immigrant Whites, and lastly by African Americans and Mexicans. Most discrimination was experienced by the two latter groups.

In his historiography and sociological study on the subject, Robert Catlin's (1993) *Racial Politics and Urban Planning: Gary, Indiana 1980–1989* suggests that the devolution of Gary from a once booming steel-mill city to one now ravaged by poverty and urban decay was due largely to conflict based on race (African American vs. White), political affiliation (Democratic vs. Republican), and public and private sector tensions. The author contends that major revitalization plans for the city were purposely thwarted due to race-based decision making, political and economic gatekeeping, and partisan pettiness that overshadowed professionalism and potential mutual benefits for Gary and the region. Central to the problems was the inability of the predominately White private sector as well as suburban and state governments to work with predominately African American local officials. Even as Gary declined around them, elites seemed unable to compromise and reach consensus about the future of the city. Catlin argues that, without key alliances, the city was virtually left to fend for itself and could not withstand the postindustrial recessionary periods of the 1970s and 1980s. He further argues that the two-fold goal of Gary's opponents was to diminish the city's racial, economic, and political power base, while simultaneously providing support for nearby Merrillville and suburban Lake County, such that Gary would be economically dependent on surrounding, predominately White areas.

It would appear that xenophobia, in addition to variations of both "old fashioned" and aversive racism manifested throughout the history of Gary; negative race relations were particularly acute.[43] With the former type of racism, Gary's minority residents contended with physical and verbal mistreatment, especially when they sought redress. The latter form of racism was evident as Whites sought to avoid interaction with African Americans and Mexicans during all but the most inopportune times. Theoretically, segregation and covert discrimination waned with the victories of the Civil Rights Movement.[44] However, their cumulative effects cannot so easily be repaired. Ironically, history suggests that working-class conflict, fueled by native, White power elite formed a wedge between African Americans, Mexicans, and immigrant Whites that served the interests of private and certain public sector leaders at the expense of groups with potentially greater class-based commonalities than the perceived race-based alliances posited by White natives toward White immigrants. These macro-level political, economic, and social changes would influence how postindustrial urban spaces in Gary would develop.

#### CHAPTER TWO

Space Usage and Cost Differentials in Gary, Indiana: Counting the Costs

Economic Entrepreneurs and Urban Enterprise

Gary's history as a leading steel manufacturer, regional retail site, and employment mecca for conscientious racial and ethnic minorities and White immigrants stands in stark contrast to current conditions. The city's evolution speaks to the theme of "structure and agency," when one considers the interplay between societal forces, both public and private, that influenced the outmigration of enterprises needed to sustain the tax base and generate revenue to support the city as well as residents' views, choices, and responses in the wake of increased poverty. This chapter focuses on how economic spaces were shaped and used to effect shopping opportunities and subsequent cost differentials in Gary and neighboring suburbs. I compare and contrast key transitions that took place that influenced the availability of businesses and services in the city and surrounding areas. Of particular interest is how the presence or absence of private-sector driven business establishments (use of urban space), such as retailers, large grocery stores, and other service providers, are related to the economic and noneconomic costs residents incur.

Research suggests that there are two primary levels on which issues of "agency" should be considered—the ordinary and the elite. Ordinary citizens impact society privately in their patterns of consumption and publicly in grassroots movements and other collective endeavors to bring about change. In these instances, everyday persons without customary forms of power associated with wealth or influential networks gain momentum and bring about change *en masse* or indirectly as a result of their similar interests and choices. In contrast, elites express private choices in the form of investments and publicly via policies of the state. Unlike the former group, the latter take advantage of wealth, status, and power relations to effect change. In doing so, economic, political, and social coalitions often result in societal-level changes that greatly influence ordinary people. Although this book focuses largely on the localized effects of urban poverty, it is important to place the transition that took place in Gary within a larger context that considers the influence of elites inside and outside the city. Several timely resources inform our understanding of the relationship between ordinary and elite agency and the types of structural changes that ultimately led to poverty in Gary.

Government and private sector activity have been shown to be inextricably linked to globalization, systemic economic changes in urban spaces, and subsequent poverty among many of its residents. The attraction of African Americans to unions, a desire by corporations to sidestep equal opportunity requirements by avoiding minority hires, as well as stereotypes and prejudices have served to increase the proportion of unemployed and poor African Americans in urban areas. Conclusions by Wilson (1996), Squires (1994), and others show that deindustrialization and disinvestment in cities have eliminated jobs, reduced education and public service revenues, and increased the socioeconomic division between predominately minority inner cities and White suburbs.

Understanding the use of urban spaces in Gary can also be informed by Logan and Molotch (1987), who suggest the commodification of place in cities. The authors posit that the dynamics of *exchange value* (use of cities primarily for financial gain) and *use value* (reliance on cities primarily as places of residence and community, where residents fulfill material and nonmaterial needs) meet in cities. They further contend that human agency can serve as a force to counteract potentially negative societal forces focused on exchange rather than use value. Cities are said to be stratified based on the ease with which they attract capital. As such, the city is a growth machine influenced by various entrepreneurs, but ultimately controlled by structural speculators who conceptualize, shape, and determine the future of urban spaces. This latter group employs strategies to form alliances with elites in social, political, and economic circles including local newspapers, utilities, and transportation officials to stimulate more growth and hence increase exchange value for personal gain. However, these benefits often infringe upon the lives and lifestyles of residents and can undermine their quality of life. Logan and Molotch (1987) contend:

The elite can mobilize the government to bolster growth goals. Governments can also help coordinate the roles of diverse members of the growth coalition, securing the cooperation of local entrepreneurs in ambitious growth projects. Cities, regions, and states do not compete to please people; they compete to please capital—and the two activities are fundamentally different. (pp. 35, 42)

Furthermore:

Those in control of the top places use place status to maintain privileges for their locations, often at the expense of the lesser locales. Often with the help of place-based organizations, they manipulate transportation routes, secure desired zoning, and keep out unwanted social groups . . . The desire for growth creates consensus among a wide range of elite groups, no matter how they might be split on other issues. (pp. 49–52)

In response, residents may also take part in the entrepreneurial process and evoke their agency in matters that threaten their use value. In addition, mutuality can arise, as elites and residents enlist each other in endeavors related to both use and exchange value. With economic growth, the authors postulate a *multiplier effect* that takes the form of in-migration of labor and demand for ancillary goods and services. Thus the out-migration of manufacturers from Gary meant the subsequent decline in the growth machine and departure of industries and residents who relied on this enterprise. Industrial shifts from central locations tend to disproportionately affect racial and ethnic minorities who are most likely to reside in cities, less apt to hold managerial and professional positions, more likely to experience longer periods of under- and unemployment, and tend to hold less equity in businesses. In addition, many urban residents lack the transportation to get to new suburban jobs, are less able to move when companies relocate, or are often unaware when new suburban jobs become available. The result is continued employment and income disparities as evidenced by indicators such as poverty and unemployment rates, labor-force participation rates, and family income.

When spending power is examined, according to the 2004 report by the Selig Center for Economic Growth at the University of Georgia, African Americans have an estimated buying power of about $688 billion. However, African Americans are said to spend over 90 percent of their earnings outside the African American community and to control less than 2 percent of the wealth and resources in the United States.[1] The question remains, given the potential revenue from African Americans, why has Gary, Indiana, been unable to maintain or restore a viable economic base? Using Logan and Molotch's (1987) concepts, what key players have influenced the *growth machine* called Gary, Indiana?

Disinvestment in Gary, Indiana

Fueled by private sector investors, suburbanization became more prevalent in the 1950s. Not only did the city witness fewer new business enterprises, but existing companies and professional offices began to close or move their headquarters outside the city. Before 1950, downtown Gary hosted thriving private businesses, retail chains, and entertainment establishments. Gary was considered a major regional retail hub with between 14,000 to 16,000 retail jobs downtown. By 1965 this figure had fallen to 9,000.[2] Downtown Gary's primary retail competitor was the Village Mall (now referred to as the Village Shopping Center) located on over 40 acres between 35th and 37th Ave. of Grant St.[3] Built in 1953, "The Village," as it was commonly referred to, was Gary's first enclosed retail center, where customers could travel by car and have access to numerous stores in a centralized facility. The approximately $5.5 million venture included an over 200,000 square foot center that housed more than 32 stores, a bank, a loan company, and a mortgage company, and employed over 500 persons. Flagship stores such as J.C. Penney, Kroger, and Kresge provided retail and grocery shopping under one roof. To accommodate Whites who had begun the exodus from central Gary, 500 single-family homes were also built to the North and South of the shopping center. As noted by Vertrees and Gengler in the October 1953 *Gary Post-Tribune*:

> The developers said that the center will go a long way toward keeping Gary out in front as the top shopping area in the industrial Calumet region. They expect it to fill the needs of residents who are shifting to the fringe areas, away from downtown living communities. A survey indicated the project may draw from an estimated 250,000 persons. (p. A7)

Residents and persons outside the city who used to frequent downtown were drawn to the newness and convenience of The Village so much so that only 6,000 retail jobs remained in Gary after 1960, and about 25 percent of residents were shopping outside the city.[4] Competition from The Village shifted a significant amount of revenue from outside the downtown area, but the new retail facility was still part of metropolitan Gary and thus benefited the city economically. This cannot be said about latter forms of retail disinvestment. It has been suggested that, unlike other cities that were experiencing business losses due to suburbanization, Gary officials failed to respond quickly in attempting to counteract these changes by providing alternatives to attract and retain customers. By 1976 The Village housed 33 stores, businesses, and restaurants, including a Gary National Bank branch, a medical building, and an insurance company; downtown Gary seemed unable to compete with the shopping center in terms of accessibility, availability, and affordability of goods and services.

In addition to the economic changes the city was experiencing, political conflict continued to mount between Mayor R. Hatcher and the predominately African American city government and the White private sector and state officials. Hatcher's 1971 defeat of Andrew Williams, who had been largely supported by the private sector, was said to exacerbate an already-tense political climate and resulted in plans to develop a shopping mall in nearby Merrillville, Indiana. Initially named Southlake Mall, the current Westfield Shoppingtown includes over 150 retail and specialty stores and restaurants, including upscale flagship retailers Carson Pirie Scott and L. S. Ayres and mainstays Sears and J. C. Penney (the latter two chains previously had locations in downtown Gary or The Village). In addition, as a shopping, entertainment, and retail service provider, Westfield is relatively self-contained. It houses a day spa, a police substation, and a travel agency and is flanked by a movie theatre, full-service bank, automobile dealerships and repair shops, upscale and discount furniture stores, home improvement chains, several discount superstores, and smaller strip-mall establishments. Catlin (1993) chronicles the business exodus from Gary:

> By 1978, the three anchor department stores and over one hundred retail establishments in downtown had either closed altogether or moved to the new malls and nearby strip centers, taking their tax dollars with them . . . Other enterprises followed the retail stores from downtown to the suburbs. Both major banks constructed new headquarters facilities there. A new hospital opened, soon to be followed by almost 90 percent of Gary's white and Asian physicians. The 300-room downtown Holiday Inn closed and essentially

reopened in Merrillville. It is estimated that between 1970 and 1980, almost $600 million was spent on this construction, all by the private sector . . . by the early 1980s black shoppers from Gary accounted for almost one-quarter of all sales there . . . Meanwhile, the number of business establishments in downtown Gary fell from over 500 in 1960 to less than 40 in 1979. Corresponding numbers of employees in retail trade downtown fell from 10,000 to only 300. (p. 27)

The mall and adjacent retailers currently comprise an approximate 5-mile span and represent the closest full-service shopping center to the city of Gary, as well as the largest site for retail employment options. And although The Village currently houses 40 businesses, it is no longer viable competition for suburban retailers and has experienced its own retail devolution. Anchor department stores, national stores, and upscale specialty shops have either closed or relocated to Merrillville and have been replaced by smaller discount retailers, Asian-owned establishments and eateries, and "five-and-dime" stores. The inability to consistently fill major retail space has also resulted in empty stores (refer to chapter 4 for more information on The Village's transition).

In the aftermath of massive economic out-migration, on any given day, there are only approximately 2,000 employees, primarily government employees, and visitors in downtown Gary.[5] In 2000 labor force participation in the city was approximately 55.9 percent as compared to 66.3 percent and 65.7 percent in Merrillville and Portage, respectively. Using Logan and Molotch's (1987) terminology, structural speculators had succeeded in creating an economic haven that not only drew revenue from surrounding areas in Indiana and Chicago, but literally drained Gary's economic resources and related jobs and placed the city at the mercy of suburban businesses. The effects of business out-migration were apparent to Gary residents, particularly during the early periods, when there were few public transportation services to the new mall areas.[6] In the wake of the exodus of businesses and residents, a *Gary Post-Tribune* commentator offered a cautionary assessment and suggestion:

It is difficult—no, impossible—to accept the theory that this is the way things ought to be: decorative, impressive structures in Merrillville with top-rate merchandise—and in Gary, whatever is left. Is it impatience, or simply the unwillingness of those merchants to become involved in (a) urban

growth or (b) a city that is predominantly black in population? Whichever the case, it is a shame. And the only thing
that would be more of a shame is for Gary residents to patronize stores that have abandoned the city. Some may still
be naïve enough to think it doesn't matter where they shop
and believe that, if Gary can't deliver, one should go to Merrillville. But as a practical matter, they should realize that
the tax dollars from the businesses they support elsewhere
do not go to improve Gary schools and streets and parks and
all other manner of municipal services. Corporation chains
can never take Gary seriously as a place to locate major
businesses as long as Gary shoppers will travel to Merrillville. (Williams 1978, p. B1)

In further contrast to the economic upswing experienced in the
suburbs, today, downtown Gary has been virtually abandoned (refer
to Figures 2.1–2.17 of Gary and surrounding areas). Although local
governmental agencies are housed there, noticeably absent are major
retailers, supermarket chains, movie theatres, entertainment establishments, and major professional headquarters. A few independ-
ently owned retailers and fast-food restaurants remain on streets
that were once replete with businesses. The city is dramatically different from its previous state as the site of over 1,000 Black-owned
businesses with sales in excess of $99 million annually.[7] The eco-
nomic transition that occurred in Gary parallels changes that took
place in other urban centers such as Detroit and Flint, Michigan.
Cities unable to quickly respond to the effects of postindustrialization
and disinvestment were hurt the most and set off a chain reaction ultimately resulting in what Wilson (1996) describes as "basic neighborhood institutions are more difficult to maintain: stores, banks,
credit institutions, restaurants, dry cleaners, gas stations, medical
doctors, and so on lose regular and potential patrons" (p. 44).

Table 2.1 provides an overview of current economic indices for
those areas most affected by the economic transition that occurred in
Gary, Merrillville, and Portage, Indiana (I also include information
for the predominately White district of Gary called Black Oak, because it factors in subsequent chapters). In addition, national and
statewide statistics and those for Indianapolis, Indiana, are provided as additional points of comparison. All seven sites have similar male/female representation and average family sizes. However,
economic indicators suggest that overall, Gary (and Black Oak)
residents are less economically stable than U.S. residents in general

Table 2.1
2000 Census Demographics for Gary, Indiana, and Other Reference Areas

Variables	US	Indiana	Indianapolis
Demographics			
Population[+]	281m	6.1m	781,870
% Female	50.9	51.0	51.6
% African American	12.3	8.4	25.5
% White	75.1	87.5	69.1
% Hispanic	12.5	3.5	3.9
Average family size	3.1	3.2	3.0
Income and Poverty			
Unemployment rate	3.7	3.3	3.8
Median HH Income ($)	41,994	41,567	40,051
Median family Inc. ($)	50,046	50,251	48,755
Capita Income ($)	21,587	20,397	21,640
Poverty rate (individual)	12.4	9.5	11.9
Poverty rate <18 below	16.1	11.7	16.2
% Families below poverty	9.2	6.7	9.1
% Families w/ children <18 below poverty	13.6	10.2	13.8
% Families w/ children <5 below poverty	17.0	13.7	17.2
% Female HH	26.5	23.4	24.5
% Female HH w/ children <18 below poverty	34.3	30.4	30.9
% Female HH w/ children <5 below poverty	46.4	43.6	40.6

Sources: 2000 U.S. Census Summary File 1 (SF 1), 2000 U.S. Census Redistricting Data (Public Law 94-171) Summary File, Profile of General Demographic Characteristics: Census 2000 Summary File (SF 1), Race and Hispanic or Latino: Census 2000 Summary File, Profile of Selected Economic Characteristics: Census 2000 Summary File 3 (SF 3).

Figures for Black Oak only reflect census tract 411, because all residents in this tract are Black Oak residents. Several other tracts include some Black Oak residents (412, 413.01, and 115), but are excluded here due to difficulty accurately identifying such persons.

(continued)

Table 2.1 (*continued*)
2000 Census Demographics for Gary, Indiana, and Other Reference Areas

Variables	Gary (Bl. Oak)	Merrillville	Portage
Demographics			
Population[+]	102,746 (3,042)	30,560	33,496
% Female	54.2 (49.3)	52.3	51.5
% African American	84.0 (0.1)	22.9	1.4
% White	11.9 (90.0)	69.7	92.5
% Hispanic	4.9 (18.3)[ψ]	9.7	9.9
Average family size	3.3 (3.4)	3.1	3.1
Income and Poverty			
Unemployment rate	8.3 (5.0)	2.9	3.2
Median HH Income ($)	27,195 (31,156)	49,545	47,500
Median family Inc. ($)	32,205 (30,189)	56,355	54,316
Capita Income ($)	14,383 (12,368)	22,293	20,146
Poverty rate (individual)	25.8 (16.8)	4.3	7.5
Poverty rate <18 below	37.9 (17.6)	5.5	10.6
% Families below poverty	22.2 (16.4)	2.6	5.8
% Families w/ children <18 below poverty	31.5 (17.6)	4.2	9.0
% Families w/ children <5 below poverty	39.9 (17.2)	5.6	11.2
% Female HH	38.2 (33.7)	4.5	20.2
% Female HH w/ children <18 below poverty	46.9 (35.8)	7.9	28.8
% Female HH w/ children <5 below poverty	58.7 (41.7)	8.6	37.8

Census Definitions:

Household (HH)—all the persons who occupy a housing unit. A housing unit is a house, an apartment, a mobile home, a group of rooms, or a single room that is occupied as separate living quarters.

Family—a householder and one or more other persons living in the same household who are related to the householder by birth, marriage, or adoption. All persons in a household who are related to the householder are regarded as members of his/her family. A household can contain only one family. Not all households contain families, since a household may comprise a group of unrelated persons or one person living alone.

[+] Actual US figure is 281,421,906 and the Indiana figure is 6,080,485.

[ψ] Reflects "Other" for the Black Oak district.

and other Indiana residents, in particular. The unemployment rate in the city (8.3 percent) is at least twice that of the other points of reference; differences between Gary and both Merrillville and Portage are especially disparate. The greater relative proportion of unemployed in Gary and Black Oak translates into lower median and mean household incomes, median family incomes, and per capita incomes. When compared to national figures, over twice as many poor families reside in Gary than in the United States in general, three times as many as are found in Indiana, four times the rate of poverty in Portage, and almost ten times the level of impoverishment in Merrillville. Gary is experiencing substantially higher levels of poverty for every listed indicator. Additionally, there is an inverse relationship between economically more stable areas and the proportion of residents that are African American. Approximately 84 percent of Gary residents are African American; similar percentages of Whites live in Portage (and Black Oak). As compared to the remaining six locales, a disproportionate percentage of African Americans reside in Gary. It should be noted that the most severe levels of poverty are apparent in all areas for female-headed households with children under five years old; Gary and its subsidiary, Black Oak, continue to have the greatest representation. The feminization and juvenilization of poverty are national problems, particularly acute in Indiana as well, but less so in Merrillville.[8] Although the aggregate nature of census data may mask important trends, particularly, more recent urban renewal efforts in inner cities,[9] the urban challenges faced by Gary, in general, are apparent and influence costs incurred by residents, especially the most impoverished.

Effects on Secondary Enterprises and City Services

As a result of the mass exodus of key businesses, the city has also seen a marked decline in secondary enterprise, social services typically funded by city revenue, and available resources residents would avail themselves of during the daily round. Gary had a 2000 annual budget of approximately $32,390,410, and the primary source of city revenue is state and local taxes. Without sufficient funding, social services and infrastructure improvements are typically reduced. Limited social services and secondary enterprise is strikingly evident in Gary. In a city of over 102,000 residents, there is one, 583-bed medical facility, Methodist Hospital; St. Mary Medical Center closed in early 1990 (a new 361-bed Southlake branch of Methodist Hospital was opened in 1971 and is located approximately 45 minutes from downtown Gary in Merrillville).[10] There are 12 dentists, 5 nursing homes, and 8 available ambulances to support the entire city. When primary safety institutions are considered, there are about 290 regular law enforcement officers and 213 firepersons. The city hosts 4 bank chains (most with at least two branches),[11] 1 savings and loan, and 4 credit unions (the latter facilities are all affiliated with local steel mills). There are no retail chains or mega stores, no large national or regional grocery stores, no major hotel chains or large entertainment venues, and one theatre.[12] The nearest alternative establishments are located in the suburban areas of Merrillville, Portage, and Hobart.

In addition to fewer manufacturing jobs (about 7,500 steel mill jobs in 2002), fewer business headquarters are now located in Gary. Nationwide, 33 percent of persons hold managerial and professional positions; representation is 13 percentage points lower in Gary. However, the number of Gary service employees (24.0 percent) exceeds national and state averages of 14.9 percent (both), as well as those found in neighboring cities and towns of Merrillville, Portage, and Indianapolis (14.9, 16.8, 14.9 percent, respectively).[13] Gary Chamber of Commerce 2002 figures identify the largest city employers as follows; U.S. Steel-USX Corp/Gary Works (6,800 employees), School City of Gary (3,163 employees), Methodist Hospital Northlake (3,081 employees), the City of Gary (2,319 employees), Trump Casino (1,300 employees), and Majestic Star Casino (1,050 employees). Five of the six establishments (save Methodist Hospital) are unionized.[14] The type and number of jobs are also correlated with the number of residents who receive public assistance. Figures compiled by the Indiana University Kelly School of Business show that, in 2001, about 9,210 Gary families received monthly welfare support (TANF), there were 54,507 food stamp recipients that same year, and 37,173 free or reduced fee lunch recipients in 2002. Of the about 8,870 births in the city in 2000, 13.0 percent or 1,153 were to teenagers.[15]

A lower tax base and subsequent fewer funds for public schools mean that the city lags behind national and state educational benchmarks. For example, although the national SAT score is 897 and 867 for Indiana overall, the mean score for Gary is 677.[16] There are 29, 6, and 6 elementary, middle, and high schools, respectively; there are no private schools in the city. Current census data shows that only 18.8 percent of the city's population 18–24 years old are enrolled in college or graduate school: comparable figures for the U.S., Indiana,

Indianapolis, Merrillville, and Portage are, respectively; 34.0 percent, 34.3 percent, 24.7 percent, 34.9 percent, and 26.4 percent. Over 80 percent of the population aged 25 or more in these same locations have earned high school diplomas or higher; the figure is 73 percent for Gary. And twice as many persons aged 25 years or older in these areas have bachelor's degrees or greater as compared to Gary residents.[17] Given that models attributing lower educational attainment among racial/ethnic minorities to issues of personal accountability and lack of aspiration have been greatly discounted[18] minority students, particularly African Americans, have been found to acknowledge the importance of education and esteem their high-achieving peers,[19] the substantially lower educational markers found among Gary residents suggest systemic problems more than deficiencies among residents. Nonetheless, the implications for gainful employment and quality of life issues are clear. Wilson (1996) references one study that supports the relationship between education and employment challenges in urban settings:

> One-quarter of all male high school dropouts had no official employment at all in 1992. And of those with high school diplomas, one out of ten did not hold a job in 1993, up sharply from 1967 when only one out of fifty reported that he had no job throughout the year. (p. 26)

The decline in inner-city employment opportunities over the past two decades, combined with an increase in the population, especially of young African American males, ill-prepared to compete for positions in new urban growth sectors, and shifts in cities from "centers of production and distribution of goods to centers of administration, finance, and information exchange" (Kasarda 1989, p. 28) have taken their toll on African American employment potential. Thus the negative effects of disinvestment and deindustrialization are expected to be most dramatic for Gary's African American residents without minimal education.

Negative effects of large-scale economic upheaval are also apparent on property values. As the primary form of wealth for many Americans, the value of owner-occupied housing can offset other costs associated with urban living. Thus owning a home becomes an example of achieving an important dimension of the "American Dream," as well as a means of establishing creditworthiness and accumulating wealth for oneself and children. Research by scholars such as Hochschild (1995) and Wilson (1996) suggest that belief in the "American Dream" is still common among historically impoverished groups. However, according to the latter author, economic and social disorganization in urban neighborhoods undermine the housing market for those who are able and desire to own homes:

> The more rapid the neighborhood deterioration, the greater the institutional disinvestment. In the 1960s and 1970s, neighborhoods plagued by heavy abandonment were frequently "redlined"; this paralyzed the housing market, lowered property values, and further encouraged landlord abandonment. The enactment of federal and state community reinvestment legislation in the 1970s curbed the practice of open redlining. Nonetheless, 'prudent lenders will exercise increased caution in advancing mortgages.' (pp. 44–46)

The telling implications of disinvestment are also evident in Gary when property values are compared to other locations. The 2000 national median value of owner-occupied units is $119,600. The figure is $94,300 in Indiana, $98,200 in Indianapolis, $101,300 in Merrillville, and $109,000 in Portage. The median unit value in Gary is $53,400.[20] Current inner-city housing constraints involving covert redlining, the lack of low-cost homes, foreclosures, gentrification, and predatory mortgage lending also represent potentially greater costs for people of modest means. Given that, for most Americans, acquiring the needed resources to purchase a home requires delayed gratification, personal and family sacrifice, and frugality, these statistics suggest that a home may not only be more costly to maintain for some residents in areas such as Gary, but may not provide them with the economic benefits typically associated with home ownership that their suburban counterparts enjoy.[21]

New Uses of Old Spaces

Current urban renewal efforts are resulting in the gradual demolition of abandoned buildings and dilapidated infrastructure. Under the leadership of Mayor Scott L. King, city officials have also responded by sponsoring events at the newly remodeled Genesis Convention Center (opened in 1981),[22] increasing marketing of the Miller lakeshore beach area, developing a new 5,800-seat baseball stadium (including a Benigan's Restaurant) and Media Center in the downtown area, and sponsoring "The Panacea," a news magazine show highlighting positive features of the city and surrounding areas. Increased economic and social benefits are expected as a result of the new Gary Steelheads professional basketball and Gary Southshore Railcats minor league baseball franchises. As evidenced in other cities, a sports franchise can generate revenue both from residents and national interest, as well as engender camaraderie, morale, and sportsmanship among residents. However, it remains to be seen whether these teams will generate the type of economic and noneconomic benefits franchises have provided in other cities, or whether the costs will outweigh the benefits. Logan and Molotch (1987) note:

> Atlanta's professional sports organizations have been estimated to be worth over $60 million annually to the local economy. But a local team does much more than the direct expenditures imply: it helps a city's visibility, putting it 'on the map' as a 'big league city,' making it more noticeable to all, including those making investment decisions. It is one of 'the visible badges of urban maturity.' (p. 80)

However, the authors acknowledge that not all such endeavors have fared as well:

> New Orleans used the development of the Superdome 'to set the stage for a tourist-based growth strategy for the future development of downtown.' The facility ended up costing $165 million (instead of the projected $35 million), and has had large annual operating losses—all absorbed by the state government. (p. 79)

Other major related infrastructure improvements include the Gary-Chicago airport and new condominiums in the downtown area near the Adam Benjamin Metro Center. Organized efforts also exist to stimulate enterprise in the downtown area and provide business-related resources to residents. Under the Urban Enterprise Zone, incentive programs that include financial and tax credits, employer credits, tax abatements, and other perks are available to residents who start businesses in the city's empowerment zone.[23] In addition, The Lakeshore Employment Training Partnership (LETP) provides job-training and educational testing services to identify and improve skills of current and potential employees for existing businesses.

Such efforts to stimulate enterprise, support existing businesses, and better prepare residents to be more competitive are viewed as responses to the current industrial and commercial inactivity in downtown Gary.

Truck terminals represent a secondary, somewhat less visible business enterprise. Because Gary provides access to several major thoroughfares, including Interstates 65 and 94 and is less than 300 miles from major cities such as Chicago, Toledo, Indianapolis, Detroit, and St. Louis, it has become a logical stopping point for long-distance truck drivers. There are currently six truck terminals in the city.[24] The inherent transient nature of this mode of driving, as well as possible concerns about drug-trafficking and prostitution associated with the trucking industry[25] must be weighed against the potential benefits of revenue for the city and jobs for residents, particularly, the working class.

Tourism and Gaming

Some consider recent tourism efforts linked to casino boat entertainment to be a viable revitalization industry in Gary. In the 1990s, five independent casinos, Trump, Majestic Star, Harris, Horseshoe, and Blue-Chip, began to service the greater Indiana area; Trump and Majestic Star casinos are located in Gary proper. Casino entertainment and its partnerships represent potential benefits to the city due to employment opportunities, job training, capital influx, infrastructure improvements, scholarship programs, and residual revenue from secondary businesses. According to 2002 Gary Chamber of Commerce figures, Trump and Majestic Star casinos are the fifth and sixth largest employers in the Gary area.

According to Trump's Casino and Hotel's economic agreement, they, "made a significant commitment to invest a minimum of $153,000,000 for economic development in Gary and Northwest Indiana throughout the year 2001."[26] In addition to lodging revenue from the 300-room hotel opened in 1998, the casino pays sales and property taxes to local and state government and generates secondary revenue for contractors and vendors. The organization also provides scholarships to graduating high school students, purchased twelve police automobiles, and contributes to various local charities and community improvement efforts. The casino was intricately involved in the construction of the downtown baseball stadium and related infrastructure improvements. It is estimated that the casino has an annual payroll of about $29.3 million. When specific financial inflow to Gary is considered based on jobs for residents and taxes, roughly 45.3 percent of the Trump workforce are Gary residents (66.7 percent are minorities and about 58.7 percent are females).[27] Further review of the employment structure shows that the majority of positions are held in gaming (340 employees as of Dec. 31, 2000), slots (115), security (102), and casino cage (122), and the average hourly wage for these posts is about $7.00–$8.00. Thus, although the casino is located in Gary, the majority of the employed are nonresidents and of those Gary residents employed by Trump casino, most hold lower-paying positions. Additional casino-provided data show greater percent tax outlays to the state as compared to Gary:

> As of December 31, 2000 Trump has paid $145.4 million in wagering taxes of which $24.2 million was allocated to the City of Gary, and $121.2 million was retained in the Indiana State Treasury to reduce income taxes, property taxes, and automobile excise taxes state wide. Throughout the year 2000, Trump paid $28.6 million in wagering taxes, with $4.8 million going to the City of Gary and $23.8 million to the state. (Trump Casino 2001 Progress Report, p. 6)

Since the Trump enterprise began, roughly $64.5 million in wagering and admissions taxes and license fees were disbursed to the City of Gary; the State of Indiana received about $137.2 million during that same period. Thus of the over $200 million allocated to the city and state, Gary received about 38.9 percent. In addition, about $155.8 million has been allocated for city and statewide economic development.

The Majestic Star Casino opened in June 1996 and currently expenses are approximately $160,682,000 in salaries and benefits; the average yearly wage and benefit package is $28,000. About 70 percent and 61 percent of employees are minorities and female, respectively.[28] From June 1996 to December 31, 2000, the casino paid about $140.5 million in direct gaming taxes to the State of Indiana, $6 million in property and sales taxes, and $2.6 million to the State of Indiana to subsidize state policing due to casino activity. In addition, of the $42.6 million in admissions taxes[29] for this same period, $14.2 million was paid to the city, $14.2 million to Lake Country, and the remainder to other state organizations.[30] A summary of the economic inlays for this gaming enterprise is as follows:

> Since June 6, 1996 through December 2000, The Company
> Majestic Star has paid in excess of $140.5 million to the
> State of Indiana in the form of gaming and admissions taxes.
> Of this amount, approximately $39 million was returned to
> the City of Gary by the State of Indiana. This amount is in
> addition to the $19.9 million in economic payments remitted
> directly to the City of Gary by Majestic Star Casino. The
> City of Gary to date has allocated approximately $44 million
> dollars received on behalf of Majestic Star Casino. (Majestic
> Star Casino Community Impact Report, p. 8)

Since Majestic Star's inception, Gary has directly or indirectly received about 31.3 percent of the remits based on state and local gaming agreements. And although research suggests the importance of
education in improving the life chances of the poor, of the amounts
designated for city enhancements (such as infrastructure and municipal development), less than $1 million was allocated for educa-
tion development.[31]

While the short-term economic benefits of casino entertainment
appear to be positive, it remains to be determined whether, in the
long-run, this mode of tourism is actually an asset or a liability. This
enterprise represents a potential liability, if residents attempt to address their economic problems by gambling, the city experiences increased gambling-related crimes, or the somewhat precarious social
fabric of the city declines. Studies show the economic and social
problems associated with casino entertainment and gambling that
take the form of addiction,[32] benefits to owners and not residents,[33]
regulatory problems,[34] casino-related crime, [35] and the tendency of
some casinos to market to the elderly or underaged.[36] Much of the
research on the subject illustrates how nonlocals and sponsoring
businesses benefit most while, overall, residents are often at a loss.[37]

It is clear that both Trump and Majestic Star[38] enterprises provide primary and secondary economic benefits to the city. Structural
speculators were able to develop alliances within the city, and most
importantly, at the state level, to support this business venture. And
although the resulting city enhancements and renovations do improve and beautify the city and quality of life for some residents (example, Genesis Center renovations, infrastructure improvements),
as active entrepreneurs and structural speculators realize, the
changes also make the area more appealing to potential gaming
customers and thus inevitably benefit the casinos. And, although
Gary bears the brunt of most costs (water pollution, possible gam-

bling related crime, potential increased gambling by residents), the state of Indiana receives a greater percentage of gaming-related taxes as a result of the enterprise, and nonresidents benefit more from job creation than do persons from Gary. Furthermore, through state-heavy allocations of these gaming-related taxes, Indiana appears to be *spreading the wealth* to other locales, but few of the costs.

Predicting the Benefits of Urban Renewal

Only time will tell whether recent efforts at economic revitalization in Gary are successful. Annual, marketing-friendly progress reports tend to focus on aggregate revenue figures that often mask indirect costs to the city and residents in the form of air and water pollution, infrastructure abuse, and crime that can ultimately result in further economic and social problems. Urban improvement efforts, especially those associated with tourism and attracting new, large businesses and private investors will also be tied to perceptions of the city.[39] This means addressing negative national and regional perceptions of the city that, some posit, are media driven and influenced by depictions from statewide, predominately White political detractors.[40] Media influence cannot be underestimated. Images of the angry, violent African American male and crime-infested crack neighborhoods resonate with many persons outside urban settings who are informed about racial and ethnic minorities largely by the evening news and television shows (refer to the *Media in Black and White* [1997] by Dennis and Pease for various analyses of purposed presentations of minorities in various mediums). Such incomplete portraits, combined with the very real results of poverty that cannot be ignored,[41] often encourage fear in a society seemingly plagued with concerns about violence from without and within.[42]

A comprehensive cost-benefit analysis of potential and existing business ventures in Gary must consider economic as well as noneconomic indices for entrepreneurial *elites*, whose business decisions are largely driven by profit margins and *ordinary* citizens concerned about their cities, neighborhoods, and families. Avenues must also exist for ordinary citizens who desire to become entrepreneurs and for elites to champion community services efforts and philanthropy. Squires (1994) provides evidence of successful business ventures between the "elite and ordinary" that benefit both. This latter option helps insure that benefits as well as costs are shared. It is also important to assess whether business ventures provide gainful employment to residents and the number and types of such jobs, whether and how the social climate and secondary businesses are affected, and the impact on infrastructure. However, whether urban renewal efforts are achieved, Gary's economic revitalization will continue to be undermined, as long as the majority of its revenue is generated by business owners who are nonresidents, and income generated by its predominately African American residents fails to turn over in the city. And a significant percentage of the city's revenue will continue to turn over outside its boundaries, as long as residents must travel to suburban locales for the majority of their shopping and service needs.

Figure 2.1. Downtown Gary. Genesis Convention Center, Gary, IN (2003)

Figure 2.2. Downtown Gary. Broadway, Gary, IN (2003)

Figure 2.3. Downtown Gary. Broadway, Gary, IN (2003)

Figure 2.4. Downtown Gary. Broadway, Gary, IN (2003)

Figure 2.5. Service in the City. Downtown Bus-Rail Station (2003)

Figure 2.6. Urban Decay. Fifth Avenue, Gary, IN (2003)

55

Figure 2.7. Urban Decay. Fifth Avenue, Gary, IN (2003)

Figure 2.8. Urban Renewal Efforts. New Sports Stadium in downtown Gary, IN (2003)

57

Figure 2.9. Urban Renewal Efforts. Site of new Emerson Townhouses in downtown Gary, IN (2003)

Figure 2.10. Urban Renewal Efforts. Site of new elementary school in Gary, IN (2003)

Figure 2.11. Urban Renewal Efforts. Gary Southshore Railcats Stadium, Gary, IN (2003)

60

Figure 2.12. Gary's Business Enterprise. Village Shopping Center, Gary, IN (2003)

Figure 2.13. Gary's Business Enterprise. Grocery store in Gary, IN (2003)

Figure 2.14. Gary's Business Enterprise. Grocery Store in Gary, IN (2003)

Figure 2.15. Gary's Business Enterprise. Discount Store in Black Oak (2003).

Figure 2.16. Casino Entertainment. Trump Casino, Gary, IN (2003)

Figure 2.17. "Southlake" Mall, Merrillville, IN (2003)

#### CHAPTER THREE

Differential Goods and Services
to Feed a Family:
Who Pays the Costs?

The day-to-day challenges and choices in urban settings are directly correlated with historical and current structural changes. As presented earlier, factors such as globalization, the shift from manufacturing to service occupations, out-migration of working-class and middle-class families, both African American and White, and businesses, increased social and residential isolation and segregation, and discrimination are primary factors that have resulted in increased urban poverty. And although residents in urban areas such as Gary, Indiana, may not be fully aware of all the intricacies of economic restructuring, they are acutely aware of its toll on their cities and neighborhoods.

In William Julius Wilson's book *When Work Disappears*, Chicago urban residents wax nostalgic about the demise of neighborhoods that were once economically and socially stable and organized. Residents now speak of the inability to locate gainful employment, decline in infrastructure, increased crime, and changes in the norms and values of their neighbors. Their responses overshadow the observations of even the most astute ethnographers and are all the more harrowing because they are lived experiences. Although not the focus of Wilson's study, one of the direct results of the exodus of manufacturing plants in Chicago inner cities was the subsequent decline in local enterprise. According to Wilson's observations: "In 1986, North Lawndale, with a population of over 66,000, had only one bank, and one supermarket; but it was also home to forty-eight state lottery agents, fifty currency exchanges, and ninety-nine licensed liquor stores and bars."[1] Wilson's observation about the exodus of such enterprise is the focus of this chapter.

This chapter assesses dimensions of structure and agency within the context of urban poverty by examining the quantity and quality of service providers in Gary, Indiana, and surrounding areas, how their absence or presence influence shopping choices, and the economic and noneconomic costs residents incur. Of particular interest is the availability of and access to basic food staples and services, whether resources differ based on the racial composition and poverty level in these areas, and the choices and strategies residents use to feed their families. Using census data, pricing data, and direct observations of area service providers, as well as in-depth interviews with African American, White, and Hispanic residents from varied socioeconomic statuses, findings show that, regardless of the racial makeup, residents in more impoverished urban areas incur a variety of economic and noneconomic costs and often make industrious decisions to secure food stuffs and other staples. This analysis of one dimension of urban living is in the tradition of a small body of research that focuses on detailed accounts of various costs and budgeting problems incurred by the poor and near poor.

The chapter concentrates on access, availability, and costs of basic goods and services at grocery stores. I focus on this topic, because food expenses are necessities for all families, regardless of race, class, or household composition. I examine the following types of questions: what types of grocery stores are located in Gary? How do these establishments fare when compared to their counterparts in a nearby city and town? What types of economic and noneconomic costs do Gary residents incur for basic food and staples? Does the poverty level of the area affect the economic and noneconomic costs incurred? Do available resources differ in predominately African American versus predominately White neighboring areas? Will costs differ in areas with different racial/ethnic make-ups, but similar poverty levels? Will differences exist between the percentages of median household income spent on food for each city/town? What choices, strategies, and coping mechanisms do residents use in light of structural constraints? Are there sociopsychological implications of exposure to certain costs?

In summary, this chapter examines the number, types, and quality of grocery stores in the areas and whether they differ based on: 1) poverty level in the area and racial composition and 2) city and suburban locale. Next, expenditures associated with "making groceries" for a family of three in these areas are itemized by comparing hypothetical purchases at stores to demonstrate cost differentials. Substantive comparisons are also made between expenditures and median household incomes for each city/town. Responses and strategies from residents and direct observation are used to illustrate some of the types of economic as well as noneconomic costs that are incurred. I conclude the chapter with a discussion regarding how these findings can inform state and local municipalities that must address the relationship between poverty, race/ethnicity, and service providers on both a short and long-term basis.

Adapting to Poor Urban Conditions

Research on adaptivity in urban centers focuses on the choices, albeit limited, residents make in the face of poverty. This body of research identifies social forces that limit economic stability and mobility and ways residents negotiate uncertainty, compares and contrasts experiences across racial/ethnic groups, and profiles strategies using rich descriptions of daily challenges. The experiences of impoverished women in general, and women of color, in particular, are often central. Scholarship suggests the importance of female-led, domestic networks and extended families that provide financial and emotional support by sharing public aid, goods, and services and providing informal day care. Women are also known to stretch their incomes via informal jobs, obtain money from community groups and charities or live in communal family units to share expenses and childcare responsibilities.[2] Agency for men and women alike can take the form of a willingness to work at low-wage jobs, delay gratification, and make sound decisions based on economic constraints.[3] More recent findings show various tiers of helping and social services in urban, poor communities, where residents make choices about contact and cooperation based on mutual exchange over time.[4] As reported in earlier chapters, deficiency theories directly or indirectly posit limited self-efficacy and poor choices on the part of the impoverished.[5] The few studies specific to Gary, Indiana, focus on the political choices of residents or their limited economic agency as a result of poverty.[6]

Several touchstone studies speak directly to this chapter's emphasis on specific, itemized household expenses and strategies. In "Work, Welfare, and Single Mothers' Economic Survival Strategies," Edin and Lein (1996) shed light on the problems of 379 White and African American single mothers. All receive welfare—some are employed in the underground economy—all are poor. The mothers use various strategies to *stretch* their incomes such as "generating extra income by working at side jobs and by obtaining cash from network members, community groups, and local charities" (p. 254). Without such alliances, the survival of most of their families would be questionable. The authors' work extends traditional research on welfare and the importance of welfare reform by tabulating basic household expenses and income to show the economic constraints poor women experience and coping mechanisms they employ. The former scholar's earlier work specific to the Chicago area provides similar findings regarding the inadequacies of the welfare system and the length women will go to feed their children.[7] Both studies are singular in their attempt to detail, as well as quantify, some of the costs associated with sustaining a poor family. Furthermore, by chronicling the experiences of impoverished single mothers in terms of household budgets and "dollars and cents," they present a reality to which many readers can relate.

Similarly, Jarrett (1994) acknowledges the economic challenges faced by single parent African American women and focuses on the adaptive features of their families. The author suggests that the current desire to explain poverty and female householders using cultural versus structural frameworks fails to acknowledge the agency of the women, as well as their ability to create alternative family patterns in response to economic marginality. By presenting the nuclear family as the standard, Jarrett asserts that researchers fail to recognize the strengths found in some poor, single-parent families. Furthermore, she uncovers mainstream dictates toward traditional marriage and family juxtaposed with a reality that a lack of economically stable potential partners and other negative experiences make such dreams implausible. In these instances, women adapt by taking on the role of father and mother, tapping into resources via extended families, and accepting limited, in-kind support from men who are willing to provide paternal assistance. The themes of coping mechanisms, survival strategies, and common sense decisions based on limited options resonate throughout the three studies. This chapter is in the spirit of their work on detailed accounts of choices, costs, and strategies to acquire basic goods and services—especially for parents who are attempting to provide for children.

Feeding a Family

Store Locations and Neighborhood Poverty Concentration

References to Gary and the predominately White district of Black Oak,[8] as compared to the neighboring city and town of Merrillville and Portage (reported in Table 2.1) present a portrait of urban decay forwarded in Catlin's (1993) and earlier studies on inner-city challenges. These areas were selected as points of comparison, because they are referenced in subsequent comparative analyses on retailers and businesses, and they are inextricably linked economically.

In Map 3.1, I present a typology of the grocery stores frequented by respondents.[9] Store locations are provided, as well as poverty rates of the neighborhoods (i.e., census tracts) in which each store resides. The two values reflect the percentage of families and individuals, respectively, living below the poverty level within a given neighborhood. A review of the typology provides an example of concentrated neighborhood poverty in Gary as compared to nearby areas. Grocery stores located in close proximity to downtown Gary tend to be part of moderately or ghetto-poor neighborhoods. Poverty rates decline as locations move further away from Gary. For example, Store 3, near downtown Gary, is located in a ghetto-poor neighborhood with family and individual poverty rates of 40.9 percent and 46.8 percent, respectively; Store 4, approximately thirteen blocks away, is part of a moderately poor neighborhood (27.6 and 30.0 percent), and lower poverty is evident in the neighborhood surrounding Store 1 (13.4 and 15.7 percent); neighborhood poverty is minimal in the Merrillville area in which Store 13 is situated (2.8 and 5.0 percent). The two Black Oak stores, like many of the Gary grocery establishments under review, are also located in moderately poor neighborhoods. What remains to be determined is whether concentrated neighborhood poverty and race/ethnicity affect important features of the grocery stores respondents frequent.

Grocery Store Costs: Product Line Comparisons and General Trends

Structural constraints are shown to influence grocery shopping choices and prices for Gary residents. Prices and total costs for: 1) available items and 2) all items[10] are presented in Table 3.1. A direct relationship exists between whether a store is in Gary, Indiana, and higher overall grocery prices (unless specifically mentioned, further reference to Gary includes the Black Oak district). Neighborhood poverty rates are also directly related to higher costs. Prices are generally cheaper as one travels away from the city and are cheapest in predominately White, suburban areas. The relationship between location and economic costs are evident. Although the amount varies based on family size and level of extended family support, most persons spend about $296.00 monthly on groceries. However, Gary residents spend substantially more money on groceries as compared to their counterparts outside the city ($320.08 versus $272.25).

However, prices do not differ based on the racial composition of similarly impoverished areas *within* the city of Gary. Total costs for the two stores in Black Oak (mainly White residents) are not significantly different from those in similarly economically constrained areas of the city where the majority of residents are African American. At first glance, it may appear that two Gary stores have the lowest prices to feed a family of three (Store 8 at $34.26 and Store 11 at $29.10 for available items only). Further review shows that their lower relative total prices are because they do not sell produce or fruit. When total prices are compared based on all items under study, in general, stores within the city tend to have the highest prices and mega or "superstores" outside the city tend to be most affordable. The highest prices for all items are found at Store 8 ($68.89), located in Gary; the lowest prices are found at Store 17 ($47.65), located in Portage. In addition,

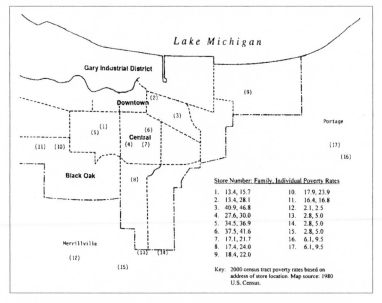

Map 3.1. Store Location and Neighborhood Family and Individual Poverty Rates: Gary, IN, and Surrounding Area.

Table 3.1
Grocery Prices to Feed a Family of Three for Stores in Gary, Black Oak, Merrillville, and Portage, Indiana
(N=17)

Stores	1	2	3	4	5	6	7	8
General Profile								
Location/Size	G(S)	G(M)	G(M)	G(S)	G(M)	G(S)	G(M)	G(S)
Staples								
Milk (gallon)	2.29	2.99	2.99	2.99	2.97	2.99	2.89	2.99
Bread (loaf)	.99	.89	1.19	1.99	1.49	1.19	.50	.99
Margarine (4)	.79	.99	.99	.79	.82	.69	.89	1.00
Eggs (lg. dozen)	N	.99	.89	.99	.79	.99	.99	1.29
Fresh Fruit								
Apples (5 lbs)	N	2.95	1.48	N	2.98	1.65	3.95	N
Oranges (5 lbs)	N	2.95	3.11	N	3.74	3.32	3.45	N
Grains								
C. Flakes (18 oz)	2.99	3.99	1.59	2.50	1.12	4.79	3.99	3.59
Oatmeal (42 oz)	2.29	1.99	3.79	3.48	1.19	2.49	1.39	N
Sugar (5 lbs)	2.99	2.89	2.29	1.99	1.89	2.39	1.89	2.39
Flour (5 lbs)	1.99	1.99	1.89	1.59	1.49	2.29	1.49	2.19
Canned Goods								
Tuna (6 oz)	.89	1.19	.69	.69	.69	.99	.99	.99
Beans (14.5 oz)	.59	.89	.50	.69	.63	.89	.69	.99
Carrots (14.5 oz)	.79	.59	.99	N	.69	.89	.69	.99
Corn (14.5 oz)	.89	.79	.59	.59	.69	.89	.59	.99
Fresh Meat								
Chicken (1 lb)	.89	.89	.99	1.29	.69	.99	.40	N
Gr. Beef (1 lb)	1.39	1.79	1.79	1.40	1.49	1.29	N	N

Total Costs to Feed a Family of 3 (in dollars):

	1	2	3	4	5	6	7	8
Available Items:	53.05	67.14	63.27	56.08	55.54	64.41	40.66	34.26
All Items:	60.72	same	same	65.65	same	same	56.66	68.89

Notes: Location/Size: G=Gary, B=Black Oak, M=Merrillville, P=Portage: S=Small, M=Medium, L=Large: N=None (store did not sell that item)

All Items: Total to feed family of 3 based on entire list and substituting average prices for missing store products (in brackets)

Detailed definitions are provided in the appendix.

(continued)

Table 3.1 (*continued*)
Grocery Prices to Feed a Family of Three for Stores in Gary, Black Oak, Merrillville, and Portage, Indiana (N=17)

Stores	9	10	11	12	13	14	15	16	17
General Profile									
Location/Size	G(M)	B(S)	B(S)	M(L)	M(L)	M(L)	M(L)	P(L)	P(L)
Staples									
Milk (gallon)	2.49	1.99	2.99	2.39	2.49	2.29	2.29	2.14	2.29
Bread (loaf)	.99	.99	1.19	.99	.45	.99	1.69	.89	1.19
Margarine (4)	.75	.99	.99	.75	.75	.47	.69	.73	.69
Eggs (lg. dozen).	.89	1.29	.99	.89	.79	.89	.75	.69	.89 [.94]
Fresh Fruit									
Apples (5 lbs)	2.99	6.00	N	3.39	3.49	2.50	3.00	3.35	2.50[3.09]
Oranges (5 lbs)	3.36	5.00	N	4.15	3.99	3.61	3.33	3.11	4.15[3.64]
Grains									
C. Flakes (18 oz)	1.49	1.93	2.24	1.79	1.49	1.55	1.55	1.29	1.39
Oatmeal (42 oz)	1.99	1.69	N	1.89	1.39	1.79	2.29	1.86	1.79[2.09]
Sugar (5 lbs)	1.39	1.99	2.59	1.79	1.49	1.29	1.69	1.58	1.29
Flour (5 lbs)	1.19	2.49	1.69	1.19	.99	.79	1.39	.97	.79
Canned Goods									
Tuna (6 oz)	1.19	1.29	.99	.69	.39	.59	.51	.59	.50
Beans (14.5 oz.	.39	.79	.79	.39	.33	.49	.37	.58	.50
Carrots (14.5 oz).	.62	.79	.79	.89	.33	.33	.65	.50	.85[.71]
Corn (14.5 oz)	.39	.89	.49	.39	.33	.29	.37	.39	.50
Fresh Meat									
Chicken (1 lb)	2.00	.79	N	1.09	.89	.69	1.19	.98	.89[.98]
Gr. Beef (1 lb)	1.39	1.29	N	1.09	1.59	1.59	1.79	1.99	.89[1.60]

Total Costs to Feed a Family of 3 (in dollars):

Available Items:	65.27	63.18	29.10	53.84	50.58	49.05	60.05	57.58	47.65
All Items:	same	same	63.72	same	same	same	same	same	same

Notes: Location/Size: G=Gary, B=Black Oak, M=Merrillville, P=Portage: S=Small, M=Medium, L=Large: N=None (store did not sell that item)

All Items: Total to feed family of 3 based on entire list and substituting average prices for missing store products (in brackets)

Detailed definitions are provided in the appendix.

the *highest priced* store outside of Gary (Store 15, $60.05) is still cheaper than most of the stores in Gary.

Lower overall prices at suburban locations tend to be driven by the *lower relative costs* of canned goods and staples. Stores outside Gary also offer more goods and services. Options include greater numbers of name brand products and, in most cases, availability of lower-priced generic product lines. And while Gary stores do provide some generic products, none have generic product lines as do stores in Merrillville and Portage. Stores in Gary also have limited or no options in terms of fresh produce and fruit. Although every store in Merrillville and Portage sells fruit and produce, Stores 1, 4, 8, and 11 in Gary do not sell fruit, and the latter two stores do not sell produce. In several instances, when fruit is available (Store 10), prices are substantially higher. And in comparison to the other stores under study, a relatively higher number of aisles in the Gary and Black Oak locations are dedicated to inexpensive, less healthy snack items, such as potato chips, candy, donuts, cookies, and canned soda.

However, some of the smaller stores in Gary have reputations for certain products and/or prices. Thus residents with access to cars can save money or get better quality goods and services on selected items outside their own neighborhoods. For example, Store 1 has limited items in general and higher overall prices, but is mentioned by two respondents as a good place to "buy good, cheap meat," and Store 11 is known for selling cigarettes cheaper than many other stores. By establishing a reputation for specific products, some locations have created somewhat of a market niche that benefits residents who travel there specifically to purchase certain items, but may result in overall higher costs for less mobile customers who must purchase higher-priced staples there as well. Stores that offer a wider array of goods and services to enable persons to maximize their dollars are located in White suburban areas; there are no such comparable stores in Gary.

Although substantial price differentials are apparent for stores inside and outside the city, it is important to assess whether store prices are significantly different from each other (see Table 3.2). As mentioned earlier, some stores in Gary do not sell certain products; this had to be taken into consideration during significance testing. Therefore, results are presented first for those stores for which all items were available (12 stores), followed by results for the entire sample of 17 stores using mean prices for unavailable items. As noted in Panel 1 of Table 3.2, total prices are significantly different based on store size, overall racial composition of locale, and when

Table 3.2
Mean, ANOVA, and Household Percentage Results for Grocery Prices by Store Size, Race, and Race* Area in Gary, Black Oak, Merrillville, and Portage, IN

Panel 1: Stores w/All Items (N=12)	All Items	Available Items	Sig.
Store Size:			
Small (N=2)	63.80 (0.87)	na	All items**
Medium (N=4)	62.81 (5.09)	na	
Large (N=6)	53.13 (4.93)	na	
Racial Make-up of Area:			
African American (N=5)	63.13 (4.47)	na	All items**
White (N=7)	54.56 (5.89)	na	
Race and Area:			
Gary: Not Black Oak (N=5)	63.13 (4.47)	na	All items**
Gary: Black Oak (N=1)	63.18 (—)	na	
Merrillville & Portage (N=6)	53.13 (4.93)	na	

Panel 2: All Stores (N=17)	All Items+	Available Items	Sig.
Store Size:			
Small (N=6)	64.43 (2.73)	50.01 (14.91)	All items**
Medium (N=5)	61.58 (5.20)	58.38 (10.84)	
Large (N=6)	53.13 (4.93)	53.13 (4.93)	
Racial Make-up of Area:			
African American (N=9)	63.06 (4.57)	55.20 (11.45)	All items**
White (N=8)	55.71 (6.34)	51.38 (10.52)	
Race and Area:			
Gary: Not Black Oak (N=9)	63.06 (4.57)	55.52 (11.45)	All items**
Gary: Black Oak (N=2)	63.45 (0.38)	46.14 (24.10)	
Merrillville & Portage (N=6)	53.13 (4.93)	53.13 (4.93)	

Panel 3: Annual Food Expenditures as a Percentage of Median Household Income (2000)

Area	Median HH Income	Mean Annual Cost	% HH Income
Gary (N=11)	$27,195	$3,030 (all items)	11.14$^{\psi}$
		$2,583 (available items)	9.50
Black Oak (N=2)	$31,156	$3,046 (all items)	9.78
		$2,215 (available items)	7.11
Merrillville (N=4)	$49,545	$2,456	4.96
Portage (N=2)	$47,500	$2,528	5.32

Note: Standard deviations provided in parentheses. **Significant at $p<0.05$ based on ANOVA results. +Mean values are substituted for missing products to calculate total price. Mean annual cost in Panel 3 calculated by multiplying the average costs of the stores in each area by 48 (weeks). Panel 3 store costs for Gary also include the two Black Oak stores. ψBecause it would also be useful to determine how much further median income in Gary would stretch based on food expenditures in the three other areas, I calculate the % HH Income using the mean annual costs from the three other sites and the Gary median income figure ($27,195). Gary residents who purchase food (all items) in Black Oak, Merrillville, or Portage would spend 11.20%, 9.03%, and 9.30%, respectively, of their median household income as compared to the 11.14% incurred by shopping in Gary.

race and local are considered simultaneously. Thus larger stores (average price of $53.13) tend to provide lower prices than their smaller ($63.80) and medium ($62.81) sized counterparts. In addition, stores in predominately White, mainly suburban areas have lower prices ($54.56) as compared to those in areas where the majority of residents are African American ($63.13). However, no significant difference in total prices is apparent between stores in Black Oak and other areas in Gary.

When all 17 stores are considered in Panel 2, findings show a significant difference between the prices for the entire list, "All Items," based on store size (Note: cross-store comparisons for "Available Items" costs are insignificant and are influenced by the absence of certain products in Gary stores.). In addition, statistically significant differences continue to exist based on the overall racial composition of the areas in which the stores reside. Lastly, an examination of the prices by race *and* locale show no significant difference between costs for available items, but continued differences when all 16 items are considered. And prices for stores in White suburbs are lower than both those in Gary and Black Oak.

Because the small sample sizes and subsequent smaller subgroups preclude definitive statements about the statistical results, it is important to determine whether these cost differentials translate to more tangible differences. In Panel 3, I cost out these weekly amounts for an entire year and compare them to the median household incomes in the four areas to compare the percentage of household income spent on food. Even when comparisons are made based only on "available items," shopping at Gary stores means that almost twice as much of the median household income of Gary residents would be spent on food (9.50 percent) as compared to Merrillville (4.96 percent) and Portage (5.32 percent). A similar pattern is evident for Black Oak shoppers, and percentage differences between the four sites are even more substantial when all food items are considered. It is also important to assess whether median income in Gary would, in fact, *stretch further* if residents shopped in the three other areas. Hence I calculate the percentage of household income based on the mean annual food costs from the three other sites and the Gary median income figure ($27,195) by taking the ratio of these figures provided in Panel 3. Findings suggest that Gary residents who would purchase food (all items) in Black Oak, Merrillville, or Portage would spend 11.20 percent, 9.03 percent, and 9.30 percent of their median household income, respectively, as compared to the 11.14 percent incurred by shopping in Gary. Thus Gary residents with lower incomes

Table 3.3
Direct Observation Results of Stores' Characteristics

Store Profile	1	2	3	4	5	6	7	8	9
Location/Size	G(S)	G(M)	G(M)	G(S)	G(M)	G(S)	G(M)	G(S)	G(M)
Security	Camera, Mirrors	Camera	Guard	Camera	Guard	Mirrors	Mirrors	Mirrors	Guard
# Aisles	4	8	11	7	8	7	8	6	8
Service	N	N	Y	N	N	N	N	N	Y
Cust. S. Locale	Closed	Closed	Closed	Closed	Closed	Closed	Closed	Closed	Closed
Clean	N	N	Y	Y	N	Y	N	Y	Y
Cluttered	Y	Y	Y	Y	Y	Y	Y	Y	N
Distance (min)	5	5–7	5–7	7–10	10	10	10	15	15
Parking	N	Y	Y	N	Y	Y	Y	N	Y
Bank	N	N	Y	Y	N	N	N	N	N
ATM	Y	N	Y	Y	Y	N	Y	N	Y
EBT	Y	Y	Y	Y	Y	Y	Y	N	Y
WIC	N	N	Y	N	Y	N	Y	N	Y
Generic Line	N	N	N	N	N	N	N	N	Y
Fresh Fruit	N	Y*	N	N	Y	Y	Y	N	Y
Fresh Meat	Y	Y*	Y	Y	Y*	Y	Y*	N	Y
Reputation	Cheap meat	None	None	Human hair	None	Vendors	H&B items	Hair care	None
Amenities/ Other	Lotto		Lotto, vendors, cart bars	Vendors, 3 aisles for hair care		Phone cards, vendors, $ orders	Cashed checks, $ ord.	3 aisles for hair care	curr. exch.
Notes		Brown meat*	On bus line	Felt Unsafe	Bacon = $5.29, brown meat*	Fruit prices, 2 aisles snacks, near projects	Odor from meat*, very dirty	Dirt on cans	EBT broken, cart bars,

Notes: G=Gary, B=Black Oak, M=Merrillville, P=Portage; S=Small, M=Medium, L=Large; Parking=lot sufficient for 5+ cars; Generic: Y means store has a generic product line; Cust. S. Locale: Closed=Bulletproof or glass enclosed area; Distance=from downtown Gary, IN, by car. Detailed definitions are provided in the appendix.

78

Table 3.3 (continued)
Direct Observation Results of Stores' Characteristics

Store Profile	10	11	12	13	14	15	16	17
Location/Size	B(S)	B(S)	M(L)	M(L)	M(L)	M(L)	P(L)	P(L)
Security	Mirrors	MIrrors	Video	Video	Video	Video	Video, Guard	Video, Guard
# Aisles	6	5	12	20	17	15	33	18
Service	Y	N	Y	Y	Y	Y	Y	Y
Cust. S. Locale	Open	Closed	Open	Open	Open	Open	Open	Open
Clean	Y	Y	Y	Y	Y	Y	Y	Y
Cluttered	Y	Y	N	Y	N	N	Y	N
Distance (min)	15	15	20	20	25	25	30	30
Parking	N	N	Y	Y	Y	Y	Y	Y
Bank	N	N	Y	Y	Y	Y	N	N
ATM	N	Y	Y	Y	Y	Y	Y	Y
EBT	N	Y	Y	Y	Y	Y	Y	Y
WIC	N	N	Y	Y	Y	Y	Y	Y
Generic Line	N	N	Y	Y	Y	Y	Y	Y
Fresh Fruit	Y	N	Y	Y	Y	Y	Y	Y
Fresh Meat	Y	N	Y	Y	Y	Y	Y	Y
Reputation	Bait	Cheap cigs.	Mega	Mega	Mega	Mega	Mega	Prices
Amenities/ Other	Bait, firewk, alcohol, lotto	Calling cards, fax, keys	Deli	Florist, cleaners	Food court	P.O., deli, bakery, clothes	Deli, bakery, clothes	Deli, bakery lotto
Notes	2 aisles snacks, 2 aisles alcohol	Mainly snacks		Very clean	Kid's events, visible cust. service	Visible cust. service	Visible cust. service	

Notes: G=Gary, B=Black Oak, M=Merrillville, P=Portage; S=Small, M=Medium, L=Large; Parking: lot sufficient for 5+ cars; Generic: Y means store has a generic product line; Cust. S. Locale: Closed=Bulletproof or glass enclosed area; Distance=from downtown Gary, IN, by car. Detailed definitions are provided in the appendix.

would benefit economically by shopping in the suburban locales of Merrillville and Portage (or having comparable shopping venues in their area). Although it is difficult to completely untangle the influences of race and place, these data show that shopping in the more impoverished locale of Gary (and Black Oak) translates into both higher grocery prices and greater food expenditures as a percentage of median household income.

Store Environment, Features, and Amenities: Intangible Costs

The majority of the stores in Gary can be considered small (i.e., Mom and Pop or corner stores) or medium in size; on average, stores have 7 aisles of products (see Table 3.3). In contrast, larger stores with more products and amenities are located outside of the city. Direct observation reveals stark differences in store environments. First, regardless of locale, smaller stores tend to be cluttered and crowded with narrow aisles. Several stores in Gary are particularly unclean, smell of rotten produce, and have visible dust-covered items on the shelves. Smaller stores typically have limited or no customer parking. Two Gary stores stand out due to the steel grocery cart constraints at the entrance/exit that prevent customers from using carts to push their groceries to their cars. And while all 17 stores have some type of security system, stores in Gary are more apt to employ visible, armed guards and more visible security measures, such as mirrors, throughout locations. Suburban stores are more likely to use less obtrusive surveillance equipment, such as cameras. At most Gary and Black Oak stores, items such as health and beauty products, cigarettes, and over-the-counter medicines are typically shelved behind glass or bullet-proof customer service areas. Customers do not have direct access to such items. Customer service agents usually speak to persons through a small opening in a window. This is not the case at one of the stores in Black Oak or any of the suburban stores and is attributed by respondents to higher crime in Gary. One Gary female resident notes concern about shopping at a local store known for quality, reasonably priced produce:

> I remember going there and getting meat. I would not go in there because there's always a lot of—it's next to a liquor store, so there's always a lot of drunk men outside—always asking for money when we come in and stuff. So of course I

never go at night. I always go during the day and I never take my daughter with me.

The stores in Gary also differ from those in surrounding areas based on the type and quality of amenities offered. The most common form of amenities offered in the Gary stores are Electronic Benefit Transfer (EBT) machines, lottery tickets, money order services, Black hair care products, and human hair. It is common to see vendors selling jogging suits, tee shirts, socks, and music CDs outside establishments. The two stores in the nearby Black Oak area do not have vendors outside, but customers can purchase lottery tickets, keys, fireworks, and at one location, live bait. As one travels outside the city, the available amenities increase and improve. The majority of suburban stores offer the aforementioned amenities, such as EBT machines, lottery tickets, and money orders, as well as services such as delis, bakeries, florists, ATMs, and food courts. The largest stores provide full-service banks, cleaners, and auto-repair facilities. Thus customers at the latter stores are able to purchase groceries and run other household errands at the same location.

Transportation Challenges and Costs

Although the majority of the stores within Gary can be accessed via public transportation, several structural constraints are evident. Stores 5, 6, and 7 in Gary are in walking distance to public housing, apartment complexes, and schools. On several occasions I noted women and teenagers walking towards or standing at nearby bus stops with grocery bags. The four mega stores located in Merrillville can also be reached by public transportation, but travel time averages about 45 minutes one-way. (Approximate cost is $2.50 roundtrip for adults plus the cost of transfers. For the 16 routes, buses run every hour from 5:00 a.m.–10:00 p.m., depending on the route. Passengers must have exact change.) The two stores in Black Oak are not easily accessible by public transportation, and the Portage stores are not accessible by public transportation. A White female Portage resident notes:

> I've been on assistance here and I've been on assistance there [Chicago Heights] and you can go to a store that's, you know, in walking distance, you know, 2 seconds away from your house, and you can spend more there than if you got on

> a bus and went somewhere because they are so outrageous
> with their prices. They don't make it very easy for you to
> survive if you don't have a car or money for the bus.

Most of the stores in the sample can be reached from downtown Gary
by automobile in no more than 30 minutes (approximate cost for gas
is $2.50 roundtrip[11]). For example, the Black Oak stores are 7–10
miles from one of the larger suburban stores. In this respect, residents with running automobiles can have access to the prices, options, and amenities available at suburban stores. Respondents who
realize that prices at local stores are higher may be unable to alter
their shopping patterns due to transportation problems. For example,
an 18-year-old Hispanic single mother of a 3-month-old baby prefers
to shop at a discount grocery store located 25 miles from her home:
"Del Ray Farms . . . it's less expensive there than it is at Sterk's,
but it's hard to travel because I don't have transportation." Persons
without automobiles, especially those who must take children on
shopping trips, face timing, logistical, and practical challenges. The
following comment by a Gary resident represents the general sentiments by the majority of respondents: "People who have cars got it
made. They can go to the good stores and get good sales. People who
don't are at the mercy of these little Mom and Pop stores that over-
charge" (grandmother of 2). In general, Gary residents travel a
greater distance to shop for groceries. Subsequent comments show
that residents who are able to travel to stores further away from
Gary to save money seem to have increased risk of poor service.

Customer Service and Customer Interaction

The decision to frequent certain grocery stores is often influenced
by product quality and prices. However, persons can also be influenced by customer service. This section focuses on experiences of respondents and direct observation at stores in Gary and in White
suburbs to investigate possible noneconomic costs to feed families.
First, responses are mixed in regard to customer service at the stores
in Gary. Most respondents do not experience differential treatment.
The most frequently mentioned concerns are related to the limited English spoken by attendants who shelve food at stores in Gary and delays associated with EBT card purchases. However, a common theme
emerges among respondents who receive public assistance and/or
WIC acknowledging differential treatment and stares by check-out

clerks and other customers at stores *outside* Gary. A 27-year-old, African American mother comments on her experiences at a large store in a White suburb:

> At Super K-Mart, only a manager can ok a WIC voucher and so you have to tell them up-front that you're paying with a WIC voucher and then, like the people behind you are like 'uhm' [sighing] because you have to wait for a manager to come to do your transaction. Then they have to say [over the store loudspeaker], 'we have a WIC voucher on aisle 1.' I haven't started WIC again because of what I have to go through emotionally just to use the WIC voucher. They always give me a hard time. 'Cause you would think the stores would let you get the most expensive because the government is gonna pay them for it. But instead they were making you get the cheapest. I don't understand that.

In this instance, although she is still eligible, the respondent has chosen not to use her WIC options based on poor store treatment. Other comments by this respondent also suggest that stores may have latitude in terms of which foods are available for public assistance and WIC customers or attempt to limit the types of purchases such customers can make. An African American male SSI recipient notes:

> Ah, when I first became disabled I received vouchers, food vouchers, ah, meal vouchers, medical vouchers—they treated like, you know, like, ah, you sure you're not playing a game [i.e., trying to take advantage of the system]? You know, ah, because, ah, I don't know, you know, we got so many people that, you know, just, I don't know it wasn't comfortable for me. Definitely not comfortable . . . Yeah, I think that—well, I don't think it, I know it. They'd say, well, you know what, the voucher's only gonna pay for this, so you could use this, but the voucher's only gonna pay for this, so this is all we can give you.

A White mother who lives and shops in the White suburb of Portage echoes similar sentiments about her experiences on public assistance:

> People sigh, you know. When you're on food stamps, you shop differently. I know I would get as much as I could at one time—so I'd have like one or two carts and just do it all

and then I'd pull out the full stamps and then you could feel
people's eyes and I'd look at their eyes and they're sighing—
the people, not the cashiers.

But an African American male from Gary notes his past interaction
with some White cashiers in White suburban stores:

When I paid with food stamps I noticed that the cashier
would really, you know, kind of give me the glance up and
down, you know, look me over and then look at what I purchased. And they don't never say it, but they look kind of
like, you know [expletive], 'you're purchasing these snack
items, you should really be spending your money better.' I
don't get that now that I pay with cash.

Another African American female notes a slightly different experience at a suburban store:

One time I was trying to use my debit card—any card you
use goes through the same machine. The guy is steadily
pressing 'welfare' and then he says 'your card's not going
through'—and I know my card's going through because it's
payday. Then he finally realized that I didn't have a welfare
card. So because few Black people shop out there, they tend
to assume you're on welfare.

Another African American married mother of two notes differential
treatment at suburban stores: "Sometimes at certain stores the
cashiers act like they don't want to wait on you. They be abrupt
when you asking questions and try to make you hurry up, and it'd be
like they want to get you in and get you out." In contrast, a White father of two who currently resides in the suburbs recalls growing up
impoverished and its affect on his family. He associates earlier
grocery experiences with his current frugal lifestyle:

I remember not getting a lot of things. You know, didn't get
a lot of fresh fruits and vegetables. Got canned or frozen.
Didn't get any—like sweets. Breakfast cereals, things like
that, we might get one big box. You know, and my brothers
would always eat it before I got a chance. I remember when
we would pay for it with food stamps, it seemed to be kind of
embarrassing. And I—I didn't—I don't know that it was—I
don't *know* that it was embarrassing. It just seemed, even as

a child that, ah—it seems like my mom was—it seems like she was treated differently.

Other respondents have not experienced differential treatment by customers in predominately White stores, but they have witnessed it. A 49-year-old Hispanic man, who receives governmental disability support, mentions such cases when he travels outside East Chicago, Indiana, to Hammond to grocery shop:

> My neighborhood stores, the clerks there, they treat me well there. It's only like when they don't have the products I want, I'll go to Hammond. I'm not treated different, but maybe I've seen other people treated differently. You know, in the line, it takes a little longer than if you're just giving cash. 'Cause when you give 'em the card, they gotta process it through the machine and it takes longer and some people get frustrated cause of that. 'Cause you gotta stand and you're waiting there.

Although most respondents who either experienced or witnessed poor customer service or customer interaction say the situations involved poor treatment of racial/ethnic minorities by Whites, a 45-year-old African American female resident of East Chicago who receives SSI has had a somewhat different experience:

> Well, I don't mean to be racist, but like a lot of Hispanic stores, they put people in front of you when you've been standing there waiting. And those stores like Sterk's, they're mean to the customers, to the elderly, to the handicap, or whoever. They don't be very courteous. And you find some good people, but that's mostly what a lot of people in my neighborhood are complaining about, we go to the neighborhood store which is a different nationality from us and they do make a difference.

Direct observation results also illustrate another possible problem for public assistance recipients who shop in Gary. During a visit to Store 5 on March 9, 2002, I noted a check-out delay in which a customer had insufficient funds on her EBT card to purchase her selected items. The customer initially seemed embarrassed, but later became irate, began to argue with the cashier, and refused to decide which items to put back. The verbal altercation delayed check-out for other customers in line and only ended when a security guard arrived. Subsequent conversations with several respondents suggest this type of scene occurs frequently at stores in Gary, when card holders forget how much "credit" is remaining on their EBT cards or know that the amount is insufficient, but somehow hope the system will allow them to make purchases. In such instances, the check-out attendant becomes the target for misplaced emotions, other customers contend with delays, and the actual customer experiences embarrassment, anger, and frustration.

These representative experiences suggest different customer service based on store locale. For some Gary residents who shop in White suburbs, the combination of insensitive check-out clerks and impatient customers seem to create a potentially negative climate and lengthy check-out delays for WIC and EBT shoppers and delays for other shoppers as well. Shoppers on public assistance often feel that they are being pointed out and unfavorably judged for being poor. In these instances, the choice to frequent suburban stores may result in stigmatization.[12] However, those respondents who note differential customer service and delays report that they continue to frequent suburban locations in order to save money. In contrast, EBT shoppers with insufficient funds may have a different type of negative experience. Thus, for different reasons, "making groceries" can become a necessary, but potentially embarrassing, negative experience that affects the shopper, other customers, and store employees.

Agency and Feeding Families

The lived experiences cited here also support agency-based theory on how some residents in poor urban areas make prudent, practical choices to survive deleterious conditions. Respondents, in general, attempt to maximize their limited incomes, and Gary respondents, in particular, also attempt to work around limited stores in their areas in order to stretch their money. The most common strategies include: using coupons, buying in bulk from warehouse stores, and comparison shopping based on store mailers. Most shop for groceries twice weekly. The majority of respondents (79.2 percent) acknowledge buying generic products, yet most augment such purchases with certain name brand products, usually based on requests by their children. This last strategy enables some parents to feel that, in spite of their poor or near-poor statuses, they aren't depriving their children of certain treats. An African American mother of a two-year-old girl who is separated from her husband struggles to balance her budget but comments:

I only buy name brands for the things for [child's name], like Dreft, juice, fruit snacks. Otherwise, I buy generics. And I go to Super K-mart because they do price comparisons, price matching, so that takes longer—shopping is about 1–2 hours and check out is about 30 minutes—that means you can bring in anybody else's sales ads and get that sale price. Even though it takes longer, it's actually more economical than going all over to those other stores, when I can get them [products available at the other stores] right there at Super K-mart.

One less impoverished African American father of a son earns about $25,000 annually. He lives in Gary, but grocery shops elsewhere and notes the discipline he needs and his strategy to budget for groceries: "I shop at Ultra . . . I travel between 7–10 miles . . . and sometimes to Sterk's . . . if they have a better sale . . . I try to go in and out and I go to the aisles where—I pretty much know where most of the stuff is. So I just go straight to it and try to avoid getting stuff I didn't come in for." A similar strategy, that includes budgeting a specific amount for groceries and using coupons, is used by a White father of two teenaged children:

Coupons—yes. I cut them out of the paper, or use the receipts that were given to me in the store. Or cut them off the boxes or off packages they're in. I just go there and whatever's cheapest, and that's whatever's within the budget, then that's what I'll spend. But if it's, if there's something I want and it's higher priced than normal, I won't buy it.

A married African American mother of two also structures her shopping trips and is mindful of differences in prices and quality:

Oh, yes, yes I do—I do write out a list. And I check the sale pages to see what there is on sale. I use coupons when they're available . . . Ultra is a little bit cleaner than Value Mart. The cashiers—their attitudes are different. Usually, Ultra is the better selection rather than the neighborhood store because their prices are usually higher.

Strategies also affect the types of groceries purchased. Female respondents acknowledge purchases such as chicken wings and legs, canned vegetables, tuna, boxed macaroni-and-cheese dinners, oatmeal, generic breakfast cereals, and eggs that are easy to prepare, less expensive, and that can be stretched to feed a large family.

Those with access to a car travel to larger stores to save money, those without cars try to find transportation with a friend or family member and may take periodic trips to mega stores to purchase staples in bulk to last long periods of time (usually a month). The most commonly shopped discount locations are Ultra and Aldi (41.7 and 20.8 percent of respondents, respectively). Respondents from Merrillville and Portage do not shop at Mom and Pop stores, and older Gary residents do so only to buy emergency items such as milk and bread or to purchase snacks for their children. One long-time Gary resident notes: "You see the stores in Gary? If you want to get good food—and meat—you have to go to Merrillville. Now I might buy canned goods [from stores in Gary], but not no meat" (grandmother with annual income under $25,000). Younger single mothers are the most likely to spend larger sums of money monthly on food and snacks at smaller neighborhood stores. One White, divorced mother of three who earns under $10,000 a year notes: "Yes, I shop at a neighborhood store . . . for milk, bread . . . if something runs out." An African American single parent and Gary resident limits shopping at neighborhood stores for the following reason:

> Usually when I go there—oh I usually go to the corner store down there, to cash my check, and then I pick up little items like milk, cheese, and bread, stuff like that. But it's only like 7, 8 blocks from the house. I don't never spend no more than like maybe 10 dollars. 'Cause it's a lot more expensive. I can get 39 cent bread at Aldi's and they bread is like 79, 89 cents for one loaf [at the neighborhood stores].

For some, grocery shopping involves planned trips to several stores as illustrated by an African American single mother of a four-year old son: "Ultra, Wise Way, Aldi. Well, I start on 30 [Highway 30], at Aldi, and I come on back and I hit them as they come . . . every time." A 30-year-old African American single mother of a small boy is the sole income-earner ($25,000) in a household of five. She spends about $2.00–$4.00 daily at a corner store on snacks. However, most respondents chose not to spend their money this way.

Regardless of race/ethnicity, single mothers rely heavily on extended family to augment their food budgets. Family members provide monetary support for purchases or periodically donate "high ticket" food items and related products such as fresh produce, disposable diapers, children's favorite snacks, and health & beauty products to help respondents make ends meet. However, some respondents note their personal pride during months they do not have to rely on family members to purchase groceries: "My father, he kind of keeps a close eye on me. If he sees that I'm having a hard time this week or this month, he will give me like $50 to help me get through" (White single mother of three). An African American mother acknowledges help from her mother, but also contends:

> I know that I have a lot of family support, but typically White people have more financial support to give than Black families. So our support is different, it's more, you know, the babysitting, and I think they [Whites] are more knowledgeable about certain services that are available to them than Blacks around here.

"Culture of poverty" theories that emphasize defeated, lazy, uninformed persons who make poor choices stand in stark contrast to these results that show poor and working-class persons who make informed decisions about shopping, make concessions and delay personal gratification for their children, and even contend with potentially negative experiences to feed their families. Common themes suggest the importance of: avoiding higher-priced name brands (except for their children) and stores with higher prices, purposed shopping to prevent impulse buying, buying in bulk, stretching one's money by purchasing food that can be "stretched" over several meals, frequenting suburban stores that offer the best deals, and, when necessary, accepting assistance from extended family.[13] These data suggest that respondents often negotiate around structural limitations out of necessity and adapt their behavior accordingly.

Some Solutions to Feed Families

In general, respondents tend to cope with certain noneconomic costs, such as added time on public transportation, juggling shopping and children, insensitive check-out clerks, and impatient customers in order to save money at larger, White suburban stores. However, some Gary residents exhibit angry resolve or provide solutions; others feel powerless as individuals to bring about change. Most of the solutions focus on proactive behavior by *residents* in Gary to demand structural changes by officials, politicians, and local organizations. An African American mother of one considers the implications of collective action:

> There's been a lack of education and a lack of resources, 'cause, you know, you're talking about food, so if you boycott the stores here, you'll have to go to the stores in Merrillville and Portage. The poorest people are affected the most because those who have alternatives, go to the better stores.

She continues:

> First it's gonna take a change in mindset of the people, that we think of the bigger picture instead of immediate gratification. And then you'll have to start boycotting the stores that are, you know, below standard and that sell below standard items, and then probably some type of lobbying for better businesses.

And while most respondents are purposed about decisions when purchasing groceries, some seem less aware of the relationship between their choices (or lack of choices) and larger structural forces. An African American mother of two contends:

> We don't have a single main grocery store, they're all foreigner owned, while other places like Portage and Merrillville have other main grocery stores—like chains. I think that because there are so many minorities here that don't demand more, then people can just move in and exploit them. Especially the young teenage mothers, they don't realize that they have a choice and a right to quality products and services.

The above respondent suggests the need for political and social empowerment and collective action on the part of Gary residents to combat structural problems. However, some respondents embrace a "blame-the -victim" *viewpoint*, in which responsibility for inadequate grocery stores is largely placed on residents, even though research shows how such situations are largely shaped by social structure rather than individuals' lack of understanding or hesitancy to demand more.

Food and Service Providers in Urban Centers

In this chapter, I have attempted to examine some of the economic and noneconomic costs associated with grocery shopping in Gary, Indiana, and neighboring areas. I focus on grocery store expenditures, because they represent basic costs that all families, irrespective of race/ethnicity, age, and class, must incur. Gary and neighboring areas provide an ideal setting to study the intersection of race, place, poverty, and feeding families. This analysis is an attempt to advance theories on structure and agency in poor urban areas by specifically and empirically illustrating the negative influence of structural constraints (locale-driven prices) on the food shopping choices of Gary residents. Although this analysis only compares one aspect of urban life in a specific area, it shows how some residents incur costs daily that may undermine their ability to make better use of their already limited funds. In general, Gary residents tend to spend more for food each month than do non-Gary residents. And while these cost differentials can be partially attributed to differences in saving strategies, the findings show that they are also influenced by the lack of availability of lower-priced grocery stores. Furthermore, these results suggest that certain choices may already be made for some urbanites in Gary. Thus agency, especially that of poor persons who live in impoverished areas, is severely constrained by a variety of structural forces that include isolation, racial inequities, and poverty.

These findings do not support "culture of poverty" studies that suggest aberrant attitudes and behavior. To the contrary, respondents' micro-level decisions confirm agency-based theory. Most persons are quite industrious and purposed in their strategies to save money, live frugally, sacrifice, shop for the best prices, and make compromises to feed their families. Most respondents invoke agency and behave proactively *in spite of* structural constraints. However, attitudes about their experiences vary. Some are ambivalent; those who only shop at severely overpriced, ill-conditioned stores in highly segregated areas have no point of comparison to expect more. Others blame complacent residents rather than macro-level forces. But most residents who are angry about the inadequacy of Gary stores still find themselves reluctantly traveling to the larger stores in White suburbs to save money. This latter response appears to be a form of "situational adaptivity" Wilson (1996) suggests occurs in poor urban settings. In this instance, some Gary residents are aware of their shopping constraints and the higher prices they pay, and many express anger. However, the situation becomes a private problem rather than a public one that is addressed (albeit in a limited manner) using strategies and coping mechanisms.

The economic costs for many Gary residents are clear. Persons tend to pay more for groceries (in general and as a percentage of median household income) and have fewer options in terms of quality and quantity of locations, products, fresh produce, and related amenities. Substantial differences are evident based on the racial composition of areas, neighborhood poverty level, and proximity to Gary; prices are cheaper in predominately, less impoverished White suburban areas. However, prices in neighboring, predominately White, Black Oak *are not* different from those in most other Gary stores. Thus differential access to resources and services based on *place more than race* means that, regardless of race, being poor or near poor can translate into different expenditures and experiences, based on whether one lives in an urban or suburban setting. However, race and place generally intersect, as minorities and the poor are disproportionately represented among urban residents and in poor neighborhoods. In addition, given that the suburban stores are located in predominately White areas, and *both* African American *and* White stores in Gary are underserviced, this suggests the institutionalized nature of racism that can also overshadow the experiences of poor Whites in its wake. These findings illustrate the relationship between concentrated neighborhood poverty and store quality in that Gary stores, regardless of the race/ethnicity of most residents in the locale, tend to be located in moderate or ghetto-poor neighborhoods.

Some may suggest that, in spite of higher prices, an absence of such stores in Gary would put residents at an even greater deficit. It may also be suggested that these cost inequities are simply reflective of higher overhead for urban grocery stores, supply/demand needs, or an unstable tax base that would not sustain larger grocery stores in Gary and that these findings are not linked to race. And while the supply/demand issue appears to make sense (because businesses follow money), one would expect the density of population in urban centers like Gary to increase market interest enough to offset profit concerns related to the additional costs of security, lost carts, or administrative costs associated with WIC/EBT customers. However, studies illustrate how racism fuels the relationship between predominately African-American cities and White adjacent local governments, state and federal agencies, and the private sector that tends to translate into underserviced urban centers.[14]

These results also show the importance of considering noneconomic costs. Possible implications of limited fresh products, poor treatment by some service providers, time loss associated with using public transportation, surveillance-intense settings, anger, feelings of impotence, and feelings of stigma, embarrassment, or shame suggest that the toll of life in some urban centers exceeds monetary considerations and further supports the need for more research on the sociopsychological implications of urban life. And while it may be easy to minimize the negative effects of some of the noneconomic costs presented in this chapter, they are often amenities taken for granted in other neighborhoods.

Several possible options may address these inequities. Short-term, Gary and Black Oak residents would benefit from organized transportation to larger stores via subsidized vanpools or church-organized vanpools. Long-term, macro-level remedies must include improving the tax base by providing incentives for potential businesses, encouraging small business growth and other entrepreneurial ventures, and informing local community and political leaders to lobby for changes in local stores.[15] Although a variety of systemic changes are needed, many of the basic economic and noneconomic costs studied here could be remedied by opening a large, multipurposed store on a central public transportation route in Gary (i.e., Walmart, K-mart, or Target Superstores). Such a location would provide jobs, more affordable product lines, amenities such as a low-cost pharmacy, a bakery and florist, as well as clothes and household goods. Berner and Forest (2002) suggest the benefits of such "superstores" in poor and near-poor rural communities and urban areas; other scholars point to their ability to create jobs during recessionary times.[16] However, contradictory studies point to problems of low-wage unions, union busting, poor treatment of workers forced to work off the clock, and possible negative effects on Mom and Pop stores.[17] And while residents in urban and nonurban areas alike must contend with the reality that food production and distribution in this country lies in the hands of the private sector, research on successful public-private partnerships that are profitable as well as civic minded[18] suggests that remedies to address the problem of inadequate and insufficient food service providers found in Gary and similar cities are tenable.

CHAPTER FOUR

Differential Goods and Services
to Clothe a Family:
Who Pays the Costs?

Much of the research on economic problems in urban areas focuses on the broader implications of being without financial security, rather than specifically how residents use their limited funds. With the exception of research by Edin and Lein (1991, 1996), Jarrett (1994), Chaisson (1998) and several others,[1] less attention has been given to the consumer culture of poor and near-poor urban residents. However, several recent ethnographies examine urban consumption patterns. In *Black Picket Fences: Privilege and Peril Among the Black Middle Class*, Pattillo-McCoy (1999) explores the importance of adorning and accessorizing the body for some African American youth and correlates their behavior with conspicuous consumerism. The author suggests that, in a society fueled by materialism as a marker of success, less prudent spending decisions by some African Americans can result in more dire consequences as compared to their White counterparts. In the chapter, "Nike's Reign," the sports shoe is considered, by large segments of "Groveland" youth, to be a marker of cultural authenticity and cutting-edge fashion sense. By specifically targeting youth fascinated with sports figures as symbols of success and prosperity, Nike and other retailers exploit the constrained economic standing of African American youth who, "use those fashions to resist and reinterpret their racially marginalized position" (Pattillo-McCoy 1999: 148) in White society and to establish hierarchies among themselves.

Similarly, Chin (2001) analyzes the spending patterns of African American children who reside in Newhallville, Connecticut, in *Purchasing Power: Black Kids and American Consumer Culture*. Her results illustrate the potentially negative effects of consumerism on impoverished children, who are bombarded by media images of materialism that most are unable to attain. Like Pattillo-McCoy, Chin is interested in the ways in which certain segments of the African American urban populace negotiate space, race, and class as consumers. The latter author situates 10-year old children as the central figures to examine the social and cultural implications of their spending habits and the structural forces that constrain their agency and active involvement in consumer culture. Unlike the youth profiled in *Black Picket Fences*, Chin's respondents' continued exposure to poverty often results in more frugal, responsible, young consumers who often contribute their extra money to help purchase household necessities. The author questions prevailing generalizations about unwise spending among the poor and concludes that impoverished children are often constrained in their consumption patterns, requests, and expectations.

Each of these studies examines aspects of the African American urban experience based on a different theoretical lens, yet both illustrate the effects of leveled aspirations, as well as ways in which spending patterns can reflect restraint, resistance, and, in some instances, compliance with market forces. Similarly, I am interested in examining spending patterns among poor and near-poor residents in and around Gary, Indiana. However, I explore consumerism for adult heads-of-households, who have the direct responsibility to clothe and care for many of the types of children and youth profiled by Chin and Pattillo-McCoy.

This chapter continues the examination of goods and service providers in Gary and suburban Indiana, but focuses on retailers and related businesses that sell clothing, household items, and larger home products. The analysis concentrates on frequented retailers, store in-migration and out-migration patterns, as well as the specific experiences of Gary residents and their counterparts in nearby areas. As in chapter 3, I consider availability, access, affordability, and the quality of businesses, and whether they vary by urban or suburban locale, with the intent to compare and contrast the everyday economic and noneconomic costs incurred. I examine the following types of questions; what types of retailers are located in Gary? Have the number and type of retail establishments changed over time? How do these establishments compare to similar establishments in nearby suburban areas? What types of economic and noneconomic costs do Gary residents incur to clothe their families? Do available resources differ in predominately African American versus predominately White neighborhoods? What choices, strategies, and coping mechanisms do residents employ during the daily round, and how do they make sense of their experiences?

*Retail Transitions and Their Influence on Shopping
Options in Gary*

As suggested in chapter 2, two primary business shifts had the most negative effect on retail and related enterprise in Gary—first, the migration of stores from the downtown area to The Village Shopping Center in Glen Park, followed by the exodus of stores from the latter facility to Westfield Shoppingtown (referred to by many respondents using its earlier name, "Southlake Mall") area in Merrillville. Each of these transitions was marked by a similar pattern. With the decision to relocate, large retailers initially maintained a smaller operation at the former site, typically selling discount-priced, returned, or catalog items, while opening a larger location in the newer facility, where better quality goods and services were sold. Eventually, the smaller sites were closed. Sears and Montgomery Ward provide examples:

> Sears maintained a skeleton operation in its downtown structure, reducing both the quantity and quality of its merchandise. Ward has just completed a clearance sale to bring in a lesser grade of stock for limited operations at its Gary store. The largest store in downtown Gary was Sears, making it a distressing sign of urban flight and community abandonment when its windows and doors were finally boarded. (Williams 1978, p. B1)

Stores that maintained streamlined locations indirectly seemed to forewarn Gary residents of their preferred customer base and pending closings.

Just as businesses in downtown Gary experienced decreased activity and declining profits after the Village Shopping Center opened, "The Village" saw similar downturns with the opening of the Southlake Shopping Mall. Large retailers such as Montgomery Ward and J.C. Penney opened new stores in the mall area, but maintained locations in The Village with significantly altered merchandise. Just as Sears had eventually phased out its downtown location, Ward followed suit several years later at its Village location. The following example, presented in a 1978 article in the *Gary Post Tribune*, summarizes the transition:

> Montgomery Ward announced today that its Village Shopping Center store in Gary will change its merchandising format and become a center for goods at reduced prices . . .

> conversion of the Village Store will enable us to offer a broad
> range of overstock merchandise at special prices. The pre-
> sent Village operation will continue as is until shortly before
> the Merrillville store opens at Century Plaza at U.S. 30 in
> Broadway. (p. B5)

Williams (1978) comments on the Ward transition: "The fact that
the quantity and quality of merchandise will be no match for what is
shipped to the Merrillville store again serves as a reminder of the
Sears pattern" (p. B1). In like fashion, other retailers downsized
their Village operations and simultaneously opened large stores in
or near the Merrillville mall. Each store eventually closed its Village
branch. JC Penney was the last department store to be located in
The Village, but by 1995, its location had been replaced by a discount clothing store. Gary residents were urged to respond to the
mass business and retail exodus:

> No boycott is necessary. Gary citizens don't boycott stores in
> Ypsilanti, Michigan, or Little Rock, Ark. Or Trenton, N.J. We
> simply don't frequent those stores because it is too inconven-
> ient. The same logic should apply to Gary stores uprooted for
> relocation to south county . . . Additionally a sense of principle
> should be employed. "Buy in Gary" should be the battle cry in
> this war against the unfaithful . . . Merchants must identify a
> need to serve the Steel City from sites in the Steel City. Mer-
> rillville folks don't come to Gary with any degree of frequency.
> If they did, Sears and J.C. Penney's would still be the anchors
> of Gary's downtown community. (Williams 1978: p. B1)

However, most Gary residents did not follow this suggestion, and
suburban trade boomed, as Gary continued its retail economic decline. This meant that most residents would have to travel outside
Gary to purchase clothing, home furnishings, and big-ticket items.
In addition, much of the income earned by Gary residents did not
turn over in the city, but rather in suburban areas that did not pay
taxes in Gary.[2] Out-migration of such businesses has contributed to
the current differences in neighborhood poverty rates around the
primary shopping areas examined here. According to 2000 census
calculations, family and individual poverty rates in the neighborhood surrounding The Village are 17.9 and 23.9 percent, respectively, and comparable values for the Westfield Shoppingtown area
are 2.4 and 4.4 percent.[3]

The out-migration of retailers and other business from downtown Gary has contributed to the increased poverty in that area as well. In many cities, "Broadway" has historically been an important economic hub. This thoroughfare traditionally features a myriad of businesses, retailers, and restaurants in the downtown area; the street has also historically provided a direct route from a city's downtown business district to the suburbs. In Gary, Broadway serves as a reminder of the city's retail history (refer to Figures 2.1–2.17 in chapter 2). Buildings that once housed department stores such as Sears, J.C. Penney, and W. T. Grant, upscale retailers such as Gordon's and Cornett, the Hurwich and Howler furniture store, and other clothiers and stores are now boarded-up and abandoned.[4] There is currently one small discount retailer (Broadway Shopping Mall), four small specialty stores (House of Brevardo, Sankofa Imports, Mini Me's, and J & W Custom T-Shirts, all located in the Mecca Building[5]), Jackson optometrist, Broadway Beauty (hair and beauty supply store), California Wigs, and Tim's Drugstore located on Broadway in downtown Gary.[6] Limited pedestrian and business travel, even during weekends, suggest customers have gone elsewhere.

Because of its historic economic significance, I use Broadway as the point of reference to show the neighborhood economic transition that occurs from the central city to Merrillville, Indiana, where many previous Gary retailers have relocated (Table 4.1). Based on 2000 census figures, poverty tends to be most concentrated in the downtown area. Economic indicators, such as the employment rate, median family income, and poverty rates parallel the southern migration of businesses out of the city. The neighborhood surrounding 5th and Broadway has an employment rate of 30.2 percent, median family income of $17,273, and family poverty rate of 36.1 percent. Single-parent households and individuals in this area reside in ghetto poverty. Although the employment rate only improves by 7.5 percentage points for neighborhoods from 5th to 25th and Broadway, the poverty rate falls by half to 17.1 percent, median family income increases to $34,702, and related poverty indicators suggest a substantial decline in concentrated poverty. Moderate neighborhood poverty persists as far out as 52nd and Broadway in spite of the median family income of over $44,000 annually and a 56 percent employment rate. Similar employment rates and median incomes are evident in the last two suburban neighborhoods listed in the table. However, neighborhood poverty is minimal in the last area. A comparison of these economic indicators between 5th and 65th and Broadway (census tracts 102.2 and 424.03) shows a 25 percentage point

Table 4.1
2000 Census Economic Indicators Between Gary and
Merrillville, IN, on Broadway

Broadway Neighborhood (Census Tract)	Employment Rate	Family Poverty Rate	Single-Parent Poverty Rate	Individual Poverty Rate	Median Family Income
5th (102.2)	30.2	36.1	44.4	40.2	$17,273
10th (113)	34.9	18.4	25.4	25.0	$26,984
$15\text{-}20^{th}$(117)	33.9	19.8	27.9	25.2	$25,926
25th (120)	37.5	17.1	14.3	21.7	$34,702
$30\text{-}45^{th}$ (124)	49.5	17.4	31.2	24.0	$37,500
$46\text{-}52^{nd}$(125)	55.5	17.0	31.8	19.9	$44,207
$53\text{-}56^{th}$ (424.03)	54.8	2.8	0.0	5.0	$50,510

Source: 2000 U.S. Census Summary File 3 (SF 3), Profile of Selected Economic Characteristics

Notes:
Neighborhood = census tract. Avenues within the same census tract are grouped together.
Census Definitions:
Family—a householder and one or more other persons living in the same household who are related to the householder by birth, marriage, or adoption. All persons in a household who are related to the householder are regarded as members of his/her family. A household can contain only one family. Not all households contain families since a household may comprise a group of unrelated persons or one person living alone.

increase in the employment rate, 18- and 8-fold reductions in family and individual poverty rates, respectively, and a reduction in the poverty rate of single-parent households by a factor of 40. Lastly, the median family income increases by a factor of 3.5 between these two neighborhoods. Review of the improvement in neighborhood economic conditions as one moves away from central Gary confirms that segments of Gary's populace experience significantly more poverty than their suburban counterparts. It will be important to consider possible implications of these economic differences on shopping patterns.

As presented in Table 4.2, the current Village Shopping center differs dramatically in terms of number and type of stores as compared to earlier periods.[7] Large retailers and upscale stores, such as Montgomery Ward, JC Penney, Hudson's, Kinney Shoes, and Melick's, have been replaced by low-end retailers, those that market more trendy attire and footwear, and discount stores. Stores that were part of the original facility in 1955 or in downtown Gary, such as Goldblatt[8] and Three Sisters, temporarily returned, only to subsequently close. Space that once housed an anchor retail store (Montgomery Ward followed by Goldblatt) now stands abandoned and boarded-up. In 1992 a $2 million renovation project at The Village resulted in a new logo, marquee, and entrance signs as well as modernized outdoor lighting, interior and exterior painting, and improved landscaping and infrastructure.[9] Foot Locker and several discount stores, such as Everything's a $1.00, Rainbow Clothing, and One Price Clothing, were also new additions at that same time. Local business leaders suggest that The Village and another city shopping area, Tri-City Shopping, are experiencing revitalization;[10] many respondents in this study tend to differ in their assessment. In addition, based on direct observation, tell-tell signs of neglect at The Village are apparent, such as unadorned walls, vacant kiosk spaces, and empty or sparsely decorated store windows and entrances. Similar to many grocery establishments in Gary, most retailers have visible security personnel or equipment that was not common at the shopping center historically. As noted by an older respondent who has lived in Gary since 1968:

> We don't have any place where you could buy a washing machine, refrigerator, or furniture. You have to go to the mall. Whether you want to or not. And even if you wanted a *real nice* outfit or something, you have to go to the mall. No Sears or any stores like that are in Gary because it would take away from sales out in Merrillville. And then, if they didn't have the Gary people shopping at Southlake Mall, it would probably close . . . and they know that.

In December of 1990, political and economic leaders in the city instituted a "Celebrate Gary" campaign to again encourage Gary residents toward customer loyalty to city stores and to begin by Christmas shopping that year at the remaining stores in downtown Gary, such as Doris & Gallery Boutiques, and in The Village. The campaign also included "Celebrate Gary" buttons and other promotionals in 1991, but did not appear to generate the desired results.[11] Today, the over 50 stores and services available at The Village do not provide Gary residents with the choice to shop at department or large retailers in close proximity to their neighborhoods. Residents uninterested in trendy attire or cautious about

Table 4.2
Business In-migration and Out-migration in The Village Shopping Center, 1955–2002

THEN[+]

Department	Up-Scale	Other Retail	Shoe Stores	Children's	Grocery	Restaurants	Other Stores	Other Businesses
Montgomery Ward	Hudson's	Three Sisters	Kinney Shoes	Mellick's	Kroger	C.W. Vienna's	Ames	Gary National Bank
J.C. Penney	Mac & Dewey	Sports 'N Life	Gallenkamp Shoe			Village Restaurant	Newmode Hosiery	
Goldblatt (discount)		Regency Fashions	Florsheim Shoes				Kresge's	
			Baker Shoes				Fannie Mae Candy	
			Naturalizer				Tuxedos	
							Christian Record Store	
							Afrikan-American Book Source	

NOW

Department	Up-Scale	Other Retail	Shoe Stores	Children's	Grocery	Restaurants	Other Stores	Other Businesses
(none)	Tom Oleskers	Mimi's Fashions	Footlocker	Rainbow NYC	Aldi	C.W. Vienna's	Card-Snack Vendor	Key and Locks
		US Factory Outlets	Payless Shoe Source	One Price Clothing		Pagoda Hut	Beautiful Things	Planned Parenthood
		A. J. Wright Clothing	Foot-Action USA	Kid's Footlocker		Caesar's Pizza	The CD Depot	Medicaid Dental Clinic
		Just for You Family Clothing				McDonald's	Chatham Beauty	Check-N-Go
		Fashion Cents Clothing					Tuxedos	Mail LUV
		Simply Fashion Clothing					H & H Jewelry	Insure One
		Uptown Me					Radio Shack	Physicians Rehab.
		Rainbow NYC*					Rex-al Drugs	Gary Police
		Avenue					Dollar Bills	Shoe Repair
		Freshwear					AutoZone	Village Cleaners
		DOTS Clothing					Verizon	Fantasy Travel
								RAC Rent-a-Center

[+]Includes majority of stores previously located in the Village since 1955; includes several restaurants and businesses outside the immediate building, but still considered part of the facility. *Sells adult and children's attire.

the durability of discount fashions have few options. So while one could argue that the quantity of retail space in The Village has been relatively maintained since its 1955 opening, few would suggest that the quality of goods and services are comparable.[12] These findings should not be considered an indictment on the current retailers and discount stores in places such as The Village, nor to minimize their importance in providing shopping options for residents. However, the retail transition that has occurred in Gary serves as a reminder of the challenges residents face, as they attempt to meet the needs of their families.

Certain retail changes in Gary can be attributed to the normal ebb and flow of business enterprise under capitalism. However, such changes are often more detrimental to urban areas, in general, and the poor and near poor who live there, in particular. For example, the closing of Goldblatt in downtown Gary and later in The Village and Kinney Shoe Source and Gallenkamp Shoes in The Village reflected the downsizing or closing of these chains nationwide. The latter store closed in midyear 1986 and was replaced by a Payless Shoe Source in July 1986. The increase in the number of Payless stores, particularly in urban and poor areas, also reflects a recent trend in discount stores designed to mimic their more expensive counterparts. A broader view of retail transitions suggests that residents in places like Gary often contend with fewer retailers and stores in their immediate vicinity and are forced to either travel to suburban locations to shop or accept the products offered at discount stores. One older African American respondent is critical of the businesses that have out-migrated and blames predominately White suburban and state business and political leaders: "It wouldn't surprise me if they (business and political leaders) didn't pay businesses *not to* open up stores in Gary."

One might expect that a densely populated city would represent economic possibility for businesses and entrepreneurs because *more people* would be expected to translate into *more customers* and hence, *more profits*. This has not been the case in Gary. As suggested by results for respondents in this study (Table 4.3), Gary residents often frequent suburban stores.

Shopping Patterns by Race and Residency

This section focuses on the shopping habits of the 24 sample respondents who identified specific stores they frequent (15 African

Table 4.3
Shopping Patterns for Respondents In and Around Gary,
Indiana, by Race/Ethnicity and Residency (N = 24)

Shopping Patterns by Total Sample and Race/Ethnicity

Stores (% Yes)	Total	AA	White	Hispanic
Wal-Mart	41.7	46.7	40.0	25.0
K-Mart	20.8	20.0	40.0	0.0
JC Penney	16.7	20.0	20.0	0.0
Value City	12.5	20.0	0.0	0.0
Mall	37.5	40.0	20.0	50.0
Target*	8.3	0.0	40.0	40.0
Other	41.7	53.3	20.0	25.0
N	24	15	5	4

Shopping Patterns by Residency**

Stores (% Yes)	Gary Resident	Non-Gary Resident
Wal-Mart	33.3	50.0
K-Mart	16.7	25.0
JC Penney	16.7	16.7
Value City [+]	25.0	0.0
Mall	33.3	41.7
Target	0.0	16.7
Other [+]	58.3	25.0
N	12	12

Key: N only includes respondents who specifically identified stores they frequent.
Significant differences +$p<.10$ *$p<.05$. **$p<.01$.
AA = African American.

Americans, 5 Whites, and 4 Hispanics). Persons were asked to identify the stores they frequent to purchase clothes for themselves and
their families, average monthly shopping costs, budgeting strategies, and experiences while shopping. Regardless of marital status,
most women are responsible for clothing and household purchases.
Persons spend approximately $199.63 monthly on clothes for them-
selves and their families. Amounts range from $20.00 to $1,000.00;
these amounts vary further based on the respondent's age, family
size, and shopping philosophy and strategies (excluding the three
most extreme amounts, most families spend about $126.00 monthly
on clothes).[13] In addition, respondents from Gary spend a significantly higher amount of money on clothes each month as compared

to non-Gary respondents ($300.75 versus $98.50).[14] Most respondents suggest that a greater amount of money is spent purchasing necessities, such as socks, underwear, and tee-shirts for family members. More expensive items, such as pants, tops, and shoes, are usually purchased as needed. Although the majority of respondents seldom use coupons or write shopping lists before going shopping, they employ various strategies to save time, minimize temptations while shopping, and locate the best buys.

Respondents frequent a variety of stores, most of which are located in suburban Indiana or Illinois. Persons are more likely to shop at mega discount stores or a shopping mall, where they can find a variety of items under one roof or in one facility. The following stores are frequented most often: Wal-mart, K-Mart, J.C. Penney, Value City, Westfield Shoppingtown, and Target (Table 4.3). These six locations are used as points of reference in this chapter. First, regardless of race/ethnicity or place of residence, respondents are more likely to shop at Wal-mart (41.7 percent of respondents), Westfield Shoppingtown (37.5 percent), or other discount stores (41.7 percent). They are least likely to purchase clothes and household items at Target (8.3 percent). Differences in shopping patterns are evident when race/ethnicity and place of residence are considered. For example, over 40 percent of African American and White respondents identify Wal-mart as one of the stores they frequent most. About 25 percent of Hispanics shop regularly at this mega store chain. The data show no significant difference between shopping patterns at Wal-mart by race/ethnicity. However, while 40 percent of White and Hispanic respondents frequent Target, none of the African Americans shop there regularly; this differential is statistically significant.

While no statistically significant difference in shopping patterns is apparent by race/ethnicity when the remaining stores are considered, due to the small sample size, I think it important to consider substantive differences in shopping patterns as well. For example, only 3 of the 15 African Americans (or 20 percent) frequent K-Mart, while 2 of the 5 Whites (40 percent) do. And while no Hispanics or Whites in the sample shop at Value City, 20 percent of African Americans shop there. Finally, the data show that a substantially higher percentage of African American (40 percent) and Hispanic (50 percent) respondents shop at Westfield Shoppingtown. This statistic is of greater interest considering the majority of White respondents live closer to the mall than do their non-White counterparts. Lastly, African American respondents are more likely to shop at other retailers such as Kohl's, Lane Bryant, TJ Maxx,

Carson Pirie Scott, and Burlington, while younger African American and Hispanic respondents are also frequent shoppers at smaller, trendy discount stores such as DOTS, Rainbow, Young's, City Sports, and The Avenue.

Next, I consider possible differences in shopping patterns based on place of residence (refer to Table 4.3). Most African Americans are residents of Gary, most Whites live in suburban cities such as Merrillville and Valparaiso, and most Hispanics live in East Chicago, Indiana. However, the group is not completely homogeneous in that some African Americans reside in suburban areas or East Chicago, and one White respondent lives in Gary. In this analysis, I consider possible shopping differences based on whether a person lives in or outside Gary. The data show no significant difference in shopping patterns by residence for the following stores: Wal-mart, K-Mart, J.C. Penney, or Target. In addition, when I consider shopping patterns at the mall, data show that about 42 percent of non-Gary residents frequent the mall, while about 33 percent of Gary residents shop there. There is no statistically significant difference between the two shopping patterns. This suggests that Gary residents (most of whom are African American) are just as likely as Whites to shop at Westfield Shoppingtown, although the facility is not located in their city nor directly supports Gary's tax base.[15] Finally, findings suggest that Gary residents are more likely to shop at Value City and other smaller retailers than are nonresidents; these differences are significant.

These results are important in illustrating shopping patterns as well as the potential impact of infrequent shopping within one's community. First, the majority of the stores identified by respondents are located outside Gary.[16] To the degree that these respondents represent typical Gary residents, the results show that Gary residents frequently shop at stores outside the city. This pattern translates to lost revenue for the city, a weakened tax base, and the continued decline of the downtown and Village areas. Other intangible costs for residents include increased travel time, shopping constraints for persons with limited or no transportation, and inconvenience. It also suggests that the retail economies of many suburban areas are significantly bolstered by the limited shopping options of Gary (and to a lesser degree, East Chicago) residents. These results also show support of discount clothiers and smaller, trendy retailers in The Village by Gary residents. For these residents, Gary does provide shopping venues of interest. However, such options may not meet the clothing needs of older residents or persons with different shopping tastes.

Differentials: Products, Services, and Customer Service

Respondents from Gary appear to be varied in their shopping habits. Possibly driven by the higher representation of persons who frequent discount mega-stores known for lower prices, such as Walmart, few respondents suggest significant price differences while shopping. However, several Gary residents comment on both price and product differences based on store locale:

> The prices are higher in Gary. Even the difference of the prices between the Walgreens in Merrillville and the Walgreens in Gary. Um, the selection is different. There's more to the selection in Portage. But I do try to—I always get my gas from the Doc's Fifth Avenue Mobil, just because it's black-owned. So I always go to that Mobil. And if I have spare money and I'm gonna buy like a outfit or something, I do always check at AJ Wright [Village discount retailer] first, in case they'll have something. (African American mother of two)

Her personal response to these perceived inequities is to, when possible, support local businesses in Gary. Another Gary resident echoes a similar observation about differential products by Walmart locale: "I really like the Schererville store. They have a better selection of things. If I go to the Hammond store it's usually with my mom." Although more respondents suggest differential treatment while grocery shopping, poor treatment while clothing shopping is rarely noted and, as suggested by the following African American single mother of a son, do not appear to divert respondents from frequenting their favorite stores:

> Well I get coupons from Lerner's [Mall trendy retailer]. Sometimes, like in certain stores, when you walk in, some people will help you. But others will just look at you. You know, you have to basically ask for help. It's a mixture. They have some very friendly employees and they have some who really don't want to be there. But I guess it's their job.

Shopping Strategies and Challenges

Just as the sample women and men employ strategies to feed their families, most also make specific choices to ensure that their families are properly clothed. Strategies include shopping at discount stores known for lower prices, attempting to develop and adhere to a budget, using store layaways, and frequenting thrift and secondhand stores. For some, especially mothers with small children, strategies also include ways to maximize both time and money and juggling transportation problems. For many respondents, the most logical strategy involves shopping at mega-stores; for Gary residents, this means traveling outside the city. The following representative quotations suggest that many respondents are purposed in their choices for clothes shopping. A single White mother of three children describes her purchasing strategy:

> For my children and myself, a lot of the times, I will go to the resale shop. I will get so much more, and, you know, I can, I go when my kids are away for the weekend, and I can just really look. There's, nice things there. Cause, I can't, I can't afford to buy my kids new stuff all the time. If I do go to a store, I go in the clearance aisles. I learned a lot from my kids' grandparents. You know they took me there [to resale shops]. And I'd never been there before, and I just thought, you know, why not? They're just clothes that people partially wear, you know, a lot of them are almost new. My kids—I don't want, I *want* to teach my kids to be humble. I don't want them to think they have to have the best of everything. I can't give them that. I mean there are circumstances where, of course I'd go to the store and get them something brand new, like for a special occasion or something. But I use the resale shop as kind of like a filler, like if they need an extra shirt or a couple pairs of play clothes, or you know, things like that . . . otherwise . . . mostly Wal-mart—they have better deals.

Resale shops and Goodwill sites in Portage and Merrillville provide less expensive options and have eliminated her need to venture to the shopping mall. Similarly, a married African American mother of two resides in Gary, but frequents thrift shops and the Salvation Army in predominately White areas for bargains. She notes benefits as well as drawbacks of this choice:

> Pants, ah, you know, undergarments, everything. Whatever I want to wear. Usually it takes me like about, it take me about three hours. If I'm getting good prices, I can be in the store for hours, especially a thrift store. I come out with a

bag full of stuff—bargains . . . Yeah, but I've had experiences where white folks call me nigger.

For others, like this 35-year-old White mother of two, planned shopping trips maximize time and also minimize chances of unnecessary purchases:

> I usually know what I need to get before I even go in and I usually know the size or whether it's for me or the kids or whatever. So I usually go in, go straight to the section I need, pick out what I need, pay for it, and get out of there. [Q: Why the quick process?] I think because you don't have money. If I go in there, 'cause every once in a while I do just like to go shopping, just nose around and you always end up spending money you shouldn't spend. So if I go straight in, get what I need to get, pay for it and get out, I'm ok. I'm in trouble if I spend more time in the store.

A 40-year-old African American divorced father and Gary resident uses a similar approach:

> Usually I know exactly what store I'm going to, I already know what I'm going to get. So it's like really—about a half an hour or less most of the time. A typical shopping trip there would be something that was in the window as I was passing and say let me go check that out and see what the price is. And if it's in the range I want to spend and the material or whatever is the quality I be looking for, I'll go ahead and get it.

As illustrated by an African American mother of a small daughter, certain strategies have to do with maximizing time and juggling small children, which translates into taking advantage of a nearby 24-hour Wal-mart Superstore:

> Usually when I go shopping for—if I take her [young daughter], then I always take somebody else. Like I'll take my sister or I'll take my friends, so they can help me watch her while I'm shopping. Or at night I usually try to leave her with my mother, and then I'll go do shopping. Typically I have to go, I usually go early in the morning, about six o'clock in the morning, because she's sleeping—I can leave her with my sister. And it's not too much

of a hassle to me, cause with my sister, you know, if she gonna wake up and cause any problems, you know. Um, so that usually leaves me to be about the only person in the store. So I can run in and see what I'm getting, and then run out, because then I usually have to get home and get her ready to go to school when I do. So it's usually kind of rushed.

Another divorced African American mother of three small children considers the layaway option an additional perk at Wal-mart. Yet she notes shopping challenges because of the number of children and their ages and the importance of child-friendly environments:

When I do take my children to the store, I don't think—like when I go shoe shopping—it's just way too much. 'Cause you have to get everybody's shoes off and shoes on. And only at Stride Rite [Mall shoe store] do they have like something for kids to do while you're trying to get the other ones sized and fitted.

A married White mother of three resides in Valparaiso and also frequents Wal-mart for many of her family's shopping needs:

I like shopping at Wal-mart, because they have everything. Like it's not just the groceries—if you need other stuff you can go and get it. You know, supplies for the kids, toys, clothes—everything like that. Um. . . . but there's usually in Wal-mart, there's a lot of people that are stocking the shelves all the time. And so they're just in your way. They really don't care that they're working and, you know, you're there to shop. So that can be annoying.

Gary respondents without access to a running automobile are usually able to visit suburban retailers by traveling with family and friends. However, one resident with transportation difficulties uses another strategy—catalog shopping. This option enables her to negotiate around her transportation constraints, but also requires high shipping and handling fees and the inability to try on clothing:

Oh, I order them. From Penney's, J.C. Penney's, and there's another catalog I get—Blair. Yeah, you know, like if I need something. Well, you know I don't wear dresses, but slacks, gym shoes, t-shirts, undies, socks. It's just about time to buy a jacket, so I'm . . . Oh well, it's easy for me. You know, I won't have to beg nobody—not beg, but try to get nobody to take me, you know.

And a White father of two works overtime in order to purchase the needs, and some of the wants, of his teenaged children:

If they want some, you know, whatever, some brand name, whatever the fad is, they can get maybe one or two of those, and they gotta get the other brand. Like my son needs some new jeans. He thinks he needs new jeans—he thinks they're short—look fine to me. So we'll get him some new jeans. That's why I'm here at midnight, to get him, make money so I can buy my kid jeans.

Another shopping strategy involves reliance on public transportation to local discount shopping centers and support from family members for transportation:

Now sometimes if I'm on my way home, I'll stop and catch it [bus] when it comes back around. But that's only like—I do that maybe once a month. Up here in Tri-City or Family Dollar—and when I know they're gonna turn around and come back, I'm gonna have a long wait . . . My parents help me when they let me use their car, you know, like if I have to run and pay a bill or something. They let me use the car and then like when I run short, they'll loan me and then I pay them back, you know, like that. (African American single mother of one)

The above comments suggest that some persons make conscious efforts to balance economic, family, and time constraints with the intent to stretch their resources. However, frugality, resourcefulness, delayed gratification, sacrifice, and other traits commonly associated with thriftiness are not evident for all respondents.

Differences in shopping patterns, views about shopping, and overall financial resourcefulness are apparent based on the age of some of the respondents. Several younger single mothers, especially those who receive substantial financial support from family members and governmental sources, appear to be less frugal shoppers and less likely to use shopping strategies. For example, a 23-year-old African

American single mother of a two-year-old son who receives SSI and food stamps and resides in subsidized housing spends about $52 monthly on rent and about $230 monthly on clothing, mainly for herself. With financial support from her mother and governmental aid, another African American single mother of two spends approximately $800 monthly on clothes: "My mother, she, um, she pays for everything. Her car—I use her car. She buys my clothes, the kids' clothes . . . I get food stamps. I get AFDC. I get Medicaid. Oh, and I get, ah, Step Ahead." In addition, price-shopping for groceries does not always translate to frugality when clothing purchases are concerned. For example, one African American single mother of a four-year-old son acknowledges extremely thrifty behavior and planned purchases when grocery shopping, but when questioned about how much she spends monthly on clothing, she admits, "I'd say about seven hundred to a thousand dollars—as much as I make."

Although the last several responses do not represent the vast majority of sample members, they do illustrate diversity of experiences and approaches to prioritizing financial decisions. Whether one believes the amounts quoted by these young respondents, their shopping choices appear disparate when compared to their current financial situations, resulting in possible undue financial burden on family members (typically their mothers) to purchase clothes and other items for their children, while they focus money on themselves. However, as compared to the attitudes and habits of most respondents, they are not the norm.

Extended Family and Clothing One's Family

The centrality of the extended family has been illustrated in earlier chapters and also appears to be an important factor in mediating economic problems for the majority of sample families. Just as Hall and King (1982), Hondegneu-Sotelo (1995), Jarrett (1994), Billingsley (1992), and Stack (1974) show the importance of family and fictive kin in maintaining poor and near-poor families, such networks often provide respondents here with needed instrumental assistance. Although several younger single mothers appear to be overly dependent on family members, the majority of respondents who receive assistance from extended family use it to augment their own strategies for maximizing resources. For example, one African American single mother of one recognizes the amount and level of family support: "Babysitting. Sister, mother sometimes. Food, my sister, my mother sometimes. Clothing.

My sister all the time. Everything else is all me. [Q: Any problems making ends meet?] Naw, not really . . . I've got a lot of family." Similar comments are noted by a married 28-year-old African American mother of two: "For clothing—my mother and my father, they buy the kids clothes quite a bit. Or, uh, to see a doctor, take them shopping. So, I really don't have to buy clothes for the kids too much." Gifts of clothing on holidays and special occasions reduce purchases during the year and can serve as a strategy to stretch incomes. A White single mother of three notes support from her in-laws: "They, um, always buy the kids things for, they'll buy them school clothes. And I think that's the only school clothes they get. They contribute—they'll always buy them suits for Easter and Christmas." A married 28-year-old African American mother makes a similar comment about clothes for her daughter. A large extended family significantly reduces such expenses: "Well, she gets clothing. I usually don't have to buy, you know like, clothes, because she gets enough clothes at Christmas time and at her birthday, from all our different family members . . . that gets her through each season . . . So I usually just end up having to get the underwear and socks and stuff." As suggested by a 27-year-old single Hispanic mother of four, some respondents limit such support to their families: "My mom, babysitting, food, clothes, everything—cousins, friends, just family." And still another African American mother of a ten- and one-year-old receives assistance from family and various agencies: "Yeah, give me, ah, clothing for my children. People have also been generous and brought things for them." Assistance by extended family to provide clothing is most central for mothers with children, regardless of marital status. Holiday gifts, children's birthdays, and thoughtful surprises by relatives that take the form of children's clothing are not viewed as extra outfits to be stored away for special occasions, but became staple attire that mothers then augment using their own funds. Most respondents who regularly receive support in this way come to include it as part of their budgetary strategies.

Other Challenges, Choices, Solutions, and the Future

For certain respondents, a discussion about shopping, budgets, and clothing their family appears to be part of a larger set of goals that includes becoming more economically stable, reducing debt, purchasing a home, and generally improving the quality of life for themselves and their children. Personal goals and objectives tend to influence purchasing patterns and the need to evaluate past and current financial decisions. The following representative comments are most common. One White single parent of three contrasts earlier periods of poor financial management with her current frugal lifestyle and plans to own her own home:

> Yes, I do have credit card debt, but I'm working on it, and I cut it up and when I get credit card things in the mail I cut them up, or anything like that, I don't do it because I'll— and, you know, the weird thing that made me stop that is be- cause there was a commercial on, and they got a credit card in the mail and they were like, where do you want to go? The Bahamas and this and that. And she's like, you know what I really want, I want a house, so they gave them some scis- sors. And I'm like, that makes a lot of sense, you know? If you really want something, you're not gonna get it with a credit card.

One married African American mother of a ten- and one-year old suggests the source of her family's present financial problems: "Um, it's been lately a lot of mismanagement of money [Q: And who man- ages the money?] . . . my husband." Still a married 28-year-old African American mother of two who admits to relying heavily on family and fictive kin mentions the impact of past poor choices and consequences over supposed structural constraints in Gary:

> When we do too much or go out to eat too much or go play bingo too much or [laughs] you know something like that, then it gets rough. Credit cards can be a challenge too. I mean, you know, you think credit cards, everybody want a credit card, so that's the reason. And the interest is like twenty-two point nine on all four of them. 'Cause it's no fun living from paycheck to paycheck—and there's nothing in the savings account . . . Just because of what we pay in rent, if we were to buy a house, something that would be ours. If we could get rid of some of the credit cards. I don't think it would have anything to do with the city. It would be personal.

The initial convenience of credit cards experienced during stable periods can evolve into economic problems due to high interest rates and delinquency fees, if one falls on hard times due to unexpected events. A White single mother comments on her credit card debt as a result of family illness and divorce:

I owe, um, two thousand. And that is only because, my credit limit was twelve hundred, and I had missed a couple of payments. The finance charge is outrageous—it's at two thousand dollars, just by finances—or, you know, the overdraft. And, I'm like, well, a thousand of that isn't even mine [laughs]. So that's something I'm working on. I ask my dad a lot about how do you—you know I want to clear up my credit, 'cause my credit isn't all that great, and most of it's medical bills, stuff like that. But you know I want to do the consolidation thing, but, or bankruptcy, I don't know. Just something I'm tossing around. My dad just says send them five dollars. So that's a lot of times what I do, if I don't send anything, I send them five dollars, and if they accept it that's five more dollars less. At least with hospital bills you don't get a finance charge, it just goes down.

Most respondents who acknowledge the importance of making prudent choices and the implications of past poor decisions tend to focus on individual initiative as the primary mechanism to experience upward economic mobility. For some, economic stability will require time and effort and is spurred by individual effort. Several respondents believe systemic changes will best help them improve their circumstances. Their suggestions to help improve life chances of the poor and near poor center on increased job provisions, improved infrastructure to attract new residents to urban locales, and lower prices for basic goods and services to help residents maximize their incomes and clothe and care for their families. The suggestion by one African American single mother and Gary resident considers both structure and agency and summarizes many of the sample members' views: "Well, a better paying job, which is what I'm about to get . . . Well, they could put more discount stores in my area."

Conclusion: Retailers and Urban Centers

The transition of retailers and related businesses from downtown Gary to suburban Gary and finally to primarily White suburban areas outside the city has resulted in the dependence of many Gary residents on neighboring cities for the majority of their clothing and household shopping needs. Current dire economic conditions in the downtown area and, to a somewhat lesser degree, in The Village area, are illustrated by the increased level of concentrated poverty in the former area that diminishes as one travels away from the city. An examination of store out-migration patterns shows that there are currently few quality retailers and no large-scale retailers or department stores in Gary. Residents must travel outside the area, typically to Merrillville, to frequent such establishments. This stimulates the economies of nearby cities and also undermines the Gary tax base when these dollars do not turn over in the city.

Findings in this chapter illustrate suburban shopping patterns by a sample of Gary and non-Gary residents. Results show that Gary residents are just as likely to shop at suburban stores as suburban residents themselves.[17] In some instances, Gary residents shop at suburban stores with greater frequency than do suburbanites. Budgeting strategies that enable residents from Gary to maximize their incomes often result in frequenting discount mega-stores. Because most of these establishments are also located in suburban areas, Gary residents who shop there also undermine possible economic benefits to the city. To the degree that these results are representative, the findings suggest that Gary shoppers play a critical role in maintaining the suburban Indiana retail economic base.

However, many Gary respondents continue to frequent local businesses such as the Village Shopping Center. In general, department and large retail stores that have relocated or closed in The Village have been replaced by discount stores and trendy, low-end retailers. Choosing to shop in these establishments retains revenue in the city, but constrains the shopping options of some residents who may wish to make purchases at department stores or other retailers that are unavailable in Gary. The ability to maintain high occupancy rates in The Village suggests the spending power of segments of the population and the ability of city business and political leaders to attract replacement stores. However, direct observation and respondent commentary suggest that the quality and type of merchandise now offered at many of the newer stores are limited and marketed primarily toward youth culture.

Downtown Gary has not fared well. There are no department stores, large retailers, or retail chains in the downtown area. Besides the one small discount retailer, small specialty stores, and sundry other businesses, the area is largely vacant.[18] Older respondents and those familiar with business out-migration from Gary find traveling to "Southlake Mall" and other suburban stores more problematic and are aware of the ramifications of continuing to *take* their tax dollars into areas that don't reciprocate by supporting economic enterprise in Gary. However, given the limited options in the city, most continue to frequent suburban stores to clothe their families and purchase large household items. The absence of department stores, furniture stores, and discount mega-stores means that the shopping choices of most Gary residents are extremely constrained by social forces seemingly outside their control.

According to Catlin (1993) in *Racial Politics and Urban Planning: Gary, Indiana 1980–1989*, business out-migration from Gary reflects a purposed attempt by primarily White suburban and state economic and political leaders to control the economic base of the city and thereby render it economically and politically impotent. For Catlin, the decision to spearhead and encourage the mass business exodus from Gary was fueled by disdain for the growing African American constituency in Gary and the refusal of African American political and economic leaders to defer to their White counterparts. Respondents who have lived in Gary since the 1970s and those privy to its history concur with Catlin's assessments. Still some, too young to witness the transition, but who notice the limited retailers and related business in Gary and abandoned sites in a once-thriving Village and downtown area have come to also suspect the connection behind the economic conditions in Gary and retail arrangements in and around the city. And some respondents appear to be less concerned about the absence of such retailers and establishments, but rather go about their daily round with the resolve that absences of these products and services are a *given* with which they must contend. From this reference point of situational adaptivity, the goal follows to save money and maximize their resources in light of these circumstances.

According to some respondents, especially young single mothers, a trip to a suburban mall is often considered a shopping outing. Trendy discount retailers in "The Village" meet many of their personal clothing needs at lower prices. Periodic trips to suburban mega-stores, usually by family members such as mothers and grandmothers, also mean their children's clothing needs and household items are purchased. Thus the 30–45-minute trip to a mall represents an opportunity to augment their wardrobes and make a "day-trip" outside Gary—seemingly with less knowledge about the broader implications for the economic viability of the city. And respondents with less favorable sentiments about suburban shopping seem to consider it a "necessary evil" based on their limited options in the city.

The unsuccessful campaigns to increase shopping loyalty in Gary may initially appear to be the result of uninformed residents without the business savvy to realize the implications of their actions. Further consideration suggests that residents may also be responding to past expectations as well as *daily round* needs. For persons accustomed to shopping at department stores, such as Sears and JC Penney, and upscale retailers, such as Hudson's, replacement retailers, such as AJ Wright, Rainbow, and One Price Clothing, may not be acceptable options—particularly if previous shopping history suggests that the former stores provide better quality, reasonably priced merchandise, while the latter stores are associated with less-expensive, but lower-quality goods. The choice to frequent the latter types of stores may be further challenged, when shoppers know their mainstay establishments are available—at the suburban mall. In these instances, store and product loyalty may overshadow loyalty to stores in Gary—especially if city officials are believed to be unable to attract and maintain the desired shopping venues. In addition, given that residents must address their daily needs (and wants) as well as those of family members, practical decisions are often made. Frequenting mega-stores that provide an array of shopping options for family and household needs at discount prices is often a response to the limited options and higher prices at local stores. Thus mega-stores enable many residents, especially the poor and near-poor, to be more resourceful and represent rational justification for shopping trips to suburban locales.

Choosing to shop solely in Gary would affect the financial standing of many suburban stores and spur economic renewal in the city, but the sacrifice would not be equally felt by all residents. More economically stable households would be better able to sustain city-shopping than their poorer counterparts. And although the long-term benefits of such collective action could result in the in-migration of retailers and others stores seeking lost suburban dollars, short-term, it appears to be difficult to convince a sufficient contingency of Gary residents to sustain such as movement.

Most respondents from Gary go about a daily round similar to those of their primarily White suburban counterparts, but without many of the amenities and conveniences suburbia affords. Detractors may suggest that the city's economic base would not support the types of retailers and stores found in the suburbs, whereas these data suggest significant spending power within the city and resident interest in expanded shopping options. Persons unfamiliar with the challenges of urban living presented here should be cautious about placing undue responsibility on Gary residents for failing to "choose" to shop in Gary (and thus boycott suburban stores), especially when their choices are quite finite, and, in some cases, undermine the ability to effectively meet family needs within their financial constraints. Business, political, and other economic leaders who reside in Gary, as well as their suburban and state counterparts, must also contend with the motives and decisions that have resulted in the current retail-related economic challenges in the city.

CHAPTER FIVE

A Tale of Three Families:
Impracticality Costs

Scholars have discovered the research benefits of first person narratives to augment traditional empirical studies. In the ground-breaking ethnography by Liebow (1967), the reader is transported into the day-to-day experiences of the central character, Tally, and in doing so, comes to better understand the challenges and triumphs of urban living for a segment of that population. Through the use of narratives and life histories, Liebow guides the reader in order to expand possibly contracted definitions of Black masculinity. This chapter is in the tradition of Liebow's work and, more recently, Pattillo-McCoy's (1999) case histories of "Spider Waters" and "Terri Jones." The three families, one African American (Tamara Davis), one White (Pat Moore), and one Hispanic (Mary Ramirez), were selected based on their experiences in and around Gary, Indiana, and their status as families with dependent children (refer to Table 5.1 for demographic profiles of each family). Unlike the families profiled in chapter 3, each family in this chapter previously lived in Gary or in an urban setting similar to Gary. Each made a decision to relocate, but continues to have close ties to urban areas. As such, they provide a unique perspective regarding out-migration challenges and choices. Each may also represent persons most likely to relocate back to cities such as Gary based on the effectiveness of urban renewal efforts. The purpose here is also to compare and contrast their economic and noneconomic experiences as current or previous residents in urban locales. Narratives are presented chronologically as recalled by the respondents.[1] I also introduce emergent themes and periodically interject observations. This slight deviation from tradition is done to provide added structure for the reader.

Table 5.1
Family Demographics and Monthly Household Expenses

Variable	Tamara	Pat	Mary
Total in Household (adults and children)	3	4	5
Average Annual Household Income	$27.5 K	$17.5 K	$32.5K
Monthly Food Amount	$250*	$75	$300
Monthly Clothing Amount	$25	$35	$100
Monthly Rent (# bedrooms)	$720 (2)	$620 (3)	$350 (house)
Gas/Utilities	$100	$109	$150
Car Insurance	$150	$82	$154
Telephone Bill	$45	$75	$50
Health Insurance	Husband	Medicaid	$40[+]
Childcare/week	$130	$50	na
Other Expenses:			
Internet		$19.95	
Car Note	$298	$0	$0
Estimated Monthly Household Income:	$2,292	$1,458	$2,708
Estimated Monthly Household Expenses:	$1,763	$1,066	$1,144
Net:	$529	$392	$1,564

Note:
[*]$175 used to purchase food for the home, remainder for day care.
[+]Children insured via Hoosier Healthcare.

The goal is not generalizability—the small sample size precludes this. However, the exploration of the everyday lives of the three families may serve to uncover common experiences and understandings that parallel current literature on poverty and urban living and also illustrate nuances within these research arenas. In general, the families are similar in terms of socioeconomic status (per capita family income). They also employ specific strategies, as they go about the daily round and incur many of the same types of costs to feed, clothe, and care for their families. However, they have varying views about poverty, urban challenges, and remedies. A summary is provided at each section end, and the chapter conclusion reminds the reader of ways in which the histories of the three families inform the larger theoretical framework and literature on the urban experience. As suggested by Pattillo-McCoy (1999), upon completion, the readers will hopefully be able "to see the world through the eyes of someone . . . using his or her unique perspective to illuminate key social mechanisms" (p. 167).

The Family of Tamara Davis

"I try to show as much support for Gary as I can, but I try not to be stupid either."

Thirty-year-old Tamara was born and raised in Gary, Indiana. Although she currently lives and works outside the city in nearby Merrillville and LaPorte, Indiana, respectively, much of her time is spent with family and friends in Gary. Tamara is one of five children born into a working-class nuclear family. Although her father could not read or write, education, hard work, and delayed gratification were stressed by both her parents. Her father was employed at American Bridge Steel, and her mother worked at a local business. Family involvement in a local Black church was central to her upbringing. Tamara earned a college degree from Indiana University Northwest, is married, and has two children, ages 2 and 10. After five years of marriage, she is currently separated from her husband; their divorce is pending. Tamara is employed as a case worker and earns between $25,000 and $30,000 annually. She and her children live in a newly renovated apartment building. The apartment is spacious, bright, and decorated primarily with furniture given to her by her mother. Photographs of her two children and sorority memorabilia provide most of the décor in the living and dining areas. The apartment is clean, but her daughter's play toys are strewn about. Tamara is visibly reflexive, yet guarded, as she speaks about her experiences as a previous resident of Gary, Indiana.

> I have three sisters and a brother and I grew up in Gary, Indiana. We grew up very religious . . . in church all the time . . . a Christian family. We grew up in a Baptist church and both of my parents attended church with us, so it was kind of instilled that this was important. And education was pushed. I remember that, close to time for graduation, I said, 'I think I'm going to go to the military.' And my mother told me, uhm, something to the effect of—'The question is not, are you going to college, but rather, what college are you going to?' So it was pretty clear that was the path that I was supposed to take. I was raised with a sense that family was important and so you stay committed to your family and a sense of community, really too—to give back to the community.

I remember when I was real little, I remember my mother working at the bank and I don't really remember my father working at that time. Then I remember when my father got laid off from the steel mill. And at first I really couldn't tell that things had changed, but as I got older we used to collect aluminum cans for money and recycle newspaper, so then I knew, that that [father's layoff] had affected our finances. I remember they use to argue about the division of labor. I think at that time, I'm pretty sure my father was laid off at that time and so my mother would say that if she came home from work the dinner should be ready and that type of thing. But then I do remember him cooking occasionally, but I only remember him cooking like two things so I'm not even sure if he could really cook. I know he did not clean. But he did do a lot of baby sitting. Even if it was just dragging the kids around wherever he was going because moreso what I remember—just going from house to house—different people, with him—and just kind of being underfoot with him and not so much as in the house.

Once I got older, I knew that we were poor. And I remember one time, these jeans had come out that had like, fake leather on the front, and everybody had some. And I was just gonna lose my mind if I didn't get any. And all my friends wanted to take these pictures together in school with these same jeans on and I remember my mother didn't have the money and I was just screaming and crying and so she borrowed the money from my aunt to get the money for me to have these jeans. And then I remember hearing her on the phone talking to my other aunt about what my aunt puts you through to borrow money from her and then I felt bad that I had put my mother through that just for a pair of jeans and so . . . we were pretty poor growing up.

Tamara's characterizations of poverty include economic as well as sociopsychological dimensions, and she is candid about including herself in the portrait.

Uhm, usually I know that it's kids who are usually poor, but I also think that, you don't have to be destitute to necessarily be poor. It's more like a mindset too or limited resources—

feeling as if you also can't get ahead—then that makes you poor too.

I think that I was poor, to a certain degree. I may not have been getting food stamps or anything like that, but if something major comes along, like when my transmission went out—if you cannot meet those things and it puts undo stress on you or even if something extra comes along—like extra childcare for a week when school is out and you can't afford to pay for it—then you're poor.

I think that I was poorer, last year, because I couldn't see a way out of it, but now I can so—that's why I said your mind-set too—because I guess then I was probably more depressed and so now that I can actually see that some things are opening up and different things are getting paid off, it's like then I don't see myself as being poor—I don't think I've arrived . . . I don't think I'm as bad off as I was before either. Well, I was struggling to pay for childcare, struggling to pay for rent and everything else, it's like the basic things, I didn't have the money to pay for.

Tamara acknowledges some of the benefits and drawbacks of marriage and education—two commonly accepted mechanisms for upward mobility.

Part of it was because my husband wasn't giving me any money and I had these two kids. Then another part of it though, I think, is this area. Even with a college degree, I'm not getting paid for having a college degree. Its like, 'well, this job requires some college' so we'll pay you what we'd pay a person with some college and so you have to take it or leave it. So it's like you've invested all this time and money into higher education, but it's not being maximized in this area.

But you still need to get an education because the majority of the jobs in this area that don't require you to have an education don't provide enough income or benefits so that you can meet your basic needs—so it's to your benefit to stay on welfare than to actually get a job. But if you had an education, it doesn't put you that much over the hump, but it does put you a little bit ahead where you could at least get a more . . . a job that makes you feel better about yourself, like you're doing something worthwhile instead of just flipping burgers or something.

In spite of previous challenges, Tamara seems confident in several life-changing decisions and also acknowledges the difficulty in making other choices. She also suggests that unique challenges may exist to maintain a marriage and rear children in an urban setting.

> I would say to go to college . . . to leave my husband last year. I think those are the two best ones. Now I think I'm kind of being paid for having a college degree, but even when I wasn't being paid, at least I knew deep down that I could always go someplace else. I knew it made me more marketable. I might not feel like it right now, but I knew, at least that that was the case, so it at least helped my self-esteem in that area.

> Well, I didn't leave for a long time, because I was thinking, ok, well then my kids are going to be poor—because he was paying the rent and Nipsco [power bill] and everything else and I knew it was going to be hard for me to pay all of that in addition to all the other things I had to pay. But then I didn't realize how much child support I would get and everything else. So actually I'm more financially secure away from him because even though he had resources, he wasn't sharing them and so when I finally left, it kind of clicked with me that the state is making him give me those resources, where before I could see the resources, but that didn't necessarily mean we [she and the children] were benefiting from those resources.

> In terms of my marriage, well we have two very different backgrounds. He grew up in a family where the father provided everything and the mother did not work and then I had two working parents. I had more education than he had, which now I think, I look back and I think that probably intimidated him and made him feel less worthy. And then, we had never planned on having kids—period. And then his son ended up living with us, which changed everything and then I ended up getting pregnant, which changed everything again. So I think he kind of blames me for both of the kids being here too . . . because like, the mother and I were having words like, back and forth, back and forth, so he kind of

feels like if I had left her alone, she never would have left the son there with us.

I would say I was married probably about two or three months before I found out that he had cheated on me before we got married. But then he swore, you know, that was when I was feeling insecure about getting married or whatever, but then further on down the line, I found out that he had been cheating like all along . . . First, I don't think he was ever ready to get married. I think probably his parents were pushing him, saying that I was the right one, so then he just went along with that probably. I think that in this area, so many women are willing to just take whatever they can get—so it's like a lot of available women which plays into it. And then, a black man with a decent job—so he had extra money to give to women too—well then that played a part too.

He hasn't really said, he didn't even mention a divorce. I had to bring it up. And he's just like . . . he's not taking the initiative. So I can see that I'm going to have to be the one to get everything together. He didn't even show up for court when we had court for our daughter. So I'm going to have to take the initiative in everything . . . I plan on having a relationship in the future. I wouldn't say that I plan on getting married. I'm not saying I wouldn't, but I'm not saying I plan on it either. But I doubt I'll have anymore children. For one, I didn't realize they'd be this expensive and then, it's draining, physically and emotionally when you never get rid of them either, because the baby-sitting resources I have I usually use during the day when I'm at work, which means that I always have them in the evenings and on the weekend, which means I never get a break. And so it's taxing.

Tamara readily mentions her future plans.

There are two things that I figure I might do. I've applied for my Ph.D.—to schools to get my Ph.D. And if either one of those programs accepts me then I'll go that route and then I'd like to open up a learning facility for special needs kids in Gary. And then if that doesn't work out, I'm probably going to stick with the agency where I am now, but I'll move to another site that

we have—probably the one that's in Alabama and then relocate with this job and just try to advance in the ranks.

However, growing up in Gary, Tamara feels an affinity towards the
city and also has definite views about its current condition, and what
is needed for renewal. She is also critical of outside depictions of the
city. Yet she and her family have tended to live outside Gary.

> Well, in a way, I regret not going off to college because my
> view of things is limited to just northwest Indiana. And so I
> think if I had gone off to college I may have come back, but I
> would not have stayed had I come back, whereas now I feel
> more obligated to stay just because you haven't experienced
> anything else.

> I would consider moving to Gary, but I would have to have the
> financial ability to move to one of the better parts of Gary in-
> stead of one of the poorer areas. Gary is my home—probably be-
> cause I grew up there. And the people that I worked with . . . all
> of those people are from Gary. So even though I wasn't living in
> Gary, I still had close community ties with people from Gary—
> and it's the one area here that has the most Black people.

> Well I try to show as much support for Gary as I can, but I
> try not to be stupid either. Things like groceries would be too
> expensive to get in Gary. But I bank at a credit union and
> it's in Gary. They have a branch in Gary and a branch in
> Crown Point so I choose to use the one in Gary—trying to
> keep some business in Gary . . . Well I think that the base-
> ball stadium thing—if they could get it off the ground and
> going—has the potential to provide a lot of jobs in that area
> and the basketball team they have—if we would focus on
> other things besides just the casinos or whatever, because
> they're owned by one person, so he chooses how much he
> gives to you, whereas the other things are owned by the city
> an' we could decide how the money is spent. If the politicians
> can get the people inspired enough to support these things—
> but I don't think they've been marketed enough. I know the
> basketball teams weren't marketed enough to get people to
> participate in those activities . . . If you look at, especially
> the young people in Gary, they're wearing one hundred dol-
> lar gym shoes and outfits where the pants alone were one
> hundred dollars, so it's how you choose to spend your money.

I think there is a lot of money to be spent in Gary, but unfortunately it's not spent in Gary. You know, you go to Southlake Mall and these other places and spend your money.

Gary is presented in a way that others, and I know because I work with White people all the time, and they always say, 'You go to Gary?'—as if people are just falling down dead on every corner. When it's not that. If you're engaged in the wrong types of activities, which could happen to you in Valparaiso, Hammond, Portage, Merrillville, where ever, then you run the risk of you know, murder, or whatever. But unless you just happen to be in the wrong place at the wrong time—which most people know the wrong places—and you just never go to those places—then you are relatively safe.

Tamara is also candid about her challenges and concerns, as she attempts to make ends meet. Her extended family plays an important role in providing childcare. She feels torn about dependence on them, yet Tamara recognizes their centrality in helping her sustain her family.

The biggest thing that I have to pay for besides rent is childcare. And that's always a struggle. At least twice a month I think to myself—I should pull my daughter out and take her someplace cheaper because where she goes is one hundred dollars a week. But then I have to also think about the investment. She could be in a daycare where she's just there, you know, playing all day—and that would be about $50 or $60 dollars, which she was at one before. But she's actually in a school, so she's learning something. So I see this as an investment into her future so then you have to pick and choose what is the greater benefit. So that's always a challenge. And then anytime anything new comes up—I'd like to save for a rainy day or whatever, but something big always comes along and you have to pay for that.

When I don't have the money for her childcare, what I do is, between me and my mother and sister; we just make arrangements to keep her for that week, because I pay week to week. So if I don't have the money this week, then she just doesn't go and one of us keeps her at different portions of the day or all day . . . I'd say this probably happens about once every two months or so.

There are like two situations when my mother might keep my daughter. One is when she has already missed like two days, then I don't see the point in paying one hundred dollars for a whole week when I've missed half of the week. So those times I don't mind asking for help, because it's not like you need it, it's just a preference. But at the times when I don't have the money to pay for it and then I need you to keep her then, that's whenever it does feel kind of bad, like, 'I can't even provide childcare, you know, for my own child.' But she [her mother] never makes me feel bad or whatever. And I think that if she could keep her everyday, she would. Before I had her, my mother wasn't working mornings and so she said she would keep her. And actually when I first had her, she used to keep her everyday, but then I was only working part-time and you're talking about a whole lot less hours than forty hours a week. And then when I started working forty hours a week, she couldn't keep her anymore. I think my mother keeps her for two reasons. I think she likes spending time with her, but I think part of the bigger picture too is when she knows that I don't have any money, well then, she'll keep her.

Like I never ask my mother to keep her like, unless I have to, because I know that she can be a handful and if you've had her all week, all day long, then there's no way that I would ask you to keep her on a Saturday for me to have some time because, that's asking too much. I know she gets on my sister's nerves because she will say, 'She's getting on my nerves or whatever.' But they still try to help out. It becomes stressful—I guess this is part of wanting to keep up with the Jones, but if I see other kids with nice things and I know that their parents paid a lot of money for them—but my kids don't look bad, but they aren't in the type of things these kids are in—then I kind of feel bad. I wonder am I doing stuff right, you know, but then I just have to remind myself well, they're well cared for, they're fed, they look clean, nice and neat, and that's the most important thing . . . and then just like a stress when you almost feel like you're by yourself—because so many decisions I have to make on my own and you don't know whether you're making the right decisions or not. That's stressful in itself because you're always wondering whether this is going to be ok or not . . .

However, she quickly recognizes her accomplishments and motivators.

> I'm most proud . . . I would probably have to say—my kids. They inspire me a whole lot to keep going. You know—when things are really, really bad. Then, it's like, well I'm not just responsible for them, but because you love 'em, you want to, give 'em, be good to them—so that kind of pushes you to do more than what you normally would do.

> Because Christianity was very important when I was growing up, it gives me a sense of—even when I get down—I don't think this is where I'm going to be forever. I always feel like there's gonna be a better day for me and God has more in store for me . . . and so that I'm able to then encourage myself, even when I get down. And I'm sure that comes from my belief in God and faith that he hears me when I pray and is more concerned about my situation than I am.

Summary

For Tamara, poverty has both an economic and emotional component and is characterized by the ease with which persons are able to negotiate the daily round. Her comments suggest that poverty can be considered from a theoretical perspective, but her personal experiences provide a practical benchmark as well. Tamara followed the customary familial pattern and married before having children, yet she has not reaped many of the benefits suggested in literature. According to Tamara, fear of exposing her children to poverty prompted her to remain in a problem marriage. Human capital as a result of her college education, continued assistance from extended family, and legal intervention enabled her to leave that environment. Strong religious beliefs, learned since childhood, provide emotional support. Attitudes often considered "middle class," such as concerns about childcare, materialism, and investing in her daughter's future, are evident in Tamara's dialogue. Yet, her child-centered concerns and Christian beliefs reflect research on African American family dimensions.[2] Finally, Tamara's upbringing in Gary in a working-class, education-oriented family, combined with her formal education, both appear to have made her acutely aware of the problems, inequities, shortcomings, as well as strengths found in the city. And although she refuses to embrace pejorative views about the city, she has made a conscious decision to live elsewhere.

The Family of Pat Moore

"Poor? . . . Not me, 'cause I always feel that there is someone worse off than me."

Pat is a 29-year-old single mother of three multiracial children ages 6, 9, and 10. Pat was born in Maryland, near Washington, D.C., but has spent most of her adult life in the Indiana/Chicago land area. She grew up in a middle-class family in Dyer, Indiana, where she graduated from high school. She lived in Chicago Heights for about three years with her partner before returning to Indiana. Her parents are divorced, and she has a younger brother. Pat earns about $15,000–$20,000 annually as a community service representative and has lived in Valparaiso, Indiana, for six years. She receives less than $200 monthly in child support. Upon entering her home, it is clear that Pat takes great pains in creating an inviting atmosphere. Modestly decorated, the home is clean and color coordinated. Pictures line the walls and candles are arranged around the living and dining areas. Pat speaks candidly about her past, her choices, and the resulting consequences. She is open to discussion and appears to have thought a great deal about her experiences. Pat begins by describing her family and her childhood.

> I have a very close relationship with my dad. It wasn't like that when I was growing up. I was afraid of him. His hands looked like they were twice the size of mine . . . he was scary. And he definitely had his views on interracial relationships . . . did not like it. He called me all kinds of names and after my mom and dad divorced I think he realized he didn't have anything and either had a choice to accept my choices or be by himself. This was when I graduated from high school. I did not have any type of interracial relationship except for, I think the first guy I dated was Latino and my dad did not like it. He made racial comments and it was like, something you just didn't do. And I think that dating someone who was Latino was like right on the edge of the fence and if I would ever date someone who was Black, I'd cross over. And I think in high school I had feelings, but I couldn't do anything about them because I was living under my parents' roof so, you know, and after that then, it was

like, well, I'm an adult and I can choose what I want to choose and it doesn't matter. But he just come to my job one night and he just broke down and he apologized for everything he said and said that he loved me and whatever choice I make is the choice I make. And ever since then we've, our relationship, has built stronger and stronger.

In spite of the initially turbulent relationship with her father and their temporary estrangement, Pat considers him her strongest ally.

He's helped me through a lot, you know, a lot of struggles when I lived in Chicago Heights, especially, you know, there were probably a month or two without lights—he wouldn't hold my hand so much where he'd pay for anything, but he'd get me through it, you know, and I thank him for that because sometimes when things are handed to you, you don't work as hard. He'd make sure, like when I didn't have a car, he'd make sure I had bus money and cab fare to get where I needed to go . . . My dad lives in Dyer. That's about an hour away. He comes every Friday and every Sunday and that helps a lot just with keeping with the family atmosphere. And then there's their grandparents, well, their grandfather passed away this year, but their grandmother, they go to see her every other weekend . . . that's in Chicago Heights, about an hour away. And my mom lives . . . about five or six hours away.

When I moved here, it was a very small, one bedroom apartment. I didn't have a bedroom [furniture] for probably the first couple of years I lived here. But each year, it got a little bit bigger and a little bit bigger. I've gotten a car, my dad, he's kind of like my loan officer. He puts up the money up front, but I pay it back, like when I get my taxes back and I always do, so I know I can hold my head up when I look at him, you know. And so every year, this year, my big accomplishment was getting a washing machine and dryer, full size. And I was like, 'Mom, you know, can I judge myself by this?' It's like I never thought I'd have, a full size washer and dryer and something so simple . . . but not to have to walk to the Laundromat anymore. So it's exciting.

Pat attributes her mother and father with instilling values such as frugality and hard work to achieve goals, which tend to be economic in nature.

> My mom was the type of person that, if she wanted something bad enough, she'd get three jobs to get it and once, she wanted a pool in the back yard. And she would also use credit cards a lot and so that was always her mission, to pay off her credit cards—which she's got excellent credit. And my dad was, you know, forty dollars a week allowance for groceries for her every week, because that's what he could afford to give. And I guess with me and my three kids I think that's enough because I've learned to survive on forty dollars a week and I do one time grocery shopping and I'm done for the month. But I think, like for Christmases I always say, 'Don't expect a lot, money's tight.' But to kids, 'Don't expect a lot,' means you're maybe going to get two or three gifts, but for Christmas there'd be all kinds of gifts, but we were never set up to expect a lot. My mom always instilled, appreciate what you have and she was the lunch lady at school and my dad worked on cars. It was pretty average. I wouldn't say I got everything I wanted, but I don't feel like, I wasn't fulfilled as a child. And my mom brought me up good, with good values. You know, work hard, and appreciate what you have and don't take anything for granted.
>
> I started working when I was 13. I had 18 families that I baby sat for. During the summer I bought my own school clothes. That's where my work started. And then when I was 16, I started waitressing, so I was ready to work as soon as I could. . . . I judge myself by my accomplishments and what I accomplish year after year, you know.

After moving to Chicago Heights, Pat began dating and met the African American man who would later father her children. She recalls the problems associated with this phase of her life and the final event that precipitated her departure.

> I worked. It started out as him paying the rent and me paying the bills. But it come about where my bills were even higher than him even paying the rent and then he'd hardly pay the rent. And it was like, 'I can't do it all,'—working at Target, making maybe $7.00, $7.50 an hour, only went so

far. And having to pay childcare and because we didn't have a whole lot of money, I think at that point I didn't know what programs were out there or what I could have for childcare. Like I know here, there are so many things to help you out and get you through hard times. And the kids had very crummy childcare. I'd make their lunch everyday, make their breakfast and dinner, 'cause they were there for the 3 until 11 shift or whatever, and the lady's daughter would eat their lunch sometimes and call my kids names. And it's like, I didn't have a choice. I didn't know what to do.

When I lived with their dad, we didn't have much and it was constantly a struggle and being under him and him being like the main breadwinner, there was too much control on his part and I couldn't—I had no money for nothing, and it was frustrating and finally after three and a half, four years, I was like, 'That's enough. You're taking money from me, you're bringing me down. I can't take it anymore.' And once I got out and got away from there, I could see what I could do.

It was economic and it was abuse [her decision to leave]. He'd shove me around a lot. He'd, he punched me. He'd throw me down, you know, different things. He'd call me racial names and I did it to him once and he about broke my jaw. We could always be good friends, but if we put any type of a relationship into it, it just wouldn't work. I mean, now, we're very good friends, we're, not close, but, we get along and he's married now and everything's fine. We have a good relationship, but anything else, no way.

I think my oldest is the one who probably remembers some of that stuff 'cause he's a little bit older. He was still a little guy, but I think he still remembers. The other two were very small and they've never thought about that. And I remind him of those things because sometimes he will hit his brother and like just punch hard. And I say, 'You know, we don't do that. We don't hit.' You know, I will spank them and I will smack them with the belt, as required, but I'm not a hitter. I'm not a puncher—you know. I said, 'Remember, you can't be a guy like that. You have to control yourself. If you're that angry then find something else to get your frustration out, do not punch somebody 'cause you could hurt them.' 'Cause he'll punch his sister and I don't like the whole punching girls

thing. And I say, 'Remember, remember what your mom
went through.' And maybe that's my issue projecting on him,
but because I'm so aware of it, I don't want my boys to be like
that because that's where boys get it. They see it. And, I'm
fearful of that, so I do remind him sometimes of that because
he's got a temper. Even though he doesn't have his father's
temper per say, because of genetics, but it's learned behavior.

The reason I left him—was the final straw—is because I
was working at Target. I didn't have an account, so I had
my money stored in my room. When I thought he was taking my money, I'd put it in books and he'd find it, take it.
And sometimes I'd have my money laid out 'cause I had
bills. I'm gonna pay this to this person, this to that person—and he took $20 from me and I needed that $20 'cause
that had to go for a bill. And I told him to give it back—
"Cause you're not just taking from me, you're taking from
your kids, we gotta pay our lights, we gotta have a roof over
our heads, I'm the one that answers to the landlord, you're
not here.' And he's like, 'I don't know what you're talking
about,' and we had our one last brawl and I called the police and had him arrested. I got tired of being pushed
around—it was just enough. I never would've had this [her
current apartment], if I didn't leave.

And these kids deserve to have a chance—to see, so they feel,
I don't know . . . the Smith's, their grandparents, they have
said they'll put a down payment on a house if I come live
there. And I told them no, because their neighborhood is
nice, their street is nice, but that's not all there is—there's
the whole area of Chicago Heights. There's kids who snatch
each other's shoes and it's ridiculous. When I moved to Valpo
and then I went back to get the last of my things out of my
apartment with my dad, I came back and it was like a different world. It was kind of like 'sunshine and darkness' and
you come back and you're like, 'I lived here for four years?'
You know, I lived in that crappy apartment in a roach-
infested and, you know—that's not even how I was brought
up. It humbled me, it made me see, this is a part of life and
some things you just accept, but it's not something I'd go
back to—I wouldn't go live there. I don't mind driving them
every other weekend to go see their grandmother. I'd rather
do that than to be living across the street. I don't care if they

paid for the house or paid my mortgage and everything, I still wouldn't do it . . . the poverty. It's the liquor stores, they just set people up for failure there. When you really don't have the bus fare to go get some groceries and you go to the corner store and you're gonna spend $50 bucks on a few items. It's terrible. Why would you do that? Why would you put up a liquor store on every other corner and you know, put up this convenience store, you know, what does 'convenience' mean? Convenience for who?

Pat has experienced hardship, yet she does not consider herself poor and has a specific definition of poverty.

Poor, not me. 'Cause I always feel that there is someone worse off than me. I have a hard time taking charity and charity I mean, like, the Toys for Tots Program. They helped me out last year and this year. This year I needed it because I didn't, I haven't been getting child support like I should have. It's hard and someone had to talk me into it to do it, because, you know, you look at people, even in my job. The way they dress, the way they carry themselves, I see the same man walk up and down the street. I don't know whether he's homeless or what—he looks like it. I've always felt that there is someone worse off than you, which there is. But I don't feel like I'm poor, because I have a lot of stuff. I have a lot of things that, maybe its material items, most things, but I have a lot of blessings. And since I've moved here, things have gotten so much better.

Poor means not having your own home—having to kind of stay with people. Poor . . . it's hard to describe. Not being able to feed your family. Not being able to pay for childcare because your job doesn't pay you enough. And that's always a constant fear for me because childcare is so ridiculous, that's another thing that they set you up for failure because they make it so high, you have to get two jobs to pay for childcare.

However, Pat acknowledges a time when she did consider herself poor.

When we lived in Chicago, we had a bedroom. It was a big house and you rented out a bedroom and we paid $275 a month. That was [her ex-partner] and my first place together.

And I cried. I cried because I had just had my oldest son. And our room was so tiny and you had a dresser, a twin bed, and a closet. A community kitchen, so you put your box or bag of groceries in the refrigerator and pray to God no one ate it. Of course, you could have your dry goods or whatever in your room, as much as you could possibly fit in there along with your clothes and your shoes and your belongings and your whole life in that room . . . a wobbly lock on the door . . . a community bathroom, no laundry facilities, so most of us would take turns washing our laundry in the bathtub on a washboard. That was an experience. I think I got the most education out of that place than I ever have. I saw a man beat to death because they found out he was homosexual and seeing blood everywhere. Drugs . . . constantly, and it was, I don't know, one of those things you just step out on faith and hope you don't get in trouble for something you didn't do or you don't get killed or and I think that was my feeling on it because I've never seen anything like that. I grew up in a rural, felt like to me, all-American town. It was just, ranch house, simple, everything was clean and then I'm here—I'm in my early 20s moving into a roach-infested tiny bedroom—and this is my fate right now. So, I think that was the lowest of low out of my life.

We needed a place and I think it was something we found or he heard about 'cause it was something he set up and I couldn't live with my mom. She lived in a trailer and she could only have the people on the lease in that house and no one else . . . We even stayed in Harvey with a couple that had 10 children and we slept there. Just enough to have a place to lay my head to go to work. I still went to work through it all. My son was just born. With all my jobs I only stayed gone for three weeks. I went right back to work because I couldn't afford the benefits of being gone for six weeks or any longer.

In addition to candor about her past, Pat is clear about prudent as well as poor choices she has made.

The best decision was to leave their dad. And I think about that everyday. Even when my kids ask me, you know, 'Why didn't you marry our daddy?' and of course that's a reasonable question, but we're just good friends and that's how our relationship is meant to be. I don't regret having kids. They're my focus, because I don't think if I had kids—I don't know what I'd be doing because before, I think I was a lot more spontaneous person and now I'm just kind of, 'This is where I am and this is what I have to do.' Kids make you grow up, not everybody, but for the most part, kids put you on the right track. Moving to Valpo, was the second best thing. I was worried about moving to Valpo because I had heard about the KKK out here and I was scared to death. I didn't know what to expect. I didn't want to put my kids in danger and I had talked about it before, but I was like, 'I'm just going to have to stay here and tough it out and I lived without their dad probably for a year.' 'Cause I had a restraining order and I didn't know if he would hurt me and I was just like scared and I was like, 'Well, I did this. I put him out. Now I've gotta do some things on my own.' So, I dated two different men on different occasions. The second one, he was the reason I left Chicago Heights because he threatened me . . . he followed me to work . . . he just came to my job and threatened me and was grabbing me and I was like, 'You know, I'm not doing this anymore. I'm not being pushed around, I'm not going to be shoved around, I'm not going to be scared.' I called my mom and said, 'I wanna come home.' And I said, 'I can't do this anymore . . . I don't know what's wrong. I'm picking the wrong men or something.' So she said, 'I've just been waiting for your call.' And she came that night and just said, 'Pack whatever you can, I'm taking you to Valpo.' And she says, 'You're not going back, so I hope this is the decision that you want to make.'

One thing I regret in my life is that I wasn't able to marry the father of my children. That's what I've always wanted, you know, and it didn't happen. And I regret—I wish that I was married [Why?] . . . It's the right thing to do. That's what you're supposed to do. You're supposed to get married first, have children second and it didn't happen that way. My mom . . . she was a virgin when she got married and that's how I wanted it, but it didn't happen that way and I don't know, I just think that, I did everything backwards, I guess. And my mom had a very tight thumb on me growing up, I couldn't do anything, I couldn't go anywhere. And when I turned 18, I was out that door—and a year later I was pregnant. So I didn't listen, I thought, I'm 18, I know it all, so that's the thing I regret—not listening, not accepting what my parents had to say—mostly my mom because I thought I knew it all.

At that time I got a job at DJs in River Oaks and that's where I started to get attention that I'd never gotten before and, you know, I liked it. Someone noticing me, like, 'Wow, you're fine—and you're cute—and, can I get your number.' It was a different kind of attention and it was kind of neat. You know, I feel beautiful, I feel, and I worked for a men's clothing store and I worked around men all day and it was fun. It was the funnest time of my life . . . more Black guys. And I think, after I turned 18 and 19, that's when I really was like, 'I like this.' Black men are more suave. They're just more smooth and they don't . . . Black men are who they are and, to me at that time, they didn't try to put a spin on anything. A lot of White men that I met always tried to act like something that they're not. They just kind of would talk weird or they would act like they're putting on a show or something. And not that much longer, I was just about to be 20, and I met their father and we had gotten along really well and that's who I was pregnant by a year later after being out on my own and trying to find myself.

Abortion—no I considered putting my son up for adoption. That was what I had set to do. I had went there because I didn't know what to do and did not have a place to stay that was steady and being 19 going on to 20, I had no clue. Fortunately I didn't like the idea of that [abortion] so I went to a family center that I'd heard about and had the interview and I was getting ready to pick out the family . . . I thought this was my only option and then my mom's friend said that she could adopt my son for a year and then I could take him back and I was considering it but I was scared, it was like, 'What do I do? It's not like I'm 16 and pregnant, I'm 20, I'm an adult, I've made this choice to have this child. What do I do?' And that's when their dad came my way and I said, 'Well, I'm in this dilemma and I don't know what to do . . . ' and he was like, 'Why would you give him up? I'll be here, you know, I'll take care of him' . . . and he did. That's why my oldest son

has his last name because [ex-partner] signed the birth cer-
tificate. [The biological father] just disappeared. He knew I
was pregnant. I went through this whole thing with him
about being pregnant. He wanted me to get an abortion. I
did not. We went to a women's center and we thought that it
was an abortion clinic and it was not. It's against abortions
and they showed you this horrible, horrible video about what
happens with babies in different terms and you know, and I
was too pregnant to have an abortion because at that point it
would kind of be taking a life . . . because I fought him on it
so much because I didn't believe in abortions. And I don't
know, it's like our whole relationship kind of faded off and I
think I was in denial a lot about being pregnant. I was like,
'No I can't be pregnant. I'm just getting out in the world. I
can't do this. I'm not done partying. I'm not done having fun.'

Pat has several options relative to residency, but has decided to remain in the more rural Valparaiso rather than returning to Chicago.

I like the schools. People up here are pretty nice. And I
really like my job a lot. I don't know what I'll do with my
education—if I'll go further with it—just high school—with
my job it's not necessary to have a college education. You
can, just in terms of bettering yourself, just to have that degree under your belt, but, I don't know. I don't know if I'll
be at my job for another five years or if I'll be somewhere
else because your life could change in an instant so . . . I do
know, my dad and I have talked about looking for a home
or a house and that's something that I really, really want.
I'm not in debt that much, I don't have any credit cards, so
he said that as soon as he gets his five years in at his job,
which is this February, then we're gonna start seriously
looking for a home . . . for me primarily to live in and for
him, primarily on the weekends. He said it didn't matter
whose name it's under. The important thing is that you
have a house, so that's my next goal—to get a house. It will
be in Valparaiso because he comes every weekend anyway.
He doesn't mind the drive because he likes to see me and
the kids.

I'm pretty much a homebody. I watch a lot of TV—that's
my thing. And as far as dating, even if my dad was in the

same house, I don't know, dating's not just part of my—of the equation right now. I'm just kind of taking care of my kids 'cause there's just too many issues in terms of them right now . . . later on . . . I don't need a guy to take my attention away from that. And you know what, it happens. When you're in a relationship with somebody you don't give all your attention where it's needed—it's kind of split. So I'm just not looking and no one's looking at me so . . . [continued interests in Black men] That's my main interest, but, you know, I just, leave it up to God. If he's purple, green, yellow, Black, or White I don't know. I find both races attractive, but I don't know. But a lot of times I think about it with my kids though, because I don't—I'm really torn. It's like, 'Is being with someone who's Black the right answer?' Because I don't want my kids to grow up like, 'I'm White and maybe he's White and maybe they feel like they don't fit in or something.' I don't want my kids to feel that way, so I don't know what the right decision is. But I guess if I leave it up to God then I'll be with the right person.

Pat has also had some exposure to nearby Gary, Indiana, and comments on the city.

Well, I had a friend out there [in Gary] and I would go out and visit her. And my initial reaction to it—it's depressing. It just seems like, well there's a lot of abandoned buildings and I think that's what I look at. To me that's scary to anybody to see abandoned buildings or it looks dirty. And it's like, 'Well, why don't people work on the streets? Why isn't there someone trying to fix it up or something?' And, I don't know, I think that if some people would get together and put other things aside and put forth the effort, you know, Gary could be like it was. It could be beautiful. My friend's, the house that she lived in was, her boyfriend's, who was African American, his mother is very much into drugs. The stories I've heard, she use to sell drugs. The house has been raided like three times by the police . . . their front door is held up by a dumbbell and a chair, you know, they've lived there for so many years and never fixed the door. And my reasoning is,

'Why don't you fix it? You have a cute house. It could be a cute house.' She works, I don't know about him. He had a legitimate job off and on, that's all I know.

Gary is different from Chicago Heights because Chicago Heights has more businesses. There's more going on. In Gary, you kind of, you go in there, like off of Broadway, when you're coming off the expressway, when you just come right in and you see gas stations and liquor stores and it's kind of like a silence or something, I don't know. It's just kind of 'blah.'

Pat suggests that the economic benefits in Valparaiso are greater than her experiences in Chicago, and she has been able to locate a variety of resources to help maintain her family.

Childcare is not so bad right now. Towards the end of the year last year, Step Ahead, they cut me off. They felt that I was no longer eligible to get help with Step Ahead . . . I wasn't poor enough to get that help. So, I was like, 'I don't know what I'm gonna do.' The kids were going to the Y [YMCA]. They had been going to a private home and that was $90 a week. And then the Y was pretty close to that, $80 a week per child. And that's for about an hour per week per child, maybe an hour and fifteen minutes. But they had programs, grants, or something like that, where they would help you out. You just applied. I had no idea. And they asked you what you thought you could afford to pay. I thought, 'All they could say is no.' And that was a very hard thing 'cause I was scared to death they were gonna say no. And I said, well, I may have to be forced to make a decision that I don't want to make and that was to leave my kids at home alone with their brother—he's ten. And I was like, that was a big scare because, I know that's how a lot of these kids get in trouble out here . . . is being left home alone, because I think that some parents are forced to make that decision because they can't afford childcare.

I just talked to the lady and I said, 'I don't know what to do. Do you offer any type of programs?' I had to ask . . . at the YMCA. I had to ask because I really didn't want to leave my kids at home alone, but it was a decision I was gonna have to make, if she said no. She said, 'but they've

been doing this to a lot of families, fill out this paperwork
and just apply and we'll see what we can do for you.' And I
think I also wrote them a letter also requesting help and I
said I didn't know what to do. So, I ended up only having
to pay $50 a week for all three—and that was like the com-
bined amount. And I was like, 'OK. It's gonna be alright.'
And then, recently, since October, I hadn't gotten any
child support from their dad because he lost his job and
he's not the type to sit around and collect unemployment.
He's out there, he's gonna look for something else. He's got
a job and he's got a side job too, but the process of it going
through the courts and them getting it to me is—forever.
You know, he'll get upset and say, 'Well, why haven't you
gotten anything? I've been paying. They've been taking it
out of my check.' And sometimes it will be three or four
months, five months before I get anything. So, the Y again,
I told them that, you know, money's tight and I don't have
the extra income coming in and so she lowered it to $30
and so it's feasible. It's manageable. It's ok.

But with [her youngest son] being ADD, that's something
I think that I've been fighting with. I been having problems with him since Head Start, it's like in preschool with
being combative and not listening and not paying attention. All these different things, different behaviors, kind of
getting worse as the years went by. I'm the type of parent,
I don't believe in ADD, ADHD, sometimes just give your
kid a good swift kick in the butt and say, 'Hey, get it together.' But it's not working. He's yelling and yelling at
him and spanking him, it just isn't working for him. So the
teacher, who's very good, very patient, is like, 'I'm sorry,
but I've been trying everything and, you know, he's just
acting out in class.' So I took him to the doctor and they
had me go to counseling services and one-on-one thera-
pists and they're going to diagnose him in March. They're
gonna look at his behavior and different things to see if we
can put him on the medication. My fear was that my kid is
gonna be a zombie, you know, I don't want his personality
taken away. I don't want him to be sitting there and just
quiet. I don't want a perfect kid, I just want him to be able
to focus and not to be a struggle to do homework. It's like
pulling teeth doing homework every night.

Pat continues to set yearly goals for herself and her family. In spite of various challenges in her past, she is optimistic about their future.

> I'm most proud of this apartment. Because it's the closest thing to a home I've ever had—not including my childhood. But this place is just, the effort I put into it, the accomplishments that I make every year. I look around and I'm like, 'This is mine. This is my house.' Even if I never get a home at all, even if, for some reason, things don't work out with my dad and we don't find a house or whatever, this is my home. And, you know, I'll probably be here for the duration. And I have really great kids, you know— and my daughter. I'm very proud of her. She's my soldier. She works hard. She's a little momma. She works hard for me. She helps keep things in control. And a nine-year-old shouldn't have that attitude, but she's got a pretty good head on her shoulders . . . You don't have to accept the stereotypes . . . If you have to get three jobs to pay your bills, then get three jobs. You have to do what you have to do . . . just don't give up.

Summary

Pat's belief in the tenets of the Protestant Ethic that encourage delayed gratification, frugality, and hard work that she learned from her parents have enabled her to weather a myriad of emotional and economic problems. Although Pat's family lives below the official poverty threshold, she has embraced "middle-class" values and aspirations associated with home ownership and setting tangible goals.[3] Her views suggest an emphasis on more visible signs of poverty. However, Pat's psychological well-being appears to be healthier, because she lives in a place without visible markers of economic decay. Parallel to literature on single-parent mothers, Pat embraces more traditional views on gender roles, family structure, and the appropriate symbols of family stability[4] and candidly acknowledges the effects certain decisions have had on her ability to realize these aspirations. And although her personal goals are largely materialistic in nature, her decisions center on providing a stable home for her three children. Her family can technically be considered impoverished; Pat does not consider them to be. With the assistance of extended family and

more easily accessible resources and support systems in an economically stable, more rural locale, Pat has been able to make
ends meet, maintain a relatively positive quality of life for herself
and children, and anticipate the future.

The Family of Mary Ramirez

"I'll never be ashamed of Gary and never be afraid to go to Gary."

Mary is a 38-year-old mother of three children ages 16, 17, and
23. She was born and reared in a middle-class family in Gary, Indiana, and has lived in nearby East Chicago, Indiana, since 1988. An
approximate 15 minute drive from Gary proper, East Chicago has a
large Hispanic population, and Mary moved there after high school
to be near her mother. She's been married four years, and her husband's family and most of her friends still live in Gary. Mary at-
tended business school and has worked for the past seven years as
an insurance processor. Her combined household income is about
$30,000–$35,000 annually. Her family lives in a small, comfortable
house in a business district in the city. Photographs of her children
and granddaughter are proudly displayed. Mary's quiet demeanor
belies strong opinions about city life, in general, and her experiences, in particular. A woman of few words, she explains her life in
East Chicago, her ties to Gary, Indiana, and challenges and choices
associated with urban living.

> My mother moved here. That's why I moved here—just to
> be closer to her. That's the only reason I moved here. I have
> more family than friends here. I go there [to Gary] often. My
> husband's family is still there, so we go often to his grand-
> mother's house. I have my sister in Gary. We don't have a
> good relationship now, but she lives in Gary and my hus-
> band's family, his grandmother, we're real close. I've been
> in the family for years. He's not my kids' dad, but they treat
> us good. His sister lives there. I don't have that much fam-
> ily over there. My dad's still over here in East Chicago.
> They built a lot, but then the crime rate goes up. It's been
> getting bad and then it goes down. But they try to build up
> East Chicago. It's really nice. The mayor's been here a long

time. They've fixed it up. But the crime rate, I read about it everyday in the paper. It's really bad . . . It's two parts of East Chicago. There's the harbor part and then East Chicago that's on the other side. It's been bad for the last couple of months.

Right now I'm going through a little financial problem. Making ends meet is kind of hard, you know. And then my husband, he don't get a steady 40 hours at his job. So his pay varies—up and down weekly. And it gets hard. And then your car breaks down—that's my problem, when my car broke down, it costs so much to get it fixed, you know . . . and my daughter's a senior so things come around with her. It gets bad at times . . . I try not to think about it. And try to do the best I can. That's all I can do. And I mean, I can't do something I don't have the money to do, so, I work around it. And make it work. I don't try to get stressed out. I work in the medical field and I know what stress does to people. So I don't try to stress.

Even with periodic economic problems, Mary has specific views about what it means to be poor. She is also candid about certain decisions that drastically affected her life and subsequent choices for her children.

. . . very low income and you have to live in the projects. That's poor to me . . . No, I'm not poor. 'Cause I got a home, heat, and my kids are dressed decent, so I'm not poor . . . 'cause I always had heat, water. I figure if you have heat and water and somewhere to live and eat . . . if you eat everyday . . . I don't consider that poor.

My best decision . . . getting divorced the first time. I was married just two and a half years—more emotional problems with the man I was with and . . . he's my kids' dad and, you know, no support, no nothing, a bad decision, it wasn't my worse decision. And the best was to get rid of him . . . Having my kids young . . . I regret it now. Because I should have went on to school and did better for myself. You know, I had my kids too young and I couldn't go back. I mean I could go back to school. But it's just so hard raising kids, going to school and having to work to support them.

Mary recalls a sense of community during her years in Gary, recognizes certain urban problems in East Chicago, but also sees certain advantages in living in East Chicago.

> Just, how full Gary used to be, you know. It wasn't all that vacant spots. I used to love going to school over there. And the bus station—I remember the old bus station. I enjoyed living in Gary. Going to the parades every year, I used to love those. Just the people I grew up with, you know. We got to know everybody—Black, White, Puerto Rican, it wasn't just one color. And I'm glad I grew up there. We got to know a mixture of people. I would [move back to Gary] after my kids get out of school . . . I wouldn't mind. [Why later?] 'Cause out here, my kids adapt to the schools—just the system. Back when I was in school, I don't know how it is, I don't know no kids that go to school out in Gary, but, back then, if we skipped school and stuff, they didn't care back then. But out here, ever since my kids started going to school, if you miss school, they call your house. And I just like the way the school system runs, you know. You can go to the school whenever you want to and I'm involved with my kids. I go to school whenever I want to. I like to know if my kids are at school. And I remember skipping school and my mother never knew. But if my kids skip school, I know. There's a phone call. And I just like the school system.

Like Gary residents, the out-migration of stores and businesses in East Chicago means that Mary's daily round often requires her to travel outside the city. However, because many of the locations are closer in proximity and accessible via free public transportation, Mary still suggests a difference in the economic conditions between the two locales.

> It's still in Indiana [shopping], but like Highland. Then you gotta go all the way out to Sherrillville for the movies. It's no movie place around here no more. My bank is in Munster, closer to my job. The kid's doctor is in Gary . . . most of these places are still close.

Having grown up in Gary, Indiana, Mary remembers an earlier period of economic prosperity as well as its postindustrial decline. She also provides specific suggestions for renewal.

I'm just disappointed on Broadway. The way everything went down on Broadway. I remember being a little kid and all the stores and stuff. And I worked on 5th Avenue for a while and—just the buildings went down. They try to build it up now. Just now, are they building a new welfare office, right, on 6th and Broadway? But they redid the Sears building for that and I think that's a waste right there. They could build something else there and it's nowhere to go down there. The drug store, Tim's, that's been there for years. It's not really a real big store. I'm just so disappointed in Broadway, but building the baseball field. I don't know. I don't know if it's for the benefit of the people. They could build other things. And down, like on 13th and Broadway, that's picking up. They've got more stores down there. But they need something else. More stores to keep people in Gary . . . I go to a little convenience store, J & R, by 5th, close to 5th and Adams and that's the only store I go to. All the vacancies over there and no stores . . . And the stores they do have . . . you go in the stores and there's nobody in there. I ain't been to that, what is it—Buy Low—in so long because the last time I went in there, you would never know that it used to be, you know, a busy store—nobody was hardly in there—but it's been some years since I've been to that store.

They're building those homes in Gary over on the east side . . . those duplexes. This is more down 5th, going towards Miller . . . because, if they're not going to be low income, 'cause I figure, in Gary, a lot of people are low-income, 'cause there's no jobs around there. And to get a good job you must have went to college and it's just nothing there in Gary and if those homes are not for the low income, then, who's gonna move to Gary? And if they're gonna do something, do something for the low-income people. Build more stores, have the stores there so the people could shop there. Then provide more jobs for people. And then you don't have to go out of Gary to get a job.

I think it's everywhere. It's here in East Chicago, drugs, crime, gangs, and stuff. I don't think it's just Gary . . . just by the rumors Gary has got. They are known for their, you know, murders, by people talking, you know. But East Chicago, no I don't think it's, not like the murders or anything [the same reputation as Gary]. Just if you live here and read the paper all the time. There's a lot of negative. You always hear negative things about Gary. You don't hear about the positive things in Gary, you know, you always hear the negative . . . just the reputation Gary has in the last few years. They always had a bad reputation, it's about the same. The drugs and stuff . . . but that's everywhere, it's beginning to be a big part of people's lives . . . the reputation . . . is somewhat true . . . it's somewhat true . . . but just being a part of Gary—I mean, I never would deny that I came from Gary. I don't have no complaints about Gary. If it was to get better, I would live in Gary. I enjoyed living in Gary. That's where I met most of my people. I would live there—if it was better.

Mary points to the accomplishments of her children and considers her past sacrifices and challenges to be worth it. She notes that her eldest son is employed, and her daughter has been accepted to several prestigious colleges.

I'm proud of my kids . . . very . . . they're not drug dealers. They're not into gangs. And they're trying to make it. Like my oldest one. He's trying to make it so hard. He was brought up here in East Chicago and he was in a gang. But his life has completely changed around. He's got the little girl [his daughter] and he's working and he's buying a house in Merrillville. And then my daughter's a straight A student—trying to make me proud of her. And then the little one—he's a little problem, but only girl problems. But I'm glad, you know, I raised them so they didn't have to turn to drugs.

Her final thoughts are reflective of her upbringing in Gary, Indiana.

I'm proud of coming out of Horace Mann. My kids go to Central, but when we go to the games and stuff I always cheer for Horace Mann, you know. I'm still a part of Gary. There's always going to be a part. I know people that won't, my oldest sister, she won't even go to Gary. I'll never be ashamed of Gary and never be afraid to go to Gary. I'll go to Gary and stop at a gas station. I'll never be afraid, that's my life.

Summary

Mary's ties with her immediate family are not indicative of the extended and fictive ties suggested in the literature,[5] but her relationship with her in-laws represents a source of expressive and instrumental support. Mary acknowledges past and current economic challenges, but does not consider herself impoverished. She also recognizes lost opportunities during her youth, but has reconciled her past and focuses efforts on the well-being and future of her children. To this end, possibly relocating back to Gary is not a short-term option based on the educational benefits she believes her children enjoy in the East Chicago School System. Mary's history in Gary and continued travels to the city have enabled her to recognize gradual changes, both positive and negative, in the city. Her candid comments regarding the city's problems (crime, limited enterprise, and jobs) and potential (sense of community, racial diversity) suggest someone who continues to feel a part of the urban center. Mary is somewhat nostalgic about her upbringing there, but cognizant of the economic changes required to sustain current residents and attract potential ones to Gary.

Conclusion: Summarizing the Costs

Based on the official poverty threshold and standard economic measures of stability, these three families are, at worst, impoverished and, at best, working class. However, careful examination of the response patterns suggests attitudes and behavior typically associated with "middle-class values." They hold similar ideologies and views: the importance of children and education, delayed gratification, materialism as a benchmark of progress, a focus on individual-initiative in response to problems, and clear opinions about the city of Gary, as well as unique appropriations of common socialization patterns. Furthermore, the three families behave in similar fashion in terms of survival strategies, goals and objectives, and sacrifice for the sake of their children. The starkest difference among the families is their knowledge of the structural influences and implications of urban poverty. Several are somewhat myopic in their understanding of the effects of concentrated poverty and subtly exhibit a "blame the victim" mentality that focuses on personal initiative to bring about change. Their views may be attributed, in part, to the strong belief in the "Protestant Ethic" suggested by many of

their comments. For example, Tamara, as a previous resident of
Gary, Indiana, appears most cognizant of the effects of forces such as
racism, segregation, and de-industrialization on the city. However,
she and Pat emphasize the importance of collective action on the
part of Gary residents to bring about urban renewal. In contrast,
Mary suggests specific economic interventions to address urban decline in Gary and is more critical of city leaders than residents.

The three women seldom use terminology common to sociological arenas. However, they are aware of certain factors that exacerbate poverty and stymie chances of upward mobility. In
addition, many of their experiences and past decisions have more
far-reaching consequences, because there are fewer buffers and
resources to combat problems and seemingly more obstacles to
face. Save for the extended family, there are also fewer networks
to call upon for assistance to address major problems, particularly
those that are economic in nature. Several important themes
emerge that are supported by current urban literature. Other
findings may be important in further understanding the implications of urban living. It is clear that the three families depicted in
this chapter have faced challenges that stem largely from economic circumstances. Their attempts to combat these conditions
are also evident. And although Tamara, Pat, and Mary mention
specific economic and noneconomic hurdles, their comments are
telling in regard to various broad *costs* that many urban residents,
particularly the poor, cannot afford. I will briefly discuss more
commonly considered costs suggested by the three women that
parallel the literature, followed by less often considered issues.

What the Poor *Can't Afford:* Commonly Considered Costs

To Have a Child Out of Wedlock. For teenaged girls, having
children before they are economically and emotionally prepared typically translates into increased economic insecurity, delays in completing basic educational goals, poor parenting skills, and generally
protracted futures.[6] However, for the poor and working class, even
adult pregnancy may result in exposure to poverty or extended periods in poverty. This problem seems even more dire in areas with limited resources to support unwed mothers. For example, Pat has been
able to locate significantly subsidized childcare in her predominately
White locale, such that she can stretch her limited funds, while

Tamara appears constantly challenged by childcare concerns. Additionally, economically challenged women who give birth to children with developmental or physical problems face additional challenges in the form of medical expenses, special childcare needs, and added parenting stress. As is the case with Pat, choices relative to her employment and personal future relationships are put on hold to focus on the demands of her children, yet she is continually concerned about her ability to meet their basic needs. Similarly, Mary notes delays in personal goals, such as returning to school or possibly relocating to Gary, in order to benefit her family.

To Get Divorced. Literature suggests that many women experience downward economic mobility after divorce (refer to chapter 1 for more information on this subject). For poor women, the problem is often more acute. As attested to by Pat, even if child support has been formally arranged via garnishment procedures, court delays can translate into an economic balancing act for women and children. Albeit a somewhat different situation for Tamara, a gainfully employed husband does not guarantee alimony or child support after separation or divorce. For Mary, Tamara, and Pat, economic concerns and the desire to maintain nuclear families prompted them to remain in physically and/or emotionally unstable marriages for the sake of their children. At the time, they did not believe they could afford to leave. But at some point, each realized she could not afford to stay. Each woman agrees that the final decision to leave was best for her and her children—even at the expense of subsequent financial challenges.

To Get Arrested. Scholars like MacLeod (1995) and Wilson (1987, 1996) show that even brief stints behind bars can translate into difficulty finding employment and integrating back into society. Longer periods of incarceration have been shown to severally limit the life chances of detainees. Any brush with the law may prove tragic in terms of limited funds for adequate counsel, obtaining bail, and placing family members in financial and emotional binds. African American males and other males of color who reside in urban settings are disproportionately represented among the incarcerated. The higher figures have also been attributed to greater incidents of delinquency and discrimination in the court systems that result in inconsistent sentencing.[7] A large number of these males are of both marrying and working age. Their absences influence their immediate families, future relationships, neighborhood conditions, and community relations (while they are incarcerated, as well as upon release), because such men are no longer available to directly take part in society in a meaningful way. While Pat's partner's experience with the law was minimal when compared to typically cited examples, his record, in addition to continued residence in an impoverished area, has meant economic hardship for him, as well as for Pat and their children.

To Neglect Education. Failure to complete high school represents a costly economic decision due to the basic educational requirements at most places of employment. But a diploma alone does not necessarily provide adequate returns to significantly transition out of poverty. Pat's position provides personal satisfaction and enables her to set and meet yearly goals to improve her apartment and quality of life for herself and children. However, it does not provide the needed economic "cushion" to address unexpected dilemmas, such as temporary lags in child support. The number and age of her children appear to preclude Pat from considering possibly returning to school in the short-term to continue her education. Thus her limited education, when combined with local resources and support from her dad enable her to make ends meet, but rarely exceed them. Similarly, Mary acknowledges lost opportunities due to limited education and strives to ensure that her children avail themselves of the benefits of a high school education, while expecting and preparing them to attend college.

A college education has been linked to upward economic and social mobility for African Americans, but it does not guarantee economic stability. Billingsley (1992) suggests that education, strong family networks, and hard work have enabled African Americans, more than other racial/ethnic groups, to progress from working class to middle class in one generation. Tamara's family's emphasis on getting a college education motivated her to complete her degree and also take some graduate courses. For her, the human capital obtained via a college education provides self-esteem, social capital, and a sense of self-efficacy. However, her desire to live and work in close proximity to Gary has limited her employment options. Positions that do not require a college education often do not reward employees a great deal for having one. Tamara is aware of her increased marketability and periodically contemplates moving to a bigger city, but chooses to remain in the area out of concern for family and because she considers Gary her "home." In addition, the skills she garnered while in college appear to have enabled her to more critically examine the conditions in Gary, yet she often feels helpless to change them.

To Become Involved with Drugs. Although not a dynamic noted within these families, research suggests the negative effects of drug involvement on upward mobility in many urban communities. Contrary to the stereotype of the large number of drug dealers made wealthy by urban trafficking, most drug dealers do so part-time and also hold down jobs in the primary sector.[8] However, limited gainful employment, peer pressure, and product availability from sources typically outside urban areas can make drug trafficking appear to be a viable option for economic survival. In addition, the sociopsychological effects of exposure to chronic poverty, crime, violence, dilapidated infrastructure, and other forms of social disorganization have been linked to increased drug use among some urban residents.[9] Thus drug involvement costs individuals and entire communities in terms of overall quality of life.

To Provide More than the Basics for Their Children. Contrary to prevailing stereotypes, these families do not spend their money on designer clothes and the latest trends for their children. Most shop at discount stores such as Wal-mart; Pat frequents thrift stores, and Mary finds bargains at the local This Is It discount store. Each averages less than $100 monthly on clothing purchases for their families and tries to make sure their children are clean, neatly dressed, and have the required supplies for school. In Mary's case, the use of school uniforms minimizes clothing expenses for her children; layaway options at local stores enable her to make such purchases. Extended family often becomes important to help subsidize larger purchases for Tamara and Pat. In Tamara's case, her mother typically purchases school clothes each year. For Pat, such purchases are made by her children's grandparents. Living on a limited budget typically involves making replacement purchases (i.e., buying new shoes once the current pair is out-grown) rather than nonessential ones. Thus necessities take precedence over wants and desires. For example, Tamara wishes that she could purchase name-brand items for her children, yet contents herself in the knowledge that their emotional and basic temporal needs are met.

What the Poor *Can't Afford:* Less Commonly Considered Costs

Just as the above noted costs are commonly suggested in research on the urban experience, several additional, less commonly considered costs and observations are noteworthy.

To Alienate Family Members. Research posits that the African American extended family is more instrumental in maintaining family stability, especially for single-parent mothers, than their White counterparts;[10] other studies show the converse.[11] This type of support is imperative for the employed mothers from the approximately 54 percent of African American women who are single parents.[12] Still other scholars contend that kin networks provide limited economic and social support to nuclear and single-parent African American families or that kin-provided childcare does not increase labor force involvement.[13] Some literature shows that employed White mothers receive greater economic assistance from extended family than their African American counterparts—who are more likely to receive in-kind support.[14] This tendency toward financial support via kin is greatest for working-class White women.[15] The extended Latino family has been shown to provide moral and economic support that fosters employment for mothers to help sustain their families.[16] Certain research points to this tendency specifically for Filipinos and Puerto Ricans.[17] As is the case for Whites and African Americans, Hispanic family and fictive- kin networks are especially important in balancing family and work in lower-status, lower-paying jobs.[18] Such networks can also help maintain a familiar environment to reinforce language and customs for children of employed women.[19]

Scholarship contends that the extended family and the child-centered nature found in communities of color provide an important buffer between negative social forces and children. These characteristics are evident, to a certain degree, in each of the three families depicted here, suggesting that dire economic conditions, even of a more temporary nature, facilitate the response of some extended families, particularly when young children are involved. Thus, cultural dictates may precipitate extended family involvement in many instances, but we should not ignore the influence of immediacy and practicality.

Extended family provides economic and in-kind support for the three families interviewed here. Pat acknowledges the centrality of her father for moral support, as well as economic support sufficient to help her make ends meet without undermining the values and experiences needed to be self-efficacious. In addition, her ex-partner's parents continue to maintain close ties through bimonthly visits, purchase school clothes, and provide their grandchildren with linkages to their African American heritage. And although Pat refuses, they have offered to purchase her a home in their neighborhood. Similarly, Tamara's mother sacrifices from her limited income to makes purchases for her grandchildren and provide Tamara with money to "tide her over." Additionally, Tamara's mother and sister enable her to work consistently by providing free childcare during periods when she is unable to afford it. During these periods, both women often rearrange their work and leisure time schedules to accommodate Tamara's work schedule.

In many ways, each family would be in dire straits without the help of extended family. For example, Tamara's "free" childcare through family members represents an "intangible" credit in her monthly budget that assists in making ends meet. Had her father remained estranged from Pat and her children, she would be without moral as well as economic support. In addition, the possibility of disengagement does not appear to be evident in the case of Pat's children and their African American grandparents, who maintain ties, not only with their grandchildren, but with Pat. Similarly, Mary acknowledges the supportive nature of her husband's family.

However, the role of extended family has implications beyond research findings and immediate benefits for the three families. We must consider the potentially negative effects *imposed on* extended family due to their involvement. First, for grandparents, toll can take the form of health concerns, particularly among the elderly, who have raised their own children and anticipate retirement and leisure time, but who must now help to raise grandchildren. These same grandparents, especially those on fixed incomes, must contend with added financial burden. Those who "informally" adopt grandchildren and other children within the family incur the costs associated with rearing children without the legal benefits of tax exemptions and credits provided to legally sanctioned guardians.[20] Next, time off from one's own employment translates into lost wages and fewer finances to pay their expenses. In these instances, economic burden is shifted from one family to another. And if the extended family members are also poor or near-poor, they risk undermining their own economic security for the sake of family members in need. And although often considered of secondary importance, the intangible costs associated with lost leisure time have direct implications on the quality of life of extended family members. For example, Tamara's mother's tendency to provide free childcare means she may be unable to participate in other activities that are important to her, must juggle her personal and professional schedule, and, as an elderly woman, expend a great deal of energy to "keep up with" small children. Lastly, it is important to consider the sociopsychological stresses of seeing family members struggle and to

only be able to provide limited assistance. Several mothers contend
that their extended families willingly make such sacrifices, yet one
wonders whether their views represent wishful thinking—a coping
mechanism to minimize guilt associated with continued reliance on
family members.

To Remain in Impoverished Areas. Even if urban residents
feel an allegiance to "home," they may be forced to make decisions in
the best interest of their families. Limited gainful employment, in
addition to a paucity of businesses and services needed during the
daily round, encourage out-migration to other locales and make it
difficult for urban centers to experience renewal.[21] Residents with
more human capital may find it prudent to relocate in order to reap
the benefits of their education and job experience. Tamara makes
a conscious effort to patronize Gary businesses, but she believes
it would be detrimental to her family to continue to live there.
Tamara's loyalty to her family and its immediate concerns would
make sense to most persons, but her decision results in the out-
migration of a resident, whose presence might help provide a stabilizing force in Gary. Mary's allegiance to Gary is temporarily placed
on hold due to the perceived inadequacy of the educational system
there. Her own high school experiences have prompted her to remain in East Chicago to help ensure that her children will get a better education. So while Mary notes the criminal element in certain
parts of East Chicago, the current benefits (better schools, free public transportation, and proximity to stores) outweigh the drawbacks.

Furthermore, the effects of poverty, both tangible and intangible, can vary greatly based on place of residency and access to resources. Pat's economic profile meets the definition of poverty, yet
she has been able to makes ends meet, in large part, due to the availability of low-cost businesses and services in her immediate area.
Furthermore, according to literature, Pat would be expected to experience less stigma as a White female resident in a more rural setting, than she would while living in urban Chicago. Her experiences
in Valparaiso also illustrate the importance of considering quality of
life issues for the poor. As suggested by Wilson (1996) and others
such as West (1993), the sociopsychological implications are often
more dire when poverty is more visible. Daily exposure to abandoned buildings, liquor stores, homelessness, crime, and other manifestations of economic and infrastructure distress may, over time,
engender despair and angst. For Pat, the intangible benefits, as she
assesses the quality of life for her children in Valparaiso, are the dif-

ference between renting an apartment in the less impoverished, more rural location rather than accepting a "free" house in a more impoverished urban area. However, visible differences in the effects of poverty may reinforce notions of "the other"—characterized by stigma of urban poverty by nonresidents who are in similar straits—and undermine efforts for collective redress by poor persons who have more in common than they imagine.

Many urban residents can't afford to leave, but neither can they afford to stay. Recent work by urban planners Grogan and Proscio (2000) point to the importance of rethinking the standards by which we measure "successful" urban renewal. Just as urban plight does not occur overnight, the authors show that it is short-sighted to expect immediate results from urban revitalization projects. They contend that conventional economic markers are inaccurate in capturing the early stages of urban renewal, and current studies often mask improvements that are not yet apparent in macro-level data. They further caution the use of a "middle-class, suburban" model to judge urban centers under transformation, because during initial stages of urban renewal, residents may not be wealthier, but their neighborhood infrastructure and general quality of life are improving due to increased social organization and civic participation to maintain the neighborhoods they have worked to revitalize. Their work informs scholars, researchers, and theoreticians of the practical, time-consuming steps required for sustainable urban improvement.

To Ignore Others' Implications of the "Marriageable Male" Dynamic. The thesis of the "marriageable male" and its correlates for single-parent families and impoverished children are informed by the experiences of these three families.[22] First, as is the case with Tamara, a gainfully employed husband does not necessarily equate to economic stability. Although her husband is legally responsible to help maintain their home, she asserts that his inconsistent financial support resulted in "poverty" in a middle-class household. Tamara does not seemingly benefit from adhering to societal dictates by earning a college education, getting married, and subsequently having children. For her, marriage meant many of the expected challenges associated with creating a family, as well as situations she more directly attributes to urban dynamics. Based on Tamara's experience, "marriageable males" in urban centers may continue to be in demand, even after they become married. Such unions may also be more vulnerable to continued pressure by male peers who are single and do not conform to monogamy,[23] severely impoverished single women who desire a relationship with an economically stable man and who are less inclined to honor the wedding vows of others, as well as husbands who recognize their "demand" and avail themselves of interested women.

In Pat's case, the desire to marry her children's father was undermined by his temper and inconsistency as a provider. Similar to Engels' critique of the proletariat husband's conflicted relationship with his wife, observations by scholars on African American male aggression,[24] and the implications of "The Prince Charming Ideal" for African American males,[25] Pat suggests that her partner had difficulty reconciling his limited abilities as provider, feelings of inadequacy due to a domineering, verbally abusive father, and the pressures associated with transitioning into adult responsibilities. In spite of physical and verbal abuse, affection combined with Pat's upbringing that encouraged marriage, motivated her to remain in the unhealthy relationship, until she realized her partner probably would not acquire the traits of a "marriageable male." As illustrated by Wilson (1996) and suggested by these two respondents, the underrepresentation of gainfully employed males, especially African American males, may result in increased tensions and conflict for persons who wish to marry, as well as for those who do decide to get married. In contrast, Mary's trials in her first marriage to the father of her children stand in stark contrast to her current marriage to an African American man who accepts her children as his own, works to provide for their family, and is part of a supportive extended family.

Unexpected Expenses or Events. Each family has had and continues to face economic challenges, yet none consider themselves poor. However, Tamara, Pat, and Mary each acknowledge concerns about addressing unexpected expenses and events. Pat's current childcare costs are low, but she fears that her children could become latchkey kids in the future should their after-school care costs increase. For both Tamara and Mary, a major car repair quickly becomes a financial burden that affects their family budgets for several months. Other events, such as illness of children, death in the family, school-related expenses, inconsistent employment, or anything that requires large, nonbudgeted finances or an absence from work could prove devastating. Thus unexpected expenses or events represent direct and tangible costs. And concerns about *if and when* such situations may arise often take the form of intangible costs, such as stress and anxiety.

To Think Primarily in Economic Terms. In spite of visible signs of neglect and other evidence of urban decay, Gary, Indiana, is "home" for both Mary and Tamara. For Tamara, connectedness to the city, friends, and family members is a disincentive to relocate to places that would probably provide better employment opportunities. And although Mary is somewhat more aware of the challenges facing the city, she continues to acknowledge a sense of community there. Mary and Tamara's personal benchmarks for success, family and education, suggest the tendency to rank intangible factors over more tangible ones. In contrast, Pat's goals and objectives tend to be more materialistic in nature, as she attempts to maintain a safe, stable home for her children. Ideological differences are also illustrated by their divergent characterizations of Gary, Indiana, definitions of poverty, and views about their current socioeconomic statuses. The use of tangible criteria and benchmarks when making assessments has its advantages in terms of specificity and measurable outcomes, but may make it difficult to consider noneconomic issues and mask benefits and potential drawbacks (example: Pat's focus on improving her domicile rather than continuing her education). Similarly, an overemphasis on subjective criteria may diminish the ability to critically assess conditions (such as, Tamara's tendency to broad-brush the extent of crime in Gary).

The ability to consider economic as well as noneconomic issues and indices may be more pressing when considering how to counteract the effects of poverty. Some writers suggest that long-term economic indicators are critical in assessing whether poverty is being abated; short-term, such variables can be misleading.[26] Using a similar approach, criteria to assess the effects of poor and near-poor conditions and subsequent improved self-efficacy by families such as Pat's, Mary's, and Tamara's would involve establishing short- and long-term financial milestones that measure changes in economic stability, as well as assessing each family's gradual improvement based on less tangible factors associated with quality of life.

To, in General, Make "Poor" Choices. The experiences of the three families presented here support literature on transitions in economic mobility, factors that exacerbate and abate poverty, and the attitudes and behavior of persons who face economic hardship. In spite of various economic challenges, the families are quite "middle class" in their attitudes and current behavior.[27] Some of their accounts suggest that the consequences of certain choices have had more long-term effects due, in part, to the nexus of ascriptive factors, such as race/ethnicity, class, and sex, as well as residence in poor areas. Thus a lapse in judgment relative to unprotected sexual activity, rejecting parental advice, involvement with reckless peers, or forgoing additional education may result in sustained detours from one's initial ambitions, as well as diminished life chances. And less than prudent decisions have potentially more dire consequences for persons from poor or working-class families, who currently experience economic challenges or live in poor areas. However, choices considered to be more prudent (such as completing college, marriage, maintaining consistent employment) do not always translate into the expected benefits due to the same types of factors. Additionally, for persons without familial or fictive support systems, any "mistake," lapse in judgment, or failure to take advantage of available opportunities can be potentially more serious. And, for many economically unstable families in urban settings, the repercussions of "poor" choices are often more difficult from which to bounce back.

Lastly, the three families face challenges found in many families—balancing work and home life, locating affordable, accessible, and available childcare, securing safe, low-cost housing, finding good schools, and solving children's health problems. However, their family challenges are often exacerbated due to household and/or neighborhood economic conditions. Each has attempted to maximize family resources, in part, by judiciously choosing their place of residency. For them, locale mitigates potentially negative economic and social challenges. In addition to many of the issues just mentioned, the daily round is facilitated due to available resources that are either nonexistent or less readily available in places such as Gary, Indiana (Table 5.2).

It may be the case that "working-class" families with "middle-class" values represent the most viable potential candidates for relocation efforts back to places like Gary—particularly those with familial and friendship ties who live in close proximity and have generally favorable histories in the city. Pat's views about Chicago Heights focused on economic conditions; Mary and Tamara expressed similar sentiments about Gary. And as employed members of families found to be adaptive, resilient, and somewhat more economically stable, the choice to out-migrate to nearby locales for previous Gary residents such as Mary and Tamara results in fewer such families in the urban center, which makes it all the more difficult to establish the critical mass of stable, working families required for sustained urban improvement and growth.

Table 5.2
Summary of Daily Round for Families

Question: Tell me about your daily round. If I name certain kinds of activities, do you generally do them in your city of residence or outside the area?

Activity	Tamara (Merrillville) In	Out	Pat (Valparaiso) In	Out	Mary (E. Chicago) In	Out
1. Buy groceries	X		X			X
2. Buy clothes (you and family)	X		X			X
3. Buy furniture/big ticket items	X		X			X
4. Go to the movies	X			X		X
5. Go out to dinner	X		X			X
6. Go to the bank		X[*]	X			X
7. Go to the doctor		X[*]		X		X
8. Go to the hospital	X		X		X	
9. Get gas for your car	X		X		X	
10. Childcare		X	X		na	
11. Buy fast food	X		X		X	
12. Buy misc. items	X		X			X
13. Work/employment		X	X			X
14. Majority of daily round	Both		X			X

Note: [*]Purposely supports Gary businesses

#### CHAPTER SIX

Sociopsychological Implications of Exposure to Poverty-related Constraints: Coping with the Costs

The daily round for most respondents appears similar to that of many heads-of-households. Activities center on attempts to make practical decisions and purchases to meet housing, clothing, and subsistence needs relative to household economic constraints; juggling multiple tasks within a finite period; and making childcare arrangements. However, for the poor and near-poor respondents, especially residents in poor neighborhoods, responsibilities are often compounded by economic and logistical constraints that can complicate seemingly routine chores and choices. A quick trip to a nearby retailer or shopping mall by a suburban mother who wishes to make department stores purchases can become a task that consumes an entire morning for a mother from Gary without such facilities at her disposal nearby. Should this same urban mother be without a running automobile and have to rely on public transportation, the task could consume an entire day. Similarly, grocery shopping at some stores in Gary result in significantly more costly purchases as compared to a similar trip to a suburban locale. Additionally, based on the experiences of some respondents, shopping trips outside the city to get better buys or better quality goods and services may result in poor treatment.

Earlier chapters primarily focus on economic costs. This chapter more closely considers noneconomic issues suggested by respondents in an attempt to uncover broader themes relative to their overall experiences. I focus on attitudes and beliefs and, in certain instances, attitudes that prompt certain behavior. The goal is to consider how Gary residents and others from nearby areas who have or continue to experience economic problems respond to their varied circumstances and make sense of their experiences. I concentrate on some of the sociopsychological aspects of life specific to the poor, near poor, and working class (who may or may not live in poor neighborhoods) and the coping strategies they employ to combat economic-related challenges. Respondent commentaries are used to illustrate cyclic effects of economic constraints and how they attempt to negotiate related uncertainty. I address some of the implications of macro-scale influences, as well as personal decisions respondents have and continue to make in order to examine how they respond to neighborhood and household economic conditions.

Sociopsychological Implications of Structure and Agency

Few respondents found it difficult to share details about the path that led to their present circumstances; others were reticent, but reflective about their pasts. Their viewpoints and experiences inform us regarding commonalities that connect seemingly disparate groups based on economic concerns. Comments can be broadly considered relative to the themes of structure and agency, suggesting that some respondents are cognizant of how their everyday lives are influenced by city and state-wide decisions beyond their immediate control, and they express specific opinions about the effects of public as well as personal choices on their lives. Despite diverse backgrounds and experiences, comments tend to center on topics germane to many adults with families—raising healthy, well-educated children, schools, balancing schedules, aspirations, and improving the quality of life for themselves and their families. However, these concerns are often compounded by pressing issues related to neighborhood and household economic problems, resulting in dialogue interspersed with the aforementioned topics, as well as concerns about economic conditions, poverty, low-cost housing, race issues, childcare challenges, coping strategies, and the ability to sustain their families.

Economic-Related Concerns and Poverty

The cities and towns in which respondents live reflect varying economic conditions. Gary's 2000 poverty rate of 25.8 percent stands in stark contrast to rates of 4.3, 7.5, and 9.1.[1] percent in

Merrillville, Portage, and Valparaiso. Other indicators of economic stability, such as presence of basic household amenities and educational attainment, also vary by location. According to 2000 census figures, 19.4 percent of Gary residents, 7.8 percent of Merrillville residents, 4.3 percent of Portage residents, and 8.3 percent of Valparaiso residents do not have an available vehicle at their disposal. The majority of residents in the four locations have telephone service in their homes. However, 5.2 percent of Gary residents do not; comparable figures for Merrillville, Portage, and Valparaiso are; 0.9, 1.2, and 1.7. Just as scholars show an inverse relationship between wealth and education,[2] census figures illustrate that higher percentages of non-Gary residents tend to have completed both high school and college as compared to Gary residents.[3] When I consider the sample respondents, the majority of African Americans and Whites have a running automobile in their household; only 25 percent of Hispanic respondents do. The majority of respondents also have a telephone. The mean annual household income of about $21,607.58 and average family size of three suggest that families of this size with employed heads-of-household are working class and live at about $7,500 above the poverty threshold ($14,129 for a family of three); the majority of families with unemployed heads-of-household are living below poverty. These differentials influence the types of economic challenges respondents face.

For suburban respondents, economic concerns tend to center on specific *household* problems, while many Gary respondents tend to face a multilayered set of concerns based on neighborhood *and* household economic conditions. But regardless of place of residence, respondents often speak of concerns about the economic stability of their families.[4] Their income-related problems are recognized in Oliver and Shapiro's (1997) analysis of economic differentials in the United States, *Black Wealth / White Wealth*. They note:

> The top 20 percent of earners receive 43 percent of all income while the poorest one-fifth of the population receives a scant 4 percent of the income . . . one in three American families possesses no assets whatsoever, and only 45 percent possess enough to live above the poverty line for three months in times of no income. (pp. 29, 179)

Working-class families, many of whom earn minimum wage,[5] can find themselves in economically precarious situations—earning too much to qualify for most governmental aid, but not earning quite enough to experience significant economic stability. Such families may theoretically be considered "nonpoor," but their everyday lives closely parallel those of the impoverished. The dynamic is often most evident for single mothers who have transitioned from welfare to work. One White single mother of three lives in Valparaiso and works as an administrative assistant since exiting welfare:

> That's something I wonder—who makes the list, or the quota, the um, what do they call it, the poverty level, you know. Who does that? Some rich guy in a mansion? You know, because they have no idea, you know? I don't—I would make it if I made forty, fifty thousand dollars a year, sixty you know, but at this point I'm not . . . People talk down on people for not having jobs or not making something of them-selves, but they say, 'oh, there's all these opportunities,' but you need a way to get there. You don't always have a friend who would be willing to take you there, or if they do they would expect gas money, you know. They just need to make things more accessible. Um, I would—they need transporta-tion out here. They need to make things, you know, big. There's always a catch twenty-two.

This frustration is compounded by the lack of transportation for urbanites to take advantage of suburban employment. Wilson (1996) suggests that urban-suburban transportation vehicles would help address this dilemma. However, many urban residents do not have this option:

> Low-wage people who don't have cars are often dependent on a relative who is willing to drop them off and pick them up again each day, sometimes on a route that includes the babysitter's house or the childcare center. Change your place of work and you may be confronted with an impossible topo-graphical problem to solve, or at least a reluctant driver to persuade. (Ehrenreich 2001: 205)

The abovementioned respondent's frustration regarding the abstract nature of current poverty criteria relative to the realities of the lives of persons for whom it is used to assess has been a point of contesta-tion among academic and mainstream writers who study poverty. Concerning the official poverty threshold as a measurement criterion, Schiller (1976) suggests: "The line we have drawn separating the poor from the nonpoor does not indicate what is enough—it only asserts with confidence what is too little" (p. 21). Similarly, Ehrenreich's (2001) undercover examination of low-wage America, *Nickel and Dimed: On (Not) Getting by in America*, parallels this academic assessment and is critical of the theoretical basis of the rate:

> The reason for the disconnect between the actual housing nightmare of the poor and "poverty," as officially defined, is simple: the official poverty level is still calculated by the archaic method of taking the bare-bones cost of food for a family of a given size and multiplying this number by three. Yet food is relatively inflation-proof, at least compared with rent. In the early 1960s, when this method of calculating poverty was devised, food accounted for 24 percent of the average family budget and housing 29 percent. In 1999, food took up only 16 percent of the family budget, while housing had soared to 37 percent. (p. 200)

The writer presents an alternative criterion that reflects basic economic needs as well as quality of life considerations:

> The Economic Policy Institute recently reviewed dozens of studies of what constitutes a "living wage" and came up with an average figure of $30,000 a year for a family of one adult and two children, which amounts to a wage of $14 an hour. This is not the very minimum such a family could live on; the budget includes health insurance, a telephone, and childcare at a licensed center, for example, which are well beyond the reach of millions. But it does not include restaurant meals, video rentals, Internet access, wine or liquor, cigarettes and lottery tickets, or even very much meat. The shocking thing is that the majority of American workers, about 60 percent, earn less than $14 an hour. (p. 213)

In addition, Sherraden (1991) critiques current AFDC eligibility standards that require recipients to be both income as well as asset-deficient. AFDC provides subsistence living such that, upon entering the workforce, most recipients are without funds to sustain their families or cushion them if they experience financial shortfalls. Such policies, in conjunction with welfare to work efforts, reduce the ranks of welfare recipients only to increase the ranks of the working poor. An employed White mother who lives in the suburbs is concerned about downward mobility from her current working-class position: "Employment-wise, I hope that the government, our county—Porter County government can, you know, keep things in line, be able to afford to pay everybody, so that people have jobs, and that we can just all, you know, have our jobs." In spite of her overall concerns about making ends meet, a White receptionist with two children who transitioned from welfare to work and currently earns $15,000–$20,000 annually suggests personal benefits of her current position that parallel Wilson's (1996) research on the tangible and intangible benefits of employment:

> When I got food stamps it was like very embarrassing, you kind of like hide 'em and take 'em out and gave them to the clerk. I do notice now they're not giving out certificates, coupons, it's kind of like a card now, so it's probably less embarrassing and humiliating to people. But I did notice there were some clerks that sort of had an attitude towards me when I used food stamps, so I feel much better now that I don't have to use those. When you're on food stamps you're buying exactly, you know, just food. Now I spend a little more, or like chips or ice cream or whatever. When you're on food stamps you want to make it look like, 'yes I'm so poor,' I'm trying to make the most out of this.

The welfare to work transition for mothers with young children often means receiving limited governmental support. Life on the cusp between self-sufficiency and dependency can result in an emotionally strained position, where one wishes to distance oneself from government aid, while still realizing its necessity to sustain their family. An African American employed mother of two comments on her experiences as a recipient of governmental assistance:

> At almost every grocery store, there's a big sign up that says, 'please notify the cashier if you're paying with WIC before she starts ringing you up.' And then you notify them and they have to flick their light up and so the people behind you know this is going to take a while. And that's just like embarrassing so I didn't even go back and get the WIC vouchers. Even though it's free food, I was just saying, 'forget it,' I'll just buy milk and cheese and everything else. It's so degrading. It hurts your self-esteem to even go to the grocery

store, you know, to even get the stuff so it's just—if you don't
have to do it, I don't think anybody would. But if you have
any type of self-respect, if you could *not* use WIC, you
wouldn't because it's really degrading.

For some who have yet to transition from governmental assistance to employment, unemployment can be viewed as a situation
to be justified. A previously employed Hispanic male from East
Chicago suggests:

Food stamps, yes, 'cause I'm studying right now and not
working. Township for rent 'cause it's all included in the
rent. But they will [provide other aid] if I need it. They asked
me already. But in order to get that, you have to participate
in the program, you know. You have to go to school or work
for them in order for them to help you out. They'll pay the
rent and everything else, but you have to work in the program. I need help for my rent to be paid and for food, you
know. If I was working, it would be alright. [Q: How long
have you been out of work?] A few years now . . . jobs are
hard to come by, everybody's looking for work. The economy's not too great right now. The economy. The city itself.
And like I said, if I had a job it would be great. But right
now, I'm studying and I enjoy it.

Regardless of their current socioeconomic status as poor, near
poor, working class, or in some instances, lower middle class, 54
percent of respondents have had some previous exposure to
poverty;[6] 29 percent currently receive AFDF support. Twenty percent of respondents are currently without health insurance, 33
percent do not have a running automobile in their household, and
54.2 and 16.7 percent, respectively, of persons spend a disproportionate amount of their monthly income on housing and food, respectively. Almost 63 percent of respondents acknowledge having
difficulty making ends meet each month. In addition, Gary residents tend to spend more each month on food and clothing than
their counterparts outside the city.[7] For many, difficult economic
times have had a sobering effect. The following comments illustrate attempts to be self-efficacious, maintain dignity in the midst
of financial hardship, and make sacrifices to provide stability for
children. According to one White mother of three:

> I've learned a lot. When I grew up, you know, if I'd pout a little bit, I'd get what I wanted, you know. And I've learned to be humble, to struggle. I lived in Chicago and we lived in a—crap, it was just, you know, horrible. I just made a point that whatever it is, I will improve myself. And even if it's a small step. And every year I'm doing something, whether it be a better car or a better place. It took me seven years to get here.

This same mother delays returning to school to focus on the needs of her children. She also reveals some self-doubt about her potential success in school. However, without additional education, it will be more difficult to provide sustained economic stability for her children:

> And that's one thing that keeps me there [at current job], right now. Not that I'm settling for that. But, until things—all my kids are in school full time, you know, then I do want to go to school, but, you know, it's just the decision I've decided to make. And that's one thing that is really hard, that I have to accept. I know when they're all older that I'll do something about it, but—but right now I don't feel it's a good time for me because there are a lot of things going on with my kids—projects and there's field trips. I don't know. Sometimes I feel like I'm making excuses for myself—that I'm scared to go to school. 'Cause I wasn't that good in school when I was, you know, regular grade school and all that. And I had a problem with keeping interested in things. So I'm a little worried about that. You know, because sometimes I feel like I am settling. I'm kind of iffy, I don't know.

Although most respondents, regardless of race/ethnicity, express concerns about financial challenges, this does not translate to comparable overall economic outcomes. Large income differentials among respondents exist based largely on whether respondents are employed or receiving governmental support.[8] Hence poor White AFDC recipients are similar in their income and wealth positions as their African American and Hispanic counterparts.[9] However, as has been illustrated in earlier chapters, place of residence tends to improve quality of life and increase the ability to stretch limited incomes for those who reside in more suburban areas.

Affordable Housing

Oliver and Shapiro (1997) also find race-based differences in income *and* wealth. The latter measure, they contend, is a much more accurate assessor of resources and the ability to improve quality of life. They suggest that over 50 percent of African American and Hispanic households have zero or negative net financial assets; one-fourth of White households do. In addition, almost 50 percent of younger households (persons aged 15–35) are in the same condition as are 72 percent of persons with high school diplomas or less and 62 percent of single-parent families. The net financial assets for African American upper-white collar workers are about $5.00.[10] Literature suggests that these disparities are influenced by the value of one's place of residence as the primary mode of wealth for many families.

Homeownership as a measure of wealth is undermined in Gary based on property values. In Indiana, 2000 census data show the median value of owner-occupied units (homes) for Gary, Merrillville, Portage, and Valparaiso are as follows; $53,400, $101,300, $109,000, and $121,700, respectively.[11] Although less than 2 percent of houses in Merrillville, Portage, and Valparaiso (0.7, 0.8, and 1.1 percent, respectively) are valued under $50,000, the figure for Gary is 45.5 percent.[12] In addition, Gary residents are less likely to own or be buying homes. Such differences suggest the effects of location on this basic wealth-generating resource. In the absence of sufficient low-cost housing, many respondents expend a larger percentage of their discretionary income on housing, leaving less money for other expenses; or they contend with subpar domiciles.[13]

In addition to median value differentials for homes in Gary as compared to neighboring areas, there is also variance in the stock of residential housing. According to the National Low Income Housing Coalition (NLIHC), affordable housing is out of reach for many.[14] Their annual compilations of the "housing wage" by state, region, and county are used to determine affordable rents. The housing wage is defined as the amount a full-time employee must earn to be able to afford a two-bedroom rental at fair-market rent without paying more than 30 percent of her or his income. Affordable rent is generally accepted to mean persons do not spend more than 30 percent of income on housing costs. Coalition figures suggest the following: "A person working full-time has to earn an average of $14.66 an hour—almost three times the federal minimum wage of $5.15—to be able to afford to rent a modest two-bedroom home . . . Indiana ranks

20th on the list with a housing wage of $10.93 . . . This is 212 percent of the minimum wage" (Fee 2002: L1).

Implications of the housing wage become more startling when one considers that, in 2001, approximately 2.24 million Americans earned minimum wage or less, and over 60 percent of minimum wage employees are family heads or their spouses (Bureau of Labor Statistics 2000). NLIHC 2002 figures illustrate the disparity between actual earnings and amounts needed to locate acceptable housing in Indiana: 1) a minimum wage employee can afford monthly rent of no more than $268; 2) a low-income household that earns $17,244[15] can afford monthly rent of no more than $431, and fair-market rent for a two-bedroom unit is $568; 3) a SSI recipient who receives $545 monthly can afford rent of about $164, but fair market rent for a one-bedroom unit is $455; and 4) an Indiana minimum wage employee must work 85 hours each week in order to afford a two-bedroom unit at the area's fair market rent.[16] Although programs such as Section 42 and Section 8 enable the poor and near poor to find affordable, acceptable housing, NLIHC president, Shelia Crowley contends:

> The gap between housing costs and income that makes rent so out of reach for families also adversely affects all aspects of family life, from affording basic necessities to achievement in school to success in the workplace. For things to improve, the federal government must re-establish itself as a leader in solving this problem. (Fee 2002: L1)

In her expose on the lives of the working poor, Ehrenreich (2001) makes a similar assessment:

> Something is wrong, very wrong, when a single person in good health, a person who in addition possesses a working car, can barely support herself by the sweat of her brow. You don't need a degree in economics to see that wages are too low and rents too high . . . When the rich and the poor compete for housing on the open market, the poor don't stand a chance. The rich can always outbid them, buy up their tenements or trailer parks, and replace them with condos, McMansions, golf courses, or whatever they like . . . the poor have necessarily been forced into housing that is more expensive, more dilapidated, or more distant from their places of work. (p. 199)

An African American mother of two from this sample echoes similar sentiments. She suggests intragroup differences among the poor, the paucity of low-cost housing (even in more suburban areas), and potential problems with unsatisfactory neighbors:

> They should lower the cost of living out there. Which I think it is so high to keep the riffraff out. But also, like they have subsidized housing, but even their subsidized—'cause I lived in subsidized housing in Gary—the subsidized housing ranges are way up higher than in Gary, so I still didn't even qualify for the subsidized housing that they have, because I make too much money, you know. But that's so that you don't have the *poor* poor, you know, out there.

Comparisons between the availability and cost of housing for Gary and nearby areas support NLIHC results and illustrate the challenges associated with meeting housing needs. According to 2000 census data, about 27.3 percent of Gary home owners spend 30 percent or more of their 1999 household income on mortgage. Comparable percentages for Merrillville, Portage, and Valparaiso are: 15.5, 16.3, and 17.7 percent, respectively. Thus Gary home owners tend to spend more of their household income on housing. Median values for gross rent show Gary residents tend to pay less money for rent ($469 monthly as compared to $704, $594, and $625 in Merrillville, Portage, and Valparaiso). However, they also tend to pay relatively more of their household income on rent. Figures show that 38.5 percent of Gary renters spend 30 percent or more of their household income on gross rent as compared to 34.3, 31.5, and 36.1 percent in Merrillville, Portage, and Valparaiso, respectively. These rates are similar, but continue to be higher for Gary residents. In addition, relative housing tends to cost more for many Gary residents, because they are more likely to be impoverished.[17] However, the average cost of shelter for respondents who receive housing subsidies is lower than their counterparts who do not. For this reason, working nonpoor respondents, especially White respondents who live in the suburbs, tend to pay more for housing and also consider housing to be their most pressing expense.

For families living below the poverty line and many who have transitioned out of poverty, the specter of economic uncertainty continues to loom large over their lives. Economic-related concerns are most apparent for families that "fall between the cracks"—between governmental support and self-sufficiency.

Their experiences support academic evidence that the current poverty threshold significantly overestimates those families that can adequately sustain themselves. In addition, working-class nonpoor and working-class poor respondents experience "spells of poverty" due to the lack of an economic buffer and insufficient income to accumulate such a buffer.[18]

Race Relations and Differential Treatment

Out-migration has been one response to actual and perceived crime and social disorganization in poor urban areas. Those for whom urban living does not engender fear, but who associate suburban life with increased employment opportunities and improved quality of life for their children, may also choose to out-migrate to predominately White suburban areas. For minority families, this means increased interaction with Whites, many of whom may not welcome racially heterogeneous neighborhoods. Group Threat theory implies that Whites may perceive increased competition by minority groups for influence and resources, when the latter become more visible in a once predominately White area. This premise suggests a direct relationship between racial discrimination and perceived increases in minority representation.[19] Similarly, Blumer's (1958) work suggests the potential for increased racial discrimination when Whites believe their group position has been threatened by a minority group. And Gaertner and Dovidio (1986) suggest a decrease in "old-fashioned racism" characterized by feelings of superiority and outward hostility toward minority groups by Whites and an increase in "aversive racism," where the latter group expresses sympathy for the victims of injustices, is supportive, in principle, of public policy that promotes racial equality, and adheres to a more liberal political stance. However, intolerance by aversive racists generally manifests in the form of discomfort, uneasiness, disgust, fear, and ultimately, avoidance, of minority groups. In this context, aversive racists would be less willing to welcome minorities in their neighborhoods. Other studies show concerns by White residents about African American in-migration and the tendency of Whites to exit neighborhoods upon arrival of African Americans.[20]

It follows that minority groups who venture into predominately White areas for employment and housing alternatives must consider the potential drawbacks of such decisions. In addition to these interracial considerations, possible intrarace conflict may arise as well. Some respondents acknowledge different race-related experiences influenced by place of residency and relocation decisions. One White mother of three biracial children has lived in an urban setting and currently resides in a predominately White, suburban area. Her past experiences have made her more sensitive to race relations:

> Some people would just say things like, you know, it doesn't matter if you're Black or White or Mexican or whatever, there's always going to be somebody who doesn't like what you do or who you represent or—you know, people—even now, people will take a double take and they'll look at my kids. They might even ask if my kids were adopted. 'No, they're mine.' In the area I lived in [urban area] it was mostly Black, and there were a lot of Latinos . . . I think maybe when I first moved there it was just a shock because I was there and you walk everywhere and I just kind of stepped out in faith and said well I've gotta become bold. You know, I can't be afraid and they can't be afraid of me. I've gotta be here and I don't have a choice.And all you can do is be friendly and show that you don't mean any disrespect or harm and then it was ok.
>
> I haven't really had too many bad experiences here. When I lived in the city, things were a little bit different, 'cause my children are mixed. And sometimes they would just kind of stop and look just for a minute and, you know, but I've never been treated really badly . . . you know. I have had a situation in the mall where I've had my kids and I had one of my friend's children who is Black and White. And an older Black lady walked by and she's like [whispered] that's a shame. And I'm like 'what's a shame? What am I doing wrong, you know?' So, I think that, ah, I have learned a lot through being, having my kids be biracial, and being a White lady in a Black community and living here. And over here they are moving more Black people out here, which I'm comfortable with that and I'm glad. You know, because I think it's gotten a bad rap out here, you know, being all White and there's the KKK, which I think there is, but they're not bothering anybody at this point. So, I just think this has taught me to be a better person—the struggles that I've gone through. Like, I don't think I'd have it any other way.

This respondent has faced twofold concerns about race, first, her receptivity as a White woman living in a predominately African American urban setting and currently, about protecting her biracial children now that she lives in a largely White area. Similarly, an African American mother of two considers relocating to the suburbs for employment opportunities, but is concerned about the childcare implications for her youngest child:

> Well, and I also know, if I worked out there at Porter County doing what I'm doing, I would make more money, but—and not that White people would abuse my child, but I'm a little bit more leery of leaving her in a White daycare than in a Black daycare. So in that sense because there aren't that many minorities, childcare is just not available out there either.

In contrast, neighborhood intraracial conflict prompts one married African American mother to leave Gary and her extended family and move to a somewhat racially mixed area in Merrillville: "Where we lived before, I had a lot of problems with, you know, kids, they act how they would at home. And therefore I didn't let the baby go out as much, like I do now. I can let her go. I haven't had any problems with fights or anything like that. They all get along." Similar sentiments are echoed from another African American single mother who relocated from Gary:

> Just because it was safer to be in Portage. Where I was living in Gary they had like shootouts and whatever. Even though, now, I did realize that the new place I just moved to, that there are several more Black people in this area than throughout all of Portage. So now I do have like the loud music again. And, um, the other night I was leaving out and the police were there, and I read in the newspaper the next day that somebody had been killed. So it seems as if they're trying to congregate all the Black people into this one—or maybe this is just one apartment complex that's willing to accept more Black people than the others.

These respondents tend to associate improved quality of life with suburban living. Directly or indirectly, some also correlate such improvements with fewer African American neighbors. Their comments suggest the possible effects of hegemony, the tendency to conflate issues of poverty with race, and the implications for inter- as well as intraracial stereotyping and avoidance.

Childcare and Raising Children

Because the majority of female respondents are mothers, issues related to raising healthy, well-balanced children and locating affordable, accessible, acceptable childcare are common concerns. According to the U.S. Bureau of Labor Statistics, although about 21.6 percent of women with children under six years old were employed in 1960, that figure increased to 55.0 percent in 2000.[21] Unmarried, separated, and divorced women are more likely to be employed than married women. Due to the disproportionate percentages of African American women who are single mothers, their workforce participation has tended to exceed these figures. Historically, African American women were more likely than White women to be in the labor force; Hispanic women were the least likely to be. Today, there is nearly equal labor force participation (57 percent of African American, 54 percent of White, 49 percent of Hispanic, and 58 percent of Asian American women), and the most rapid increase has occurred for Hispanic women.[22]

Given the economic necessity for most respondents, especially single parents, to work outside the home, most require childcare services. The government subsidized childcare program, Step Ahead, facilitates employment for many women in these circumstances.[23] Most employed mothers in this study agree about their limited childcare options. A White single mother of three initially used in-home care, but was forced to locate another provider due to rising costs:

> People don't think of all the things that are involved. Because if you have to work and you have children, you have to have childcare. And the childcare costs are sometimes ridiculous, you know. I mean, I love Miss [name of in-home childcare provider] to death, but a hundred dollars a week. And that's for each.

Extended family becomes essential for some, as suggested by this African American mother of two:

> Well my mother' ll baby-sit free, as long as I schedule stuff during the times that she's not working. And she is usually the one to take my daughter to the doctor too, whenever she needs to go for like her checkups and stuff. So that I won't have to take off work. And, she helps me a whole lot. Sometimes she pays my daycare . . . and she lets me come and do my laundry at her house.

Working-class mothers who do not qualify for programs such as Step Ahead may find themselves struggling, unless they locate a provider willing to accommodate their special needs. One African American mother of a young daughter comments:

> I think now the going rate for her age with Step Ahead, which is the state—if the state pays for the daycare—it's like $125. So most of the kids in her daycare are on Step Ahead. So the woman at first was charging me $65 a week—you know, to try to cut me a break. And then, she said once she saw that I was going to pay regularly and always bring food, 'cause I was bringing food, diapers, wipes, all that. Then, about a month and a half ago, she dropped it to $55. So she's trying to give me a break, 'cause for everybody else, she's getting $125 a month—from Step Ahead.

Some mothers who do receive child support suggest it is inadequate to cover childcare costs. An African American divorced mother of three who resides in Gary comments on her problem and provides a solution:

> I get child support, as good as it is—child support is a drop in the bucket. It doesn't—it doesn't even cover childcare . . . They don't make fathers pay enough at all. They don't have the hours at my job [scheduling problems between her job and childcare]. It would be nice to have a second income that didn't come from myself. [Q: What do you mean?] A husband.

For some women, childcare problems lessen once their children reach adolescence and can remain home alone. Although latchkey children reduce or eliminate the economic cost of childcare, they tend to increase concerns about dangers associated with leaving children unattended. One White mother of two children (one of whom is a teenager) from Valparaiso remembers her childcare challenges and sympathizes with employed women with younger children: "I don't need to pay for childcare anymore because the kids are old enough to stay home by themselves. But there is a sort of shortage of childcare and it's so expensive in this area. I received Step Ahead. Otherwise I don't know how people afford to pay for it." Although childcare problems are considered the most pressing problem for women with children, concerns about the trade-offs between an improved educational system and increased taxes, as well as role models, also surface. One White mother of three notes:

They [community leaders] had talked about the different school systems and stuff. And if they, you know, build on or do this and that, things can—the taxes get raised even more. So I guess that, you know, they're remodeling the schools. I would hope that they don't decide to, you know, go way out and decide to build a whole new school, because our taxes are gonna go up, and it's, you know, not too, too bad right now, but . . .

Just as an absence of role models in some urban areas is suggested by Wilson (1996), suburban minority or multiracial families may also face a similar problem of locating appropriate role models in largely White locations:

'Cause they've already got the fact that their dads aren't around, you know, and I don't want them to suffer because of a choice I've made. They need to know that it's not all—they're not all bad—there's good people out there. But, it's hard to find. There's not police officers, there's not firemen, there's not—And some kids say, what do you want to be? Well I want to be a fireman or I want to be a police officer or something really great. I've gone to seminars and stuff in my work. And it's a big controversy, because nobody wants to come out here, nobody wants to be the guinea pig in our society, you know? (White mother of three biracial children)

Research shows an emphasis by middle-class parents in providing opportunities for their children to obtain economic and cultural capital to be successful in life. So too, do most parents in this study.[24] However, respondents are often better prepared to provide some of the intangible forms of cultural capital rather than those benefits that require substantial economic capital.[25]

Coping Strategies

A sense of self-efficacy involves believing that one can make the most of current resources and circumstances. Realizing these objectives requires understanding the task at hand, existing constraints, available resources and options, and having some reasonable idea of the consequences of each possible option. Although respondents represent various socioeconomic positions, most possess middle-class beliefs. Research on the attitudes, aspirations, and behavior of the middle class in the United States associates members of this group with conspicuous consumption, fears about downward mobility, and a desire to maintain a comparable lifestyle to peers. A middle-class lifestyle influenced by materialism as a sign of success can translate into mounting expenses, juggling finances, and working inordinate hours to repay debt.[26] Respondents socialized toward middle-class dictates, but faced with neighborhood and/or household economic problems, often develop strategies to minimize financial constraints, such that their families can hope to attain certain markers they perceive to be "middle class." The experiences of many respondents here suggest that their criterion for middle-class status emphasizes attitudes more than behavior.[27] In addition, behavioral indicators reflect a somewhat "context appropriated" form of materialism focusing on the ability to make ends meet monthly and to provide the needs as well as some of the periodic "wants" for their children and themselves. To this end, the use of creative, nontraditional strategies is common. Additionally, for several respondents, meeting these criteria appears to be the primary measuring rod for personal evaluation more than the *source of the funds* used to meet them. Hence employed persons, as well as governmental aid recipients, strive to maintain such a lifestyle.

For example, subsidized childcare expenses enable one White welfare-to-work mother to live above poverty. Should her income exceed a certain threshold, this would mean forfeiture of this childcare support. Her short-term strategy involves refusing wage increases to avoid losing subsidized childcare. She would have to earn a substantially higher salary to pay for the costs of unsubsidized childcare—an option that is not currently feasible with a high school education. However, intangible benefits justify continuing at her place of employment:

> The only problem with that, is, I'm limited as to how much money I make. I can make fifty cents more and that's it. If I make anything higher than that—so basically if I make anything higher than nine dollars an hour, they're taken off [children removed from subsidized program]. And, which they don't realize that even if you make ten dollars an hour, that's not enough to pay a hundred dollars a week in childcare and then all the bills, you know, and you're left with ten bucks for, you know, two weeks. I have asked her [the supervisor], don't take me above that. Yeah, I have been denying a raise [laughs]. We don't get a whole lot of raises at the of-

fice. It's few and far between—but, there's a lot of perks there that work for me. You, know, we get paid personal time off, we get paid snow days. There's just a lot of things— if something's wrong with my kids, I can go, without someone saying, 'where do you think you're going,' you know. And that's one thing that keeps me there, right now.

Prioritizing debt and juggling bills is a common strategy among sample women transitioning from AFDC to employment. One African American mother currently works as a file clerk. Although her limited income frequently prevents paying the required amounts on bills, she strives to ward off going into default: "Like, for instance, when I—the checks that I get—when they were real small, I would call like the gas company to get an extension on the payment of the bill, or even like for the phone—I'd tell them I'll pay a little bit this week and a little the next week. You know, so it won't be like I'm not paying nothing." Despite budgets, planning, and juggling of expenses, most persons are ill prepared for unexpected events. A White mother of two from Valparaiso describes her strategy: "Sometimes, I mean, have a strict budget and I try to stick by it, but every once and a while I can kind of go over that budget . . . if something happens to the car or the kids need to do whatever, unexpectedly, that can really throw you off." Regardless of the income source, most respondents realize the importance of developing economic strategies. A young Hispanic single mother of one discusses her family's use of governmental support, as well as aid via extended family: "We receive $275 a month from food stamps, so we probably spend about 50 percent of that. Sometimes we spend a little bit, but then we spend, some on two weeks and some on another two weeks. My brother will give us some money here and there. Or I'll get some money from my dad—but that's rare. He's stingy [laughs]." An African American recipient of SSI suggests that maximizing her governmental support is strained due to bureaucratic problems, but notes additional avenues for assistance:

> I don't have a Medicaid card yet. The government keeps losing the—they can't find them. So I have to take some of my money from SSI and pay for the medicines I need. Some of it is like $80. Like I spend at least $30 per month on medicines. I do have some help from some companies. They will send me like high blood medicines when my doctor make a order out. And uh, the drug store, they give me a discount and give me generic products, so it can be cheaper.

Other strategies require respondents to seek out inexpensive or free opportunities to treat their children. For one African American family with two children on a tight budget, trips to a suburban mall become "play dates" rather than shopping excursions: "They have free movies that are family oriented, so I do that a lot. And then like my friends, we get together and—I will go the mall, but *strictly* to the food court where the play area is, and so then we'll let our kids play in the area, and then you just go home. And so, it's usually free." Regardless of race/ethnicity or urban/suburban locale, respondents with children tend to associate their identities as providers and caretakers with the ability to pay their monthly bills and shield their children from family economic problems. For such persons it is important to provide children with some semblance of security and protection, even when parents themselves question whether ends will be met each month. In these instances, respondents take some pride in "small victories" as signs that they are doing their best despite the circumstances. One White single mother of three provides a representative viewpoint:

> I applied for section eight when I first moved to Valparaiso, and I had gotten my second [acceptance] letter and I heard nothing after that. So I just figure, well, if I was supposed to get it, I would get it, you know. And I'm okay with paying the rent that I do, you know. I actually, I get happy when I can pay my rent [laughs]. My rent is always paid and my electrical is always paid. You know, it's just satisfying to me to be able to afford that. You know, I mean, money is tight sometimes, but I know I'm ahead . . . I have become comfortable with myself, you know, accepting who I am. I don't have to change anything for anybody.

Given that middle-class lifestyles often connote marriage and children, several married respondents from dual-earner households who can be characterized as lower middle class acknowledge the relationship between changing marital status, increased economic expenses, and the need to develop coping strategies. One married African American mother who recently had her third child comments:

> Well we've included a new member into the family. So that's the first thing—baby milk is extremely high. I'd say, I guess it's more expensive for me because first, it was me and just the 10-year-old. And, I was working, but I lived cheap, so my rent was a lot cheaper. Um, I didn't have a car note. I had a

little junky car, that made it back and forth to work, but it was mine, it was paid for. I think the more money you make, the more money you spend, and the more expenses you have. So when I didn't have that much, I made it, you know without struggling, I had change left over. I didn't do as much, I didn't go as much, I cooked a lot more at home than I do now. And I qualified for public assistance, just because of which job I had. When I started working where I work now, I was totally cut off of everything. But it didn't matter, because I could do the overtime. And when we moved, once we got married, we shot straight up [economic bracket] because of his income. But with just my income it wasn't a big deal. I mean, you know, two or three hundred dollars a month for rent. And if I wanted to do something extra, I would work a extra eight hours or nine hours or whatever and get some overtime . . . I didn't have any credit cards.

And just as combining incomes and expenses as a result of marriage can increase debt, an African American mother of two attests, divorce can result in economic strain after debt has accumulated:

Well, I'm spread thin. And I'll be starting a second job pretty soon. Usually I've worked two jobs all the time, off and on. But I have, I've consolidated all of my bills into a consumer credit counseling thing. So really all I have are the major bills and then that consolidation thing. Um, my checking right now doesn't have anything, 'cause I get paid on Friday. And my savings probably has about $35, $40.

Respondents consider the lack of gainful employment, high taxes, and limited low-cost housing to also be pressing costs they face. Although many respondents are able to juggle monthly expenses despite these challenges and provide for their families, few are able to accumulate sufficient savings or accumulate assets that will increase their personal wealth and enable them to experience other economic facets they associate with middle-class life.

Making Sense of It All

For most of the urban respondents interviewed here, concerns about dilapidated buildings, crime hazards, and drug havens are not

as grave as has been suggested in some studies and become most germane, as they consider the implications of urban problems for the
lives of their children. They and their suburban counterparts are
much more concerned about everyday financial challenges associated
with maintaining a family. In most instances, the poor, near-poor and
working-class suburban respondents face economic problems similar
to those of urbanites. However, access to suburban amenities such as
discount grocery stores, retailers, and affordable housing, typically
mean they are likely to be more effective in their attempts to care for
their families and to do so with fewer obstacles.

By and large, respondents were socialized to embrace certain
tenets of so-called "middle class" America. Most were raised in
homes that were middle class in principle, even if they were more
working nonpoor or working poor in terms of economic reality. The
majority of respondents continue to aspire to middle-class dictates,
but their aspirations are often leveled, short-term, by the sobering
reality of their economic circumstances. However, long-term, factors other than their own personal goals and aspirations appear to
order their actions and decisions. Wilson's (1996) examination of
the experiences of urban Chicago residents, most of who live below
the poverty line, informs this observation. Most persons in his study
faced neighborhood as well as household economic problems.[28]
Despite their economic circumstances, the author notes:

> Despite the overwhelming poverty, black residents in inner-
> city ghetto neighborhoods verbally reinforce, rather than
> undermine, the basic American values pertaining to indi-
> vidual initiative . . . Nonetheless, given the constraints and
> limited opportunities facing people in inner-city neighbor-
> hoods, it is altogether reasonable to assume that many of
> those who subscribe to these values will, in the final analy-
> sis, find it difficult to live up to them. Circumstances gener-
> ally taken for granted in middle-class society are often
> major obstacles that must be overcome in the inner-city
> ghetto. (p. 67)

However, his research finds that over 85 percent of respondents
are optimistic about their children's futures and believe their children will be better off than they are. In addition, over 60 percent expect their children to graduate from college—even though most
respondents have not done so themselves. Whether these aspirations reflect a planned child-rearing agenda or wishful thinking,

they parallel the views of most Gary and non-Gary respondents who are parents. My findings suggest that Wilson's (1996) assessments that inner-city values are often circumvented due to circumstances can be generalized to segments of poor and near-poor suburbia as well. Many respondents in and around Gary are also concerned about economic constraints. However, they are often more preoccupied with aspirations for their children's futures. This concern serves as a primary motivating factor in their everyday lives.

Wilson also contends that low income and unstable employment can result in a diminished sense of self-efficacy and the inability to reconcile productive values and aspirations with behavior. Similarly, Gans's (1968) historic examination of the structure versus agency debate focuses on whether the poor respond to change as well as the role played by culture in mediating change. The author suggests that, instead of either theoretical camp being correct, the solution probably "lies somewhere in between" (p. 206). He further argues that poverty research that concentrates on behavioral indictors is limited, because behavior is dynamic under different conditions.[29] Several respondents in this study admitted experiencing periods of self-doubt and defeatism, but forced themselves to move past these feelings for the sake of their children. Most parents contend that they must persevere for the sake of their children—they have no choice. Ironically, respondents who embrace a child-centered belief system[30] appear to be economically less able to maintain a standard of living to significantly improve their children's life chances. Oliver and Shapiro (1997) note: "The arrival of children can have a critical effect on resources of households: income drops . . . both net worth and net financial assets decline drastically with the presence of the first child . . . Except for the second child, the wealth decline continues with each successive child" (p. 80). Thus for many poor and working class respondents, a focus on their children's futures may be undermined by the *very presence* of children in the household. The authors continue:

> Close to one-half of all children live in households with no financial assets and 63 percent live in households with precarious resources, scarcely enough net financial assets to cushion three months of interrupted income . . . Most telling of all perhaps, only 11 percent of black children grow up in households with enough net financial assets to weather three months of no income at the poverty level. Three times as many white kids live in such households. (p. 88)

The experiences of several respondents suggest that, for single mothers, the above observation does not only apply to African Americans. A White female recalls painful experiences as a result of poverty and decisions made during her youth, yet continues to maintain her instrumental and expressive roles as a single mother:

> There have been times when I would cry. I mean, I don't know what else to do, you know? Why, you know why, why is my life this way, why did I make the choices that I made, you know? I mean, of course if I had anything to do over, it would be the choices I made. But I wouldn't choose not to have the children I have. I know for me, maybe not for everyone, but, um, they help you keep a good eye on the big picture. You know, what are you really wanting? You know, what do you want them to have? And, you know, that's hard sometimes. You know, a lot of people say, 'God, it's gonna be hard raising kids.' The hard part is not raising them, the hard part is keeping the roof over their head and keeping the big things intact. You know, the teaching them, showing them how to do this or do that, doing their homework. You know, it gets a little crazy sometimes, but it's not the hard part. It's just managing everything, and it's hard. I know that, I feel that I'm responsible for the most part.

Similar to the literature on the middle class, most respondents have economic concerns and struggle to stave off downward economic mobility. Unlike their middle-class counterparts, their concerns are typically more pressing and more pervasive. The issue becomes, not making payments for several automobiles, but locating the funds to repair an old vehicle and making transportation arrangements for the several months that will be required to save money for the repair. For respondents, middle-class concerns about home repairs are supplanted by pressing needs to locate low-cost housing in better neighborhoods. Coordinating van pools and supervising extracurricular activities for children are replaced by strategies to locate low-cost, acceptable childcare. Most respondents have middle-class ideals and exhibit certain middle-class markers when possible. Fewer have a comparable economic support system or the network to locate sufficient instrumental support when they face unexpected emergencies.

Contrary to deficiency theories and more recent paradigmatic derivatives,[31] most respondents do not exhibit present-time orientation, feelings of hopelessness, despair, inferiority, low aspirations, and fatalism, but rather appear to concentrate their efforts and resources toward the future of their children. Save several younger female single parents, most do not exhibit the ghetto-related behavior suggested of extremely impoverished urban residents.[32] In their own way, many respondents have had to adapt to situations beyond their control—those who live in underserviced neighborhoods in Gary more than their suburban counterparts. Previous experiences during more economically stable times and current instances, when reasonable economic and expressive milestones are met, serve to reinforce and remind most respondents that the short-term economic and noneconomic costs they incur will diminish, if not for them, then for their children.

Conclusion:
A Thesis on the Poor Urban Experience:
Validating Experiences

Much of recent research in urban sociology has shifted its emphasis from descriptions of the urban experience to analyses of macro-level effects of urban poverty. Given the implications of deindustrialization, globalization, hyper-segregation, and the resulting social isolation, such research is warranted. However, an indirect result of this focus has been a paucity of studies on the everyday lives of residents in urban centers. This examination of the daily round of African American, White, and Hispanic residents in Gary, Indiana, and surrounding areas is reminiscent of earlier case studies of urban life and illustrates the relationship between neighborhood-concentrated poverty and the structure versus agency discourse. I have focused on the everyday experiences of primarily poor and working-class persons. Qualitative and quantitative findings suggest varied shopping experiences based on the type of neighborhood one frequents for goods and services. In this section, I forward a thesis to describe these and other possible responses to poor urban conditions that reflect what I term *validating experiences* and *patterns of incremental integration and isolation.*

Despite structural constraints resulting in limited opportunities and resources, I contend that many residents in Gary, Indiana (and other urban areas, to the degree that they are similar to Gary) attempt to engage in thrift, are optimistic about their children's futures, make daily round decisions in less than ideal circumstances, anticipate home ownership, and embrace other attitudes and behavior typically associated with "middle class" society due largely to *validating experiences.* A validating experience can be defined as

191

a personal experience or experience of another person or group (past or present) that encourages or justifies positive and proactive attitudes and behavior. A validating experience is associated with a positive outcome and affirms and reaffirms the benefit or potential benefit of engaging in certain behavior or embracing certain attitudes. For example, because validating experiences can be tangible or intangible, parental sacrifices for possible future gains of children continually appear in this study as a potential validating experience and a mechanism to attempt to combat the negative effects of neighborhood poverty. Validating experiences reinforce positive attitudes and behavior when one experiences tangible, affirming results or anticipates such results.

I contend that residents in poor urban neighborhoods are more likely to embrace tenets, such as delayed gratification, frugality, hard work, and the importance of education, when they have had validating experiences that justify such attitudes and behavior, have witnessed the successes of others, or anticipate personal benefits. When positive results are experienced (such as saving money to purchase large household items), attitudes and behavior are reinforced. The economic and noneconomic gains of family members, friends, coworkers, and in some cases, media personalities also serve as potential validating experiences that may subsequently motivate persons to set similar goals and objectives. Consequently, the absence of validating experiences (or the potential for such experiences) acts as a disincentive.

If residents in poor urban areas have not had validating experiences or witnessed them among family members or in their neighborhoods or believe the odds of success are slim, they will be less likely to believe the benefits of positive, proactive attitudes and behavior apply to them. Thus personal experiences of the economically and socially disenfranchised undermine actual validating experiences and belief in them. Given the negative effects of neighborhood poverty in Gary, Indiana, that take the form of an absence of goods, service providers, and department stores and the presence of higher-priced grocery stores, it is important that residents have validating experiences to confirm that the "system" will and can work on their behalf, if they "do their part" (for example, work hard, live thriftily). Such experiences will justify further involvement and investment on their part. Urban residents must be able to make a clear, discernible linkage between the utility of their efforts and the likelihood of realistic, beneficial returns. A direct relationship is expected between validating experiences and the wherewithal to combat negative structural forces. The link between experiences I've termed validating experiences and positive behavior, such as hard work and obtaining an education, has been suggested in literature.[1]

The basis of my thesis regarding the importance of validating experiences is found in theories of utilitarianism that suggest that some decisions are largely motivated, not by act or motive, but by potential consequences or outcomes. If the perceived consequences represent an improvement or benefit for the person or at least not a cost, the act will likely be performed. Based on this premise, I would expect residents in poor urban locales, such as Gary, Indiana, to consider the possible consequences of their attitudes and actions to determine whether they should invest time and energy.[2] For some, if the ends do not justify the means, they are less likely to commit themselves.

However, it is my assessment that validating experiences can affect behavior more than attitudes. Thus, while persons may decide to refrain from a particular activity, it does not follow that they do not believe the activity is important or generally beneficial. The act simply appears to lack benefit *for them*.[3] Thus, for example, some Gary respondents may recognize the importance of living and shopping in Gary, yet fail to do so because they do not consider such activity personally beneficial.[4] Some may continue to anticipate validating experiences in spite of their present condition[5] or reduce their expectations or resign to present circumstances.[6] Some may simply withdraw, and still others may blame themselves or the larger society.[7] These outcomes are evident among certain respondents in this study. Given the importance of validating experiences as tools for structural and social integration and as a means of motivation, effective public policy for urban improvements should include programs that help ensure certain expedient returns for residents' efforts. Examples include: adherence and accountability by political leaders to promised urban renewal efforts, training programs that transition more quickly into gainful employment, counseling services to combat feelings of alienation and angst and address conflict management, and harsher penalties for employers who commit discrimination. These types of measures will encourage residents in impoverished urban areas (and poor and near-poor persons in general, I wager) to continue to strive and possibly increase motivation and proactive attitudes and behavior.

Revisiting the Isolation Thesis: Patterns of Incremental Integration and Isolation

Scholarship has shown that residents in high poverty urban areas often suffer from physical and social isolation that undermines the ability to locate gainful employment and experience upward mobility.[8] I argue for the need to also consider the *type* of isolation under consideration (for example, physical, social, isolation from family, neighbors, or the larger society), points of reference, and counteractive measures. For example, Ogbu (1978) suggests that poor African Americans may develop an oppositional culture (resulting in social and cultural isolation from the larger society) in response to a closed opportunity structure (physical and economic isolation). Furthermore, the author believes that such cultural markers often further isolate African Americans socially. In this instance, cultural and social isolation are generally defined based on one's position relative to members (generally White) of the larger society. Comparisons within the African American community or for the individuals themselves (Weber's notion of *verstehen*)[9] may suggest a different form of isolation or may not suggest isolation at all.

For example, although most residents in Gary are clearly physically isolated from major grocery and department stores, they attempt to compensate through the use of automobiles and public transportation. In this context, the full effect of physical isolation may also be curbed somewhat by the tendency of residents to "buy in bulk" at suburban stores, thereby reducing the chances of falling short of important items to maintain their households. In doing so, they attempt to negotiate around some of the effects of physical isolation by "segmenting" periods of isolation to minimize their influence. This strategy also provides a short-term remedy for absent providers in their immediate vicinity. Additionally, some residents, especially younger persons, have reconceptualized the issue of outmigrated stores. For them, the absence of major stores in Gary becomes less a systemic problem reflecting inequities and economic and noneconomic costs, but rather a reason for a shopping excursion to suburban malls and restaurants. These examples suggest varied approaches to defining and understanding the term *isolation*. The importance of scholarship regarding the effects of physical and social isolation in the most segregated urban neighborhoods should not be diminished,[10] but rather must also be weighed against a variety of other possible responses to life in poor urban neighborhoods.

Based on my findings, I also contend that many residents in poor urban areas experience, what I term, patterns of *incremental integration* and *incremental isolation*. Integration can be defined as the degree to which residents in poor urban areas both *are and feel* connected to their neighborhoods and the larger society. In the broadest sense, isolation reflects the absence of tangible or intangible connections or affiliations. Using this schematic, integration and isolation are two ends of a continuum and increments refer to gradual shifts between the two ends of this spectrum based on one's life experiences, behavior, and beliefs. Like validating experiences, integration and/or isolation reflect a cognitive or intangible component (whether persons feel or consider themselves to be integrated or isolated) and a tangible component (more traditional measures of isolation and integration primarily measured by indicators, such as employment, weak social ties, or spatial relationships). Both components influence one's place on the continuum. The tangible and intangible components that enhance actual and perceived connectedness are validating experiences.

For example, some residents in Gary may not feel like a part of suburban areas that they frequent to shop, due to poor service; unwelcoming suburbanites directly or indirectly engender disconnectedness for such persons as well. Similarly, Gary residents may be cognitively connected outside the immediate city (for example, are financially able to frequent suburban stores and "afford" items for their families), but disconnected in other ways (for example, be unemployed or underemployed or lack basic stores in their own neighborhoods). Also, others may be tangibly integrated in some respects (e.g., employed), but not feel integrated in others (e.g., stigmatized when they shop at suburban venues). The forms of integration or isolation will vary based on the type and extent of validating experiences. Thus validating experiences are an important mechanism through which integration and isolation are expected and manifest. This thesis suggests that there are varying degrees of integration and isolation. Levels of incremental integration and isolation are affected both by validating experiences, as well as by one's responses to such experiences. Persons "move" along this continuum, as they act and react to a variety of experiences—in this study—those related to the daily round. As earlier noted, these dynamics can be affected both by the attitudes and behavior of residents in poor urban neighborhoods and by the attitudes and behavior of those outside these locations.

Let us consider an example relative to employment experiences. The loss of a job due to out-migration of a company may result in one becoming more isolated from the employment sector and thus incrementally less integrated. A person may experience increased isolation, because job loss means loss and associated "costs"—loss of daily contact with an employment network, loss of finances, loss of structure in one's day, and possible loss of a sense of self-efficacy that employment provides.[11] This shift is tangible, because one experiences a variety of real problems. However, the experience may also bring about feelings of emotional and psychological isolation. Thus the experience brings about a shift towards the end of the continuum represented by "isolation." However, the full effect of isolation is thwarted, if one is able to locate another comparable job. If this is not possible, the incremental effects of isolation can be diminished, if decent-paying employment in the formal or informal arenas is located. The latter two experiences do not restore one to the previous position on the continuum, yet they *minimize* the incremental isolation that occurred due to job loss. Persons who can maintain some sense of self-efficacy will experience less dramatic shifts toward isolation. In addition, other mechanisms can somewhat lessen isolation or feelings of isolation (for example, validating experiences through one's children, family, friendship, or religious networks), make persons feel more integrated, and help to reestablish one's position on the continuum.

Patterns of isolation and integration can reflect various dimensions (physical, emotional, economic, social, cultural, and psychological). And although this thesis can be applied to circumstances outside poor urban spaces, its implications are potentially most dramatic when considering situations that can be associated with dramatic shifts toward isolation due to systemic forces and attenuated validating experiences. Because of urban poverty, many residents in cities such as Gary are faced with a variety of potentially negative experiences that vary in type and severity and affect their "position" on the continuum. These experiences can occur simultaneously and result in variable changes in one's position on the continuum. Certain experiences can be more devastating than others (such as job loss, inability to meet basic family needs, crime victimization, discrimination, stigmatization) and result in more dramatic incremental shifts toward isolation. And certain proactive and reactionary responses may be more effective in resulting in incremental integration (for example, in this study, optimism about children's futures, the ability to successfully complete the daily round, the ability to make "special" purchases for one's children, and periodic "splurging" during shopping outings). One's position on the continuum is dynamic, as one attempts to combat isolating effects and remain and feel connected to the immediate surroundings and the larger society. In sum, incremental integration and incremental isolation that many residents face in poor urban areas such as Gary are largely determined by the degree to which they either "bounce back" or are "set back" by a variety of structural and individual obstacles. Fruitful inquiry relative to the concepts of validating experiences and patterns of incremental integration and isolation will require researchers to not only consider what urban residents do (or fail to do), but also consider the local implications of systemic changes and examine more nuanced issues based on ethnographic studies.

My assessments of patterns of incremental integration and incremental isolation suggest that many residents in cities such as Gary represent a diverse subgroup within mainstream society. This definition transcends physicality and includes people who are aware of and, to some degree, acknowledge a broad set of expectations and beliefs typically associated with the middle class. However, I contend that these ideological tenets are acted upon in variable ways based on structural constraints and personal agency. Furthermore, whether residents in poor urban areas wish to be associated with "middle class" society or conceive that they are a part of the larger society affects whether and how they may respond to experiences that may result in isolation or integration. Similarly, whether persons outside urban spaces feel "connected" to poor urban areas will influence their support of policies and programs that affect the lives of residents in poor urban areas, particularly those who are attempting to combat isolation.

Neighborhood and "Household Effects" in and around Gary, Indiana

Given that the majority of respondents, even those that acknowledge having difficulty making ends meet, are able to somehow sustain their families, readers should be cautious about ignoring the varied obstacles persons face and the amount of time and energy it can take to meet basic economic-related household goals. Most respondents attempt to be adaptive and resilient—but a focus on their limited success stories can divert attention from the sobering reality that the vast majority of the poor and near poor face financial obstacles and will continue to do so without intervention.

These results also emphasize the importance of reconsidering the implications of the term "neighborhood." Based on their socioeconomic position, especially for single-parent mothers who have transitioned from welfare to work, suburban respondents face some of the negative effects common to residents in impoverished urban spaces. Financially constrained suburban respondents tend to live in areas with lower crime rates, less social disorganization, and increased employment opportunities. These locales also provide sanctuary from the scrutiny and stigma often experienced by residents in impoverished urban areas. However, the challenges of many female-headed households are similar regardless of place of residence, and persons may contend with welfare dependency, limited social networks, and inadequate low-cost housing. In addition, the tendency for poor and near-poor Whites to experience segregation and isolation based, not on race, but class, can exist based on the latitude of housing subdivision managers and rental property owners. As their numbers increase, such persons risk potentially becoming isolated in rent-subsidized facilities and housing complexes or in neighborhoods more likely to accept the poor and near poor. These possible outcomes suggest the need to expand the definition of neighborhood effects that tends to focus on the urban experience and overlook similar suburban dynamics.

Neighborhood poverty effects in and around Gary that take the form of limited grocery and department stores, inadequate goods and services, and higher prices are most apparent when I examine structural differences based on place. However, given Gary's racial/ethnic homogeneity, place is almost synonymous with race/ethnicity. Those costs examined at the neighborhood level provide a macro-level assessment of life in Gary and surrounding areas. However, it is also important to consider the role of micro-level or "household effects" that can influence one's ability to complete the daily round. Results here illustrate the interrelatedness of macro- and individual-level variables in understanding economic and noneconomic costs incurred.

In most instances, respondents from Gary rely on strengths within their respective households to counter possible negative neighborhood effects associated with limited goods and service providers. In this context, "household effects" reflect both financial and nonfinancial assets, such as household income and strategies to make ends meet. Household dynamics are used to buffer some of the harsher realities of neighborhood poverty. Thus, while many Gary residents may live in poor neighborhoods that face challenges, such as poverty, crime, and diminished infrastructure, the economic status, beliefs, and behavior in their immediate households and, in some instances, extended and fictive kin, may serve as a partial shield from the full impact of negative neighborhood conditions. I contend that some of the most important buffers for combating the full effects of neighborhood poverty reflect the ability of residents in poor urban spaces to take part in certain activities (considered "middle class" by some), such as successfully completing the daily round, saving small sums of money, anticipating future home ownership, and being able to purchase special items for their children and their homes. These activities can provide practical, emotional, and psychological benefits (representing validating experiences), because they may diminish possible feelings of social and physical isolation by reinforcing a sense of self-efficacy and connectedness in spite of possible physical isolation. These forms of "household effects" are reflected among respondents from Gary and surrounding areas. Although they do little to address systemic problems that perpetuate urban poverty, such household conditions can make the daily round somewhat more feasible.

As was the case for many respondents in this study, one's income may actually lie below the official poverty threshold and thus qualify one as impoverished. Yet, if one is able to engage in activities or possess beliefs not generally associated with "the poor," one may not *consider* oneself impoverished and may continue to embrace notions of hard work and optimism and attempt to behave accordingly. Neighborhood-concentrated poverty can thus be considered a powerful, static force that often overshadows the dynamic nature of individual-level experiences.

Reconsidering "Choice" in Urban Settings

Most respondents in this study can be considered proactive in their attempts to feed and clothe their families; their efforts should, in no way, convince readers that urban poverty has been arrested. The daily round decisions made by Gary residents are influenced by structural forces that have affected the number and quality of basic service providers. Many residents appear to have resolved to work within these constraints rather than attempt to change them. Hannerz (1969) and later Wilson (1996) describe the process of *situational adaptivity* as a mechanism of cultural transmission through which persons directly or tacitly embrace certain behavior based on their daily experiences. Thus social context becomes a significant force in engendering certain types of behavioral norms and expectations, when residents are continually exposed to or involved in a specific milieu.

   This concept can be applied to the experiences of segments of the population in Gary who have come to accept the current daily round choices in and around the city. Thus traveling to suburban stores for groceries, clothes, or other household items has become normative. Such persons may be less likely to question the process that has resulted in dramatic downtown vacancies and limited options in other local shopping centers. Additionally, campaigns to encourage residents to shop in the city are less effective. Based on continued exposure to current conditions, some residents have resigned to their present options and attempt to complete their daily round as expeditiously as possible within existing limitations. Others have decided to compromise by shopping in Gary when possible and minimizing suburban visits. Both groups still incur costs based on these choices, for with every shopping trip outside the city, dollars that could help fortify Gary's economy are used to strengthen the economic base of neighboring cities and towns. For younger residents, the adaptive process appears somewhat more entrenched. Such residents may have little or no frame of reference relative to the city's economic history or the direct and indirect implications of their shopping choices. For them, Merrillville shopping centers are considered quasi-extensions of Gary and places to frequent for shopping diversions and alternatives. Increased shopping options in the city are not necessarily implausible, but rather unnecessary.

   The choice to relocate to suburban neighborhoods, particularly for working- and middle-class Gary residents, results in the exodus of a critical mass of families needed for substantial economic growth. While some of the costs to the city have been presented throughout this book, family members expect to have increased opportunities for employment, better-funded neighborhoods and schools, and less crime. Possible trade-offs include separation from extended family historically known to provide instrumental and expressive support and intolerance by White neighbors. Whether decisions are primarily related to daily round shopping or reflect more dramatic choices to out-migrate, residents in Gary and cities like it must weigh the benefits and drawbacks of these decisions based on immediate and long-term family needs and perceptions of the economic as well as noneconomic benefits of each alternative. The consequences can be far-reaching in that decisions to improve life chances of family members, especially children, may result in choices that indirectly stymie urban improvement.

   The influence of exposure to poor and near-poor conditions on attitudes and behavior was most apparent for respondents with more middle-class dictates. Because the majority of respondents had been socialized in working- or middle-class homes, each possesses a specific set of markers that they attribute to the "middle class" or more broadly, to the nonpoor. Based on the assumption that no one wishes to be poor, the experiences in Gary, Indiana, depicted in this analysis suggest that negotiating impoverished conditions often reflects immediacy rather than complacency. And while most of their attitudes are indicative of more middle-class beliefs, their behavioral models are affected by household economics and, for many Gary residents, neighborhood context. It would be reductionist to suggest leveled aspirations, because most respondents appear to be optimistic, especially about their children's futures and their role in the process. Rather, I would suggest that, for some, more middle-class behavior has been *compromised* due to economic constraints. In these instances, they are attempting to regain past economic stability or attain self-determined perceptions of a middle-class lifestyle.

"Racial Projects" and Urban Economics

Given Gary's history, current predominately African American populace, and dependence on predominately White suburbia for many daily round activities, it is difficult to ignore the implications of race. Whether one wishes to support Catlin's (1993) assessment that current economic conditions in the city were driven by race-based politics and discrimination or point to other factors, various White, Hispanic, and African American respondents, Gary and non-Gary residents alike, suggest that race influences their daily round and related tangible and intangible costs. Older respondents from Gary have vivid recollections of race-based infighting among leaders over political, economic, and social control that parallel Logan and Molotch's (1987) assessment of results, when the exchange value of urban spaces is controlled by predominately White economic and political leaders:

> These conditions, resulting from the larger pattern of historical relations in production and rent collection, can then be mistaken by outsiders to mean that there is nothing worth preserving in the ghetto, making almost all black people's homelands appropriate candidates for any reuse that will serve the growth needs of the metropolis. Blaming the victims helps justify destroying their community. (p. 134)

Ignoring the implications of racism and discrimination diminishes the experiences of segments of Gary's population and makes it difficult to address issues required to build the necessary alliances needed to foster substantial urban improvements.

In *Racial Formation in the United States from the 1960s to the 1990s*, Michael Omi and Howard Winant (1994) present a theory of racial formation that can be applied to the racial dynamics that have and continue to affect Gary. According to the authors, the United States' economic, social, and particularly the political realms have been shaped by race. Change in the racial order occurs when minority groups assert agency and confront oppressive majority groups (a process referred to as a racial project). But racial domination is often exemplified and maintained by predominately White groups in power via their own racial projects. To this end, White government, economic, and political leaders must diffuse potential conflict, usually by offering minority groups moderate, often symbolic gestures of redress. Thus race is used to construct and reconstruct a variety of societal arenas.

The history of Gary suggests that race has been used to fuel political interests, create divisiveness, and undermine the economic stability of the city. Using Omi and Winant's (1994) terminology, the political polarization between Gary and suburban and state leaders that has resulted in the subsequent and systematic out-migration of critical business from Gary can be considered a racial project. The attempt by African Americans, to gain power and rearticulate their disenfranchised position, culminating with the election of Richard Hatcher as the first African American mayor, resulted in conflict with the largely White established political and economic coalitions in and around the city. Whites eventually acquiesced politically, but also responded by withdrawing major economic support from the city and subsequently creating suburban establishments that many Gary residents would be forced to frequent in order to complete the daily round in a manner to which they had been accustomed in the past.

Key African Americans in power appeared to mistrust many of their White political counterparts and had difficulty compromising as well. Political and economic conflict diverted attention from predicting and preparing the city for de-industrialization. Without replacement enterprises for an economic base intricately connected to manufacturing, in general, and steel mills, in particular, Gary was economically ill prepared and vulnerable. Ironically, the perceived political gains were eclipsed by ever-increasing economic dependency of the city on the suburban hinterland. Because of the essential nature of certain daily round activities, it appears some suburban cities and towns near Gary were not as pressed to develop replacement businesses to compensate for economic changes due to industrialization—providing goods and services to Gary residents has become their important secondary economic enterprise. However, the urban and suburban spaces in and around Gary are inextricably connected, whether residents wish to acknowledge it or not. My findings are clear—many Gary residents need suburban venues to complete the daily round. Suburban areas around the city are also economically dependent on Gary residents, who frequent grocery and department stores in their neighborhoods. To this end, Gary residents potentially hold more power than they may know.

Policy Suggestions and Public Response to Affect the Daily Round: Opportunities and Obstacles in Gary, Indiana

Government intervention and support in urban improvement projects is a common suggestion by urban researchers and community leaders who coordinate such efforts. Strategic alliances between the private sector, local grassroots organizations, and local and national government agencies are central in the urban renewal scenarios outlined by Grogan and Proscio (2000).[12] Although their depictions, at times, romanticize an obviously arduous and time-consuming process, the authors explain the need for active involvement by urban residents in revitalization efforts, the importance of incremental economic improvements, and the intangible benefits of improved quality of life for residents.

They contend that urban areas have untapped human resources that can be harnessed to help reduce poverty and make urban spaces more livable and appealing to potential businesses and potential residents. These points are germane to Gary's context, given that improved infrastructure, particularly in the downtown area, would be important to motivate in-migration by retailers and other businesses. In addition, visible signs of renewal, combined with increased policing could renew interest by middle- and working-class potential residents, especially previous residents of the city who now live in the suburbs or in nearby cities and towns, such as East Chicago and Indianapolis. Furthermore, I believe previous residents may represent the most viable candidates to which the city could be marketed, considering they: 1) have a history in Gary, 2) are more likely to have family members who still reside in Gary, 3) may have positive childhood memories about Gary, and 4) may be less likely to hold stereotypical views about the city, as compared to suburban residents. Although some research emphasizes the importance of attracting middle-class suburbanites to cities such as Gary, untapped possibilities may be found among the working-class and previous residents. Persons with an existing affinity for the city may be less likely to consider relocating to Gary a "hard-sell" for which they must receive greater "rewards" for their decision to do so. Additionally, it seems somehow disingenuous to focus concerted attention and resources to attract those persons who have out-migrated based on stereotypically driven perceptions, concerns about increased minority presence, and other questionable reasons (similar to past failed attempts to minimize White flight from integrating neighborhoods by carefully restricting the number of minority families that move in). More prudent strategies to attract residents and businesses would involve focus on overall economic improvement and marketing the city to persons who understand the potential benefits of urban living.

In *Building Communities from the Inside Out*, Kretzmann and McKnight (1993)[13] provide a manual for urban renewal that compliments academic theory, research, and policy initiatives. The authors' "capacity-focused" model also builds on the premise that urban communities contain untapped economic and noneconomic resources that, when combined with private sector support, can be used for community enrichment. They contend:

> Historic evidence indicates that significant community development takes place only when local community people are committed to investing themselves and their resources in the effort. It is increasingly futile to wait for significant help to arrive from outside the community . . . effective community development efforts . . . are based upon an understanding, or map, of the community's assets, capacities and abilities. For it is clear that even the poorest neighborhood is a place where individuals and organizations represent resources upon which to rebuild. The key to neighborhood regeneration, then, is to locate all the available local assets, to begin connecting them with one another in ways that multiply their power and effectiveness, and to begin harnessing those local institutions that are not yet available for local development purposes. (pp. 5–6)

Applying Kretzmann and McKnight's (1993) approach specifically to Gary would mean establishing relationships (and enhancing existing ones) between local businesses and community colleges, citizen's associations (such as churches), cultural groups (such as local fraternities and sororities), and labeled people (residents in poor urban neighborhoods, especially urban youth) to promote interdependence and develop "a community-building path which is asset-based, internally focused and relationship driven" (p. 10).

Of particular interest for economic restructuring is the authors' discussion of locally controlled lending institutions, such as Community Development Credit Unions (CDCUs) and Community Development Loan Funds (CDLFs),[14] that generate economic resources within the community and attract capital from outside it. The former institutions can be established through institutions, such as local churches and grassroots organizations, and are typically funded by banks, foundations, religious organizations, public institutions, and individual investors interested in taking part in community development. CDCUs provide traditional banking services in addition to possible lending opportunities for persons and groups deemed credit-risks by most banks, improved quality of life in impoverished neighborhoods, and help to reclaim abandoned and unkempt spaces.

Although their grassroots planning appears, at times, overly simplistic and belies the work required to bring about and sustain significant urban renewal citywide, Kretzmann and McKnight (1993) do provide concrete "success stories" of specific urban residents and groups that have experienced self-efficacy through personal initiative and locating community resources. Here are a few examples of community-building efforts that are applicable to the economic context in Gary:

- A CDLF provided a $40,000 loan amortized over a five-year period to a cooperative grocer to expand his neighborhood business. The grocer had been unable to secure funds through traditional banking sources.

- Housing development residents worked with citywide agencies to obtain contracts to maintain their own neighborhood housing.

- A CDCU made a $750 loan to a welfare mother to purchase furniture for a daycare center that currently bills more than $60,000 annually in childcare services.

The mother was unable to secure the loan via any other financial institution.

- Alliances between a local bank, community college, and grassroots organization provide small commercial loans to graduates of a self-employment program for business start-ups.

- A local hospital established a community development corporation with 40 neighborhood groups to redevelop 700 abandoned houses.

- A pastor was able to secure a series of CDCU loans and additional financial support from the community to lease and equip a gas station.

The above scenarios illustrate the effects of public initiative on the improvement of urban spaces, improved conditions for residents, enhanced infrastructure, and local economic growth. However, as the authors note, it is important to consider the role of the broader public and private sector in alleviating urban ills. Other scholars provide policy suggestions that are applicable to improve economic conditions in Gary. Common themes focus on decreasing economic disenfranchisement and social isolation by establishing mechanisms to alter current structural constraints via economic, legal, and political changes.[15] Although not developed specifically for the Gary, Indiana, context, such initiatives, and the following possibilities, may assist the city in experiencing and maintaining marked urban improvements.

Increased Initiatives Beyond Empowerment Zone Support. Development of an Empowerment Zone is a commonly used approach to stimulate economic enterprise in impoverished urban areas. Although empowerment zone initiatives have stimulated some business in cities such as Gary, such programs should be specifically tailored to reflect the history and specific conditions in a given urban arena. For example, Gary's downtown district has been experiencing business out-migration for over 30 years; retailers that stimulate considerable traffic have been absent for over two decades. The paucity of nongovernmental businesses in the downtown area, the length of time the area has been largely abandoned, as well as the length of time many residents have developed a daily round that includes suburban shopping, translate into increased risk of failure for smaller new businesses. Given these dynamics, the Empowerment Zone program may need to subsidize small businesses to a greater degree to buffer the risk they take to relocate in downtown Gary. The marketing campaign would be concerted and consider the implications for such businesses that have more to lose if their businesses do not prosper.[16] Expanded options could include increased tax cuts for small businesses that locate in the downtown area or in other abandoned retail sites, security provisions for a specified period, free or reduced media support, and additional government-provided seed money.

Government Assisted Cooperative Childcare Centers. Findings from this study illustrate the need for additional low-cost childcare in Gary. Alliances between city organizations and residents are possible to help address this need. For example, a local grassroots organization or church could organize the process that would include cooperative efforts between the Social Services agency, local colleges, interested single mothers who receive public assistance or subsidized childcare, the Step Ahead program, Community Development Credit Unions (CDCUs), and business leaders. In order to organize a childcare center, interested women identified by Social Services would be required to complete a childcare program at a local college and business training through the Empowerment Zone program, after which they would be eligible to apply for seed money or subsidized loans via the Empowerment Zone, CDCUs, or local banks. Additional support would be provided for groups of women who wish to renovate old warehouse space or vacant buildings in order to start their business (this latter possibility could result in threefold benefits that include increased childcare options for residents, improved infrastructure, and removal of physical eyesores). Although this option alone would not rejuvenate the city's economy, it would provide employment options for residents, help parents stretch their incomes, reduce childcare costs for some residents, especially among the poor and near poor, provide additional employment and childcare options for welfare-to-work mothers, and tap into potentially unused human resources.

Tax Cuts for Extended Family Who Rear or Provide Childcare for Children. According to Hill and Shackleford (1999) and Billingsley (1992), it is common for African American extended family members to informally adopt related and, in some instances, nonrelated children. Typically informal adoptions include grandmothers or aunts who take primary care responsibilities for grandchildren or children of younger relatives who are no longer able or willing to care for them. The former authors suggest that, in most instances, these family members, especially elderly caregivers, do not legally adopt the children and are ineligible for government assistance available to legal guardians. The increased economic strain of an additional family member lowers their overall standard of living and is not offset by available government resources. The authors contend (as well as respondents in this research) that poor and near-poor grandparents are unduly affected. Similarly, although a disproportionate percentage of racial/ethnic minority women rely on family members for low-cost childcare, tax deductions or subsidies are only provided when children are cared for via formalized channels or in a childcare facility. Expanding current income tax guidelines to make provisions for extended family members who are raising the children of relatives or providing consistent childcare will help secure caregivers for the children, generate additional household income, and affect the ability of such caregivers to maximize their resources.

Bringing Technology to the Child Support Payment Process. According to respondents in this study, the replacement of food stamp vouchers by EBT machines resulted in a more efficient process and also helped minimize some of the stigma associated with receiving government assistance. Technological advancements that include direct deposit capabilities suggest that the child support payment process would be improved if it too was automated. Just as employers, the IRS, and other businesses can access employee and customer accounts, child support payments could be automatically transferred from parent accounts to accounts established and designated for their children via a specified guardian. An automated mechanism would reduce potentially lengthy mail delays (particularly when payment revisions have to be made) and provide recipients with quicker access to funds. The following final seven suggestions specific to this research in Gary, Indiana, may also be applicable to other urban centers.

Assessing Urban Renewal Efforts and Economic and Noneconomic Costs. Based on the effects of the economic and noneconomic costs examined here and the difficulty of restoring urban areas, it is important to move beyond traditional cost-benefit analyses when considering urban renewal options. For example, the new sports stadium in downtown Gary generates revenue from Gary and non-Gary residents who attend events. However, the question remains whether revenue from periodic stadium activities offsets or is comparable to the continuous revenue that leaves the city, when residents shop for clothes, food, and other household essentials in suburban areas. A similar comparison could be made relative to the costs and benefits associated with casino entertainment. As suggested by scholars such as Logan and Molotch (1987), more critical cost-benefit analyses should ultimately consider costs *for whom* and benefits *to whom* relative to use and exchange value.

Establishing Essential Retail Trade. The need for additional retail and retail-related trade in Gary, Indiana, is apparent to break the chain of dependency between Gary and suburban areas and increase the turnover of funds within the city. As long as capital continues to exit the city, Gary residents will continue to be forced to support the financial interests of places such as Merrillville without reaping the rewards those funds could potentially provide to strengthen Gary's economy. As mentioned earlier, strategic alliances between local organizations and individuals are crucial; other urban areas provide examples of creative methods to attract retail trade and related enterprise. For example, a Chicago Community Development Corporation (CDC) with aid from a city commercial district designation program, was able to purchase abandoned property from the city. Once the property had been refurbished, the CDC was able to attract a major supermarket chain to locate on the site. The shopping addition provides another grocery store option for local residents and has helped stimulate economic enterprise in the area.[17] There is no reason to believe a similar process could not take place in Gary and involve grocery as well as retail stores.

Continue to Press Upon Residents the Importance and Urgency of Buying in Gary. The community-based "Buy in Gary" (BIG) committee of the late 1980s headed by Rev. F. Brannon Jackson and civic, religious, community, and business leaders was developed to motivate residents to spend the bulk of their dollars in the city to improve the tax base and help provide jobs.[18] Several similar campaigns have been sponsored with limited success. Given the importance of turning over money in Gary, these types of campaign efforts should continue and increase to include media reminders in newsprint, announcements during local political and social gatherings, and publicity via church and community organizations to keep the campaign before residents. Part of the process would include admitting to Gary residents that support will temporarily mean limited options for certain goods and services. Committee leaders could offset these limitations by providing information about local stores that may be unknown or undermarketed. A consistent campaign would ultimately reduce shopping traffic by Gary residents at suburban stores. The end re-sult—companies that wish to recoup lost revenue will be more likely to return to the city. Local alliances may be able to negotiate with potential vendors interested in doing so.

Establish Church Partnerships. There are an estimated 300 churches on record in Gary (Hess 2002). These congregations represent poten-tial political, economic, and social alliances. Kretzmann and Mc-Knight (1993) present various examples of ministerial alliances that have been developed to champion community efforts, such as local hiring practices and retail trade: 1) a church-YWCA partnership to provide low-cost childcare to community members; 2) a church rents space to an entrepreneur to start a children's nursery school; 3) an in-terfaith coalition negotiates concessions for their neighborhood from builders; 4) a church-Habitat for Humanity alliance results in the in-creased stock of affordable housing in a community; 5) a mega church publishes a monthly newsletter of minority businesses to promote the local economy and provide entrepreneurs with less expensive mar-keting means; and 6) a church starts its own construction company and builds affordable community housing. Other economic initiatives possible through church coalitions include: establishing local credit unions,[19] opening restaurants, and making church space available for small community start-up businesses. Interdenominational relation-ships can also be enhanced by intradenominational ones. Kretzmann and McKnight (1993) note: "Although there is often a chasm that ex-ists between city and suburb and between suburb and rural areas, churches can be at the very forefront of bridging these chasms be-cause churches have ready-made partners from their own denomina-tions in each of these areas" (p. 155). In addition to these possibilities, efforts in Gary could also include greater church-casino and church-college efforts, as well as coalition efforts to obtain government grants through proposal writing and charitable choice funds.[20] Given the number and influence of many of the congregations, a citywide church coalition could generate significant political as well as economic influence.

The Need for New Evaluative Models. Increasingly, community lead-ers with experience in urban redevelopment are suggesting that in-appropriate measures are often used to gauge urban renewal. Conventional markers, such as poverty or unemployment statistics, may be incomplete in assessing early stages of urban renewal and mask improvements not yet apparent based on macro-level data. Writers such as Grogan and Proscio (2000) caution the use of "middle-class, suburban" models to evaluate urban centers under transformation. They suggest that during the initial stages of urban renewal efforts, residents may not be wealthier, but their neighborhood infrastructure and general quality of life have improved due to enhanced neighborhood organization and self-efficacy. Similarly, urban improvements in Gary should not be measured based on suburban dictates, but based on realistic, measurable outcomes that are specific to the city's history and available resources. Kretzmann and McKnight (1993) acknowledge the need for ongoing involvement if long-term economic improvements are to be realized:

> The key to building sustainable local economies is in developing a strong resource base—both human and physical—which is appropriate for that particular community. Sporadic infusions of capital, relief financing, and dependence on external sources of expertise and aid cannot, in the long run, guarantee a thriving local economy. Many neighborhoods have experienced such neglect and economic devastation that short-term financing of special projects and programs will not go very far in helping to rebuild the local economy. In some instances, the human and physical infrastructure has to be rebuilt brick by brick.(p. 288)

Importance of Leadership Accountability. In addition to evaluating renewal efforts based on measurable, context-specific criteria, the merit of city leaders should also be examined based on specific metrics that are realistic, measurable, and outcome-oriented. When selecting leaders, residents should be cautious about partisan decision making and race-based decisions. Although African American residents experienced dramatically improved conditions with the election of Richard Hatcher in 1971, several respondents suggested that African American residents in Gary were not critical enough when assessing his effectiveness during latter terms—primarily because he was (and they were) African American. In contrast, residents should be cautious about relying on *other* ascriptive traits to identify leaders. The previous racially tense history of the city is supported in the literature. Political leaders who attempt to stimulate retail growth in Gary risk alienating state leaders and suburban business elites. This represents a potentially more grave challenge in Gary than in other cities that have already identified more diverse alternatives for economic growth or have a less-strained history of race relations. But just as residents cannot afford partisan politics given current economic conditions, they should be leery of becoming vulnerable to ill-conceived plans by potential leaders for fear of being without resources. Given the need for additional goods and service providers to improve daily round activities, it would appear prudent to elect officials for whom this is a priority and who have the initiative and networks to lobby for retailers, mega stores, grocery chains, and other economic enterprise. As elections approach, residents should vote specifically based on the progress of incumbents and the potential of opponents based on their past involvement in helping to improve the city. Additionally, leadership accountability includes proactive cohort replacement efforts, when leaders become entrenched in partisan or race-driven agendas and zero sum ideology.

Establishing Alliances. In *Race Matters,* Cornel West (1993) examines ways in which race influences the lives of African Americans, especially the poor and disenfranchised in inner cities. West suggests a stronger need for committed African American leaders and alliances with grass roots movements. Prudent leaders in Gary will realize the potential challenges associated with developing public/private alliances, especially in an area with an existing economic structure that may be satisfactory to suburban and state leadership. Challenges should also be expected relative to partisan decision making, developing cross-racial alliances, class-differences, establishing trust given previous periods of exploitation of urban spaces, and the difficulty associated with maintaining stable grassroots organizations in poor and near-poor neighborhoods. It may also be the case that some African Americans will be skeptical of the sincerity of White leadership to address their best interests. Similarly, some Whites have been shown to be less likely to support largely African American leadership and tend to withdraw political and economic support.[21] However, in addition to church cooperation with local and state businesses and organizations, multiracial, multiclass alliances are needed. Other ideas pertaining to business and community college coalitions suggest possible mutually beneficial relationships between Indiana University Northwest, Purdue University-Calumet, local technical schools, and local businesses and grassroots organizations. When establishing alliances, Kretzmann and McKnight (1993) also suggest locating a policy advocacy group in the city to provide advice and access to political power.

When Public Problems Become Private Concerns

When considerations are made regarding the implications of macro-level forces on individual decisions, residents from more vulnerable areas who face household financial problems are likely to incur the greatest economic and noneconomic costs. The nexus between neighborhood and individual economic challenges is most simply reflected in neighborhood poverty rates (for example, the more poor persons who live in a given neighborhood, the more likely that neighborhood will be impoverished). Logan and Molotch (1987) suggest other implications beyond this relationship:

> The special vulnerability of poor people's neighborhoods also stems from the low standing of their residents in the larger systems of economic and political power, not only because of their poverty but also because of the relative ineffectiveness of the organizations that represent their interests. It takes very little to set destabilizing actions into motion, and the entrepreneur has little to fear from defenders of the poor. If an entrepreneur can make only a small profit by adding a wall or tearing one down, there is little standing in the way. (p. 113)

These authors suggest that politically and economically disempowered neighborhoods, often in urban areas, are more likely to incur costs as business leaders seek to profit from their vulnerability. Additionally, businesses and other service providers in places such as Gary, Indiana, transfer economic and noneconomic costs along to residents and often subsequently abandon the locals, if they are no longer deemed profitable. Current establishments such as local grocery stores often transfer costs in the form of higher prices and substandard goods and services. Less tangible costs take the form of lower quality, limited goods and services, unclean facilities, and poor or variable customer service. Small discount retailers may provide lower-priced items, but often at the expense of quality and variety. When businesses outmigrate, persons who remain in such neighborhoods incur costs associated with a reduced tax base, lost employment,[22] abandoned buildings, fewer daily round options, and the intangible benefits associated with access to enterprise and visible signs of economic activity in the area. In the battle between the interests of urban residents and business, economic, and political leaders outside the area, Logan and Molotch (1987) predict:

> The critical fact is that in the ghetto, the pursuit of exchange values is almost totally in the hands of outsiders; the daily round is worth little to anyone with an exchange interest and the resources needed to back up those interests. The people who own and control the ghetto, through their market holdings or their bureaucratic positions, live elsewhere and thus have little stake in enhancing the use values of residents. (p. 132)

Quite possibly the most disquieting noneconomic costs associated with depleted economic and business enterprise in urban locales is the implicit suggestion by those responsible for economic transitions that Gary residents should resign themselves to inadequate or substandard conditions and decisions largely made by outsiders and adapt to incurring additional costs by availing themselves of suburban businesses. In this way, decisions made regarding the use of public spaces result in a myriad of costs that are transferred to private citizens who are generally unable to bear the brunt of them. Urban residents must consider the benefits and trade-offs associated with relocating to predominately White areas, such as separation from extended family and possible strained race relations. Yet the choice to remain in many urban neighborhoods often means that decisions about many daily round activities have already been determined.

Readers familiar with economic and business trends should be cautioned about reducing the retail transitions that have occurred in Gary to routine market fluctuations and prudent business arrangements. Historical accounts as well as respondent commentary suggest a very deliberate series of macro-level decisions by public officials and leaders in private enterprise. Their decisions have resulted in narrow shopping options for many Gary residents and dependency on suburban locales to complete the daily round. My findings suggest that Gary residents have tended to respond to these macro-level changes by viewing them largely as private matters to be addressed within each household. Thus the typical response to constrained resources appears to be to develop coping mechanisms and household strategies to work within existing constraints rather than considering the limited goods and service providers to be a systemic problem in need of solutions. Clearly attempts have been and continue to be made to stimulate economic enterprise, encourage residents to shop in the city, and bring in replacement businesses as others out-migrate (the high occupancy rate at The Village attests to this). However, I believe that few residents would disagree that there is need for increased businesses in Gary, both retail and nonretail.

The tendency for many respondents to "privatize" their response to this problem and make decisions based on household needs reflects, in part, prioritizing family needs before other issues that may be considered problematic, but not as pressing. Just as Maslow (1954) suggests a hierarchy of needs, providing food, shelter, and clothing as cheaply and expeditiously as possible may overshadow concerns relative to taking part in collective efforts to foster retail growth or continually policing public officials regarding the needs of the city. While the latter activities are potentially more time consuming and may be met with limited or no tangible success, they are critical, if residents in urban centers such as Gary wish to effectively care for their families on a long-term basis. Furthermore, continuing to privatize such problems indirectly suggests that these issues are not influenced by the larger society, and therefore redress is not a public or private sector concern. But just as the public and private sectors and, to a lesser degree, individuals were influential in decisions that have shaped economic enterprise in Gary, efforts on the part of these groups will be required to improve current conditions and move the shopping and retail problems many residents experience out of their private households. The challenge can be met using strategic policy initiatives, public and private sector investment of human and economic resources, and through the empowerment of urban residents.

The experiences of residents in Gary, Indiana, may not be unique when compared to members of other urban centers. Certain factors that led to the city's current economic challenges are not unique. In addition, daily around activities of Gary residents often parallel those found among their suburban counterparts, both poor, near poor, and nonpoor. Furthermore, most of the respondents in and around Gary exhibit middle-class values and a child-oriented ideology. The implications of neighborhood poverty, its direct and indirect effects on household expenses, quality of life, and economic upward mobility represent distinguishing features between many Gary residents and their suburban counterparts. The differences in the economic and noneconomic costs incurred and how residents negotiate the daily round represent real-world examples of the tension between social forces and individual agency that influences the life chances of men, women, and children who live in poor urban neighborhoods.

Appendix:
Data and Methodology for
Chapter 3 and 4 Analyses, Sample
Information, and Summaries Survey

Chapter 3: Analyses of Product Lines, Prices, and Services

The data presented in chapter 3 were collected from three sources. I examined census data in Gary, Black Oak, Merrillville, and Portage, Indiana, to determine population percentages, poverty rates, and racial composition. The latter two sites were selected due to their proximity to Gary in that Gary residents shop there and because of their racial homogeneity in comparison to Gary and impoverished subsections. Black Oak was selected because it is a predominately White, somewhat self-contained district in Gary that is experiencing poverty similar to that of the entire city. I wished to compare and contrast the availability and types of grocery stores and actual prices in Gary to those found in a predominately White nearby city and town with lower poverty and a predominately White district *within* Gary with similar poverty.

Part of the preliminary analysis consisted of locating and categorizing grocery stores in Gary based on telephone directories and respondent feedback. Larger grocery stores were distinguished from corner or "Mom and Pop" stores or liquor stores that sold groceries based on number of aisles and store size. Because Gary is the center of comparison in this study, all major grocery stores in the city are included, while respondents' comments were used to identify the stores in the Merrillville and Portage areas they frequented most to include in the sample. In addition, smaller stores frequented by Gary residents to purchase staples were also included. A total of 17 stores from Gary and surrounding areas were included. After the stores were identified, a three-person project team priced items and assessed the quality and quantity of goods and services available at each location. The majority of stores were visited during the week of October 20–27, 2001. I elected to visit most of the stores during the same time period to minimize possible price differences due to sales.

During each visit, hypothetical purchases were made based on a predetermined list of 16 items such as milk, bread, eggs, chicken parts, fresh fruit, and canned goods. The list included basic foods that were purchased by families in the study. Prices for name brand and generic products were recorded to determine how much it would cost to "make groceries" at the various stores. The lowest-priced name brand and, if carried, the lowest-priced generic-brand items were identified. When possible, identical brands were priced at each store. However, this was usually not possible, because few stores carried identical product lines. However, prices reflect products of the same-sized portion or weight (i.e., the lowest prices for a name brand or generic 5-lb. bag of sugar at each store). Prices were obtained such that comparisons for a "total shopping trip" could be made. The total expenses presented in Table 3.2 for each shopping trip represent the lowest possible costs at each respective store for one week of groceries for a family of three. This family size was chosen because it reflects the average family size in the four study areas. Analysis of Variance (ANOVA) tests were used to compare between and within group differences for total grocery expenditures. Substantive comparisons were also made between expenditures and median household incomes for each city/town.

Next, I examined the general features of each establishment (i.e., number of aisles, number of cashiers, cleanliness, parking, proximity to public transportation, product lines), special amenities (i.e., ATMs, copy machines, bakery), security (cashiers behind bars or enclosed areas, surveillance cameras, armed guards), or unique store features (lottery tickets, multipurpose stores). After each trip, the project team debriefed to compare notes and discuss their findings. Based on store size, each visit to price items and evaluate the location lasted 45 minutes to 1 hour. In addition, I randomly performed additional direct observation at several of the locations (Stores 3, 5, and 15) during monthly trips to Gary from September 2001 to May 2002. Detailed definitions and direct observation criteria are provided in subsequent sections of the appendix.

Appendix of Definitions for Tables 3.1 and 3.3

Table 3.1

1. Location/Size: Where grocery store is located, G=Gary, B=Black Oak, M=Merrillville, P=Portage. Store size based on number of aisles (PI determined): S=Small (1–7 aisles), M=Medium (8–11 aisles), L=Large (12+).
2. N=None: Store did not sell that item.

3. Price Conversions: In a few instances, items were available at stores, but in different sizes. Conversions were made so prices reflected the same-sized products. For example, only 24 oz. boxes of Corn Flakes were available at Store 5 ($1.49). In order to use a price comparable to 18 oz., I calculated the price per oz. ($.062) and multiplied it by 18 oz. for a price of $1.12. As another example, apples and oranges were $.59 lb. at Store 2. The conversion was made by multiplying this price by 5 to get the price for a 5-lb. bag of apples or oranges ($2.95).

4. Feeding a Family of Three Scheme: This definition was developed from respondent suggestions on the approximate amount of food they purchased/consumed weekly. The calculation reflected 2 gallons of milk and 2 loaves of bread, 1 of the following: a package of margarine (4 sticks), a dozen large eggs, 5 lbs. of apples, 5 lbs. of oranges, 18 oz. box of corn flakes, 42 oz. container of oatmeal, 5 lb. bag of sugar, and a 5 lb. bag of flour, four cans of the following: tuna, string beans, carrots, and corn, and 10 lbs. either chicken parts or ground beef. Prices reflected the lowest price (generic or name brand) for each item. Although this scheme was subjective (i.e., some families may drink more milk than others or eat more chicken and less ground beef than others and also purchase other items), it provided a consistent scheme to compare store prices based on respondent experiences. Total prices for "available items" and "all items" were to feed a family of three.

5. Available Items: The total only included those items that were available at that specific store.

6. All Items (Proxy Prices): In order to compare total prices across all 17 stores for the entire list of items, estimates or "proxy" prices were calculated for items that were not available at certain stores (for example, Store 1 does not sell eggs or fresh fruit). The proxy price was determined for missing items by calculating an average price based on prices for that item from the remaining stores. For example, to calculate a proxy price for eggs for Store 1, an average price was determined based on the price of eggs from the remaining 16 stores ($.94). This price was substituted for the price of eggs for Store 1 to estimate costs for all items. The other proxy prices were: $3.09 (apples), $3.64 (oranges), $2.09 (oatmeal), $.71 (carrots), $.98 (chicken), and $1.60 (ground beef). While this method does have limitations, it provided a conservative method to compare each store for all the grocery products under study.

Table 3.3

1. Security—Whether store used mirrors, guards, and/or video surveillance equipment as security.

2. # Aisles—The number of aisles in each store. Either posted in each aisle or counted by the PI.

3. Service—Whether store had visible customer service workers other than cashiers (Y=yes) or not (N=no).

4. C. S. Locale—Whether the customer service department was enclosed in glass or bullet-proof encasing (Closed) or not (Open).
5. Clean—Whether store had visible dust on products, paper, water, or produce blood in aisles, or odor (Y=yes, store was clean).
6. Cluttered—Whether store had boxes in aisles and/or on shelves (not assessed during nightly product shelving) (Y=yes).
7. Distance—Approximately how far, in minutes, the store was from downtown Gary.
8. Parking—Whether the store had sufficient parking for 5 + automobiles (Y=yes).
9. Bank—Whether the store had a bank on the premises (Y=yes).
10. ATM—Whether the store had an ATM machine on the premises (Y=yes).
11. EBT—Whether the store accepted Electronic Benefit Transfer cards (EBT) (Y=yes).
12. WIC (Women, Infants & Children)—Whether the store accepted WIC (Y=yes).
13. Reputation—Whether respondents noted any special products, amenities, features for the store (listed).
14. Generic—Whether the store had a generic product line: distinguished from merely offering a few generic items (Y=yes).
15. Fresh Fruit—Whether the store sold fresh fruit (Y=yes).
16. Fresh Produce—Whether the store sold fresh produce (Y=yes): * if produce was old, brown, or smelled spoiled.
17. Amenities—Special features noted by PI.
18. Other Notes—Additional observations by PI.

Chapter 4: Analyses of Retail and Related Options

The data presented in this chapter were based on data from 25 White, Hispanic, and African American respondents. Twelve respondents lived in Gary and the remaining lived in surrounding areas such as Merrillville, Portage, Valparaiso, and East Chicago, Indiana. I also included direct observations and print media. Respondents were asked to identify the stores they frequented to shop for clothes and household items, shopping strategies they used, and their experiences while shopping. This analysis focused on the primary purchasing sites identified by respondents. They were: The Village Shopping Center, Westfield Shoppingtown (i.e., Southlake Mall) in Merrillville, and other retailers in close proximity to the mall. In addition to being locations most frequented by respondents, these retailers were the most readily available stores in and around Gary. The objective of this analysis was to identify frequented establishments in Gary and suburban areas, chronicle changes in access and availability of such business in the city, compare and contrast the availability and types of stores frequented to clothe respondents' families, and present the shopping experiences of Gary residents and their counterparts in nearby locales.

ANOVA tests were used to compare between and within group differences for stores by race/ethnicity and place of residence. In order to obtain current data, direct observations of sites in Gary (example, downtown and The Village Shopping Center) and Merrillville (Westfield Shoppingtown) were made during the months of January–March 2003. In addition, both locale representatives provided detailed documentation about their facilities, and the Village facility coordinator provided extensive historical articles on that site. Retail and other historical business transitions via newsprint were also collected from January 2002 to March 2003.

Analysis of Experiences Based on In-Depth Interviews

These data were augmented by results from a series of in-depth interviews with residents from the study areas. The sample consisted of 25 women and men, 18 years old or older, who either had at least one dependent child, received SSI, or unemployment compensation. Eleven of the 12 Gary residents were African American and the majority of all respondents had at least one dependent child. Given their disproportionate representation among the poor and in Gary, the sample was skewed toward women with dependent children. There were 16 African Americans, 5 Whites, and 4 Hispanics in the sample. One African American respondent was a grandmother who had informally adopted her grandchildren. Although single and married persons were interviewed, the primarily urban locale resulted in disproportionate representation by single African American mothers. The average respondent was 34 years old, single, had a high school education, and two children. Most children were under the age of 13 years old, and most women supported a child under the age of 5 years old. Regardless of race/ethnicity and place of residence (example, Gary, Portage, Merrillville, East Chicago), most lived at or below poverty or were working class (mean family income of $21,607.58); most had access to a running automobile. Employed persons tended to work in blue collar or lower-level white collar positions; 8 respondents were unemployed. A large number of the single, divorced, or estranged mothers received some sort of public assistance [i.e., EBT (Electronic Benefit Transfer) and/or WIC (Women, Infants & Children is a subsidy program that provides vouchers for the purchase of dairy products and other related items for low-income women with small children)]. Although the sample was not random, it can be considered representative of residents who live in the study areas, frequent the stores under analysis, and who can attest to the prices, quality, and goods and services available. The majority of respondents were identified with the assistance of a project team member who is employed as a case worker in Gary. Several respondents were identified through church canvases. Only one resident from Gary asked to participate in the

Table A
Summary of Sample Variables by Race/Ethnicity

Variable	Mean or Prop.	Afr. Am.	White	Hispanic
Demographics				
% Gary	50.00	73.33	20.00	0.00
% Female	87.50	93.33	80.00	75.00
%African American	62.50	—	—	—
%White	20.83	—	—	—
% Hispanic	16.67	—	—	—
% Single	45.83	46.67	20.00	75.00
Age	33.95 (9.19)	34.60 (9.52)	32.80 (5.31)	33.00 (13.44)
# Children	1.54 (1.22)	1.07 (.96)	2.60 (.55)	2.00 (1.83)
Total in HH	3.13 (1.54)	2.73 (1.49)	4.20 (.84)	3.25 (2.06)
# Employed in HH	1.08 (0.97)	1.20 (1.01)	1.20 (0.84)	0.50 (1.00)
% White Collar Job[‡]	50.00	46.67	80.00	25.00
HH Annual Income[†]	$21,607.58	$20,513.50	$28,750.00	$3,160.75
	($21,388.91)	($18,522.12)	($19,724.67)	($2,726.32)
% AFDC Recipients	29.17	26.67	20.00	50.00
% WIC Recipients	8.33	13.33	0.00	0.00
% W/O Health Insur.	20.83	26.67	20.00	0.00
Running Car in HH (% Yes)	67.67	73.33	80.00	25.00
Take Bus to Shop (% Yes)	29.17	26.67	0.00	75.00
Purchasing Profile				
Buy Generics (% Yes)	79.16	73.33	100.00	75.00
Neigh. Store: Food (% Yes)	58.33	60.00	40.00	75.00
Neigh. Store: Clothes (% Yes)	41.67	40.00	20.00	75.00
Monthly Amt: Food	$296.17	$268.67	$365.00	$313.25
	($208.50)	($225.53)	($198.12)	($177.54)
Monthly Amt: Clothes	$199.63	$253.60	$102.40	$118.75
	($229.08)	($276.01)	($59.40)	($55.43)
Monthly Amt: Housing	$408.29	$300.67	$767.80	$362.50
	($301.66)	($249.01)	($303.47)	($96.82)
Challenges, Comments, Strategies				
Family Aid (% Yes)	66.70	66.67	60.00	75.00
Nonfamily Aid (%Y)	37.50	33.33	60.00	25.00
Highest Monthly Expense:				
Housing	54.17	46.67	100.00	25.00
Food	16.67	20.00	0.00	25.00
Transportation	8.33	13.33	0.00	0.00
Problems Making Ends Meet				
(% Yes)	62.50	66.67	60.00	50.00
City Changes Needed:				
More Jobs	29.17	33.33	0.00	50.00
Lower Taxes	16.70	20.00	20.00	0.00
Housing	12.50	6.67	40.00	0.00
Childcare	4.17	0.00	20.00	0.00
N	24	15	5	4

Key: St. dev. in ( ): [‡] Jobs such as case worker and bank teller: [†] One profile excluded due to missing data.

Table B
Summary of Sample Variables by Place of Residence

Variable	Sample Mean or Proportion	Gary Resident	Non-Gary Resident
Demographics			
% Female	87.50	91.67	83.33
%African American	62.50	91.67	33.33
%White	20.83	8.33	33.33
% Hispanic	16.67	0.00	33.33
% Single	45.83	50.00	41.67
Age	33.95 (9.19)	33.50 (9.75)	34.32 (8.99)
# Children	1.54 (1.22)	1.33 (1.07)	1.75 (1.36)
Total in HH	3.13 (1.54)	3.08 (1.56)	3.17 (1.59)
# Employed in HH	1.08 (0.97)	1.17 (1.03)	1.00 (0.95)
% White Collar Job[‡]	50.00	41.67	58.33
HH Annual Income[†]	$21,607.58	$21,558.58	$21,656.58
	($21,388.91)	($19,153.88)	($24,283.42)
% AFDC Recipients	29.17	33.33	25.00
% WIC Recipients	8.33	8.33	8.33
% W/O Health Insurance	20.83	41.67	0.00
Running Car in HH (% Yes)	67.67	75.00	58.30
Take Bus to Shop (% Yes)	29.17	16.67	41.67
Purchasing Profile			
Buy Generics (% Yes)	79.16	66.67	91.67
Neigh. Store: Food (% Yes)	58.33	66.67	50.00
Neigh. Store: Clothes (% Yes)	41.67	33.33	50.00
Monthly Amount: Food	$296.17	$320.08	$272.25
	($208.50)	($256.48)	($154.49)
Monthly Amount: Clothes	$199.63	$300.75	$98.50
	($229.08)	($289.79)	($58.59)
Monthly Amount: Housing	$408.29	$293.92	$522.67
	($301.66)	($249.39)	($315.48)
Challenges, Comments, Strategies			
Family Aid (% Yes)	66.70	58.33	75.00
Nonfamily Aid (% Yes)	37.50	41.67	33.33
Highest Monthly Expense:			
Housing	54.17	41.67	66.67
Food	16.67	16.67	16.67
Transportation	8.33	16.67	0.00
Problems Making Ends Meet			
(% Yes)	62.50	58.33	66.67
City Changes Needed:			
More Jobs	29.17	41.67	16.67
Lower Taxes	16.70	25.00	8.33
Housing	12.50	8.33	16.67
Childcare	4.17	0.00	8.33
N	24	12	12

Key: St. dev. in ( ): [‡] Jobs such as case worker and bank teller: [†] One profile excluded due to missing data.

study declined. Given that the research focus was to examine spending patterns and strategies, it was important to include parents and adult caregivers in the sample. The sample selection process was not random. I provide a demographic summary of Gary residents (as well as Detroit and Flint, Michigan, as similar "rust-belt" cities, refer to note 19 in the Introduction) based on census data to illustrate the overall similarities in the profiles of the respondents and typical residents in Gary and similar urban locales.

The majority of interviews were conducted and taped between September 2001 and April 2002 based on a series of 35 open and closed-ended questions (interview schedule provided below) with several follow-up sessions later that year. Sessions lasted 1.5–2.0 hours and took place at the respondent's home or at a location determined by each respondent. To increase intercoder reliability, two interviewers were present at the majority of sessions. The qualitative data were transcribed and coded and content analysis was used to uncover themes.

Survey on Cost and Living Expenses in Urban Neighborhoods

Please answer the following questions as honestly as possible.

1. What is your age?
2. What is your race/ethnicity? African American, White, Hispanic, Asian, Other:_____
3. What is your sex? Male or female.
4. What is your occupation?
5. What is your marital status?
6. How many children do you have living with you? _____ What are their ages?
7. How many people live in your household? _____ How many are employed at least 30 hours per week? _____
8. Have you ever received public assistance (SSI, AFDC, etc.)? If so, how long ago?
9. What is the approximate yearly household income including wages, tips, and salary?

_____ Less than $2,500	_____ $25,001–30,000
_____ $2,500–5,000	_____ $30,001–35,000
_____ $5,001–7,500	_____ $35,001–40,000
_____ $7501–10,000	_____ $40,001–45,000
_____ $10,001–15,000	_____ $45,001–50,000
_____ $15,001–20,000	_____ $50,001 or more
_____ $20,001 –25,000	_____ Refused

Grocery Shopping

10. Where do you shop for most of your food?

11. How far do you travel to shop for groceries (address if possible)? Do you ever travel outside the area to shop? Yes or no.

12. How often do you shop for food? Weekly, twice a week, monthly, other:_____

13. Do you ever buy generic products? What types?

14. Do you buy name brands? What types?

15. When you shop for groceries, what items do you usually buy?

16. Describe a typical shopping trip for groceries (do you take your children)?

17. Do you ever shop at a neighborhood store? What products do you usually buy? Describe a typical shopping trip there.

18. Approximately how much money do you spend per month on food?

19. Tell me about any unusual experiences you may have had while shopping for food (perks at certain stores, inconveniences, etc.)

Clothes Shopping

20. Where do you shop for most of your clothes (self and other family members)?

21. How far do you travel to shop for clothes (address if possible)? Do you ever travel outside the area to shop? Yes or no.

22. How often do you shop for clothing? Weekly, twice a week, monthly, other:_____

23. When you shop for clothing, what items do you usually buy?

24. Describe a typical shopping trip for clothing (do you take your children)?

25. Do you ever shop at a neighborhood store? What products do you usually buy? Describe a typical shopping trip there.

26. Approximately how much money do you spend per month on clothes?

27. Tell me about any unusual experiences you may have had while shopping for clothes (perks at certain stores, inconvinces, etc.)

28. About how much money do you spend monthly on the following:

a. Housing _____

b. Car Insurance _____

c. Health insurance _____

d. Other _____

Transportation

29. Is there a running automobile in your household? Yes or no.

30. How often do you take the bus to shop? Do you live on a bus line? Yes or no.

Other Expenses

31. Do you receive assistance from family and/or friends who help with your household expenses (food, babysitting, transportation, clothing, insurance, etc.)? Explain.

32. Have you ever gotten assistance from local organizations, churches to help with household expenses (food, babysitting, transportation, clothing, insurance, etc.)? Explain.

33. In general, of all your monthly household expenses, what costs the most (food, shelter, clothing, transportation, insurance). Explain.

34. Do you have any problems/challenges making ends meet? Explain.

35. What changes in your neighborhood, town, or city would help you the most in taking care of your household expenses? Explain.

Notes

Introduction

1. I adopt definitions of structure and agency used by William Wilson in *When Work Disappears* (1996), where structural forces are defined as "the ordering of social positions (or statuses) and networks of social relationships that are based on the arrangement of mutually dependent institutions (economy, polity, family, education) of society. Race . . . is also a social structural variable." Agency, free will, or choice is broadly defined and correlated with "values, attitudes, habits, and styles" also referred to as culture (xiii–xiv).

2. This thesis is detailed in Chapter 2. Wilson (1996) provides a detailed presentation of the subject.

3. Refer to Aponte (1991), Bickford and Massey (1991), Kasarda (1989), Massey and Denton (1988, 1993), Pattillo-McCoy (1999), Quillian (1999), and Wilson (1987, 1996).

4. Bickford and Massey (1991), Massey and Denton (1988, 1993), and Quillian (1999).

5. Waldinger (1997) for details of exclusionary hiring processes in inner cities.

6. Aponte (1991) and Tienda and Stier (1996).

7. A parallel definition for the term is posited by Giddens (1984) in his structuration theory, where agency is defined as deliberate, purposed efforts of persons, thinking and acting, alone or as a group.

8. Use of the term "mainstream" reflects broadly defined notions of overarching values and behavior typically associated with the larger society. Examples include: adherence to laws, the desire to be employed, being a hard worker, use of "standard English," and delayed gratification. These socially constructed norms, values, and behavior diversely manifest in the

larger society as well as in poor and near-poor urban settings (Drake and Cayton ([1945] 1962) and Wilson (1996).

   9. Edin and Lein (1996), Newman (1999), and Stack (1974).

   10. Drake and Cayton ([1945] 1962), Hannerz (1969), and Williams (1981).

   11. Anderson (1999).

   12. Alex-Assensoh (1993, 1995) and MacLeod (1995).

   13. Patterson (1998) and Waldinger (1997).

   14. Edin and Lein (1996) and Jarrett (1994).

   15. Lewis (1996), Mead (1992), Murray (1984), and Ogbu (1978, 1991).

   16. Also refer to McLanahan and Garfinkel (1989) and Ogbu (1978, 1991) for related themes.

   17. According to Billingsley (1992), African Americans have been able to move from working class to middle class in a single generation due largely to the benefits of education.

   18. Anderson (1990, 1999), Hochschild (1995), MacLeod (1995), Massey and Denton (1993), and Wilson (1987).

   19. The following table provides a summary of 2002 census demographic data for several "rust-belt" cities that have experienced economic challenges similar to those found in Gary, Indiana. Although differences exist, (example, Flint, MI has substantially lower African American representation), the cities are quite similar in their current profiles.

Summary Table of 2002 Census Figures

	Gary	Detroit	Flint
% Female	54.2	52.9	53.0
% African American	84.0	81.6	53.3
Average HH size	2.66	2.77	2.51
% Married	34.1	31.2	35.7
% BA degrees	10.1	11.0	11.3
% in Labor Force	55.9	56.3	58.5
Median HH Income	$27,195	$29,526	$28,015
Per Capita Income	$14,393	$14,717	$15,733
% Families Below Poverty	22.2	21.7	22.9
% Individuals Below Poverty	25.8	26.1	26.4

Chapter One

1. The poverty threshold in 2002 for a family of three was $14,348 annually and $18,392 annually for a family of four. According to census figures, the 2002 national poverty rate was 9.6 percent (7.2 million people), which represented an increase from the 9.2 percent rate (6.8 million people) in 2001. Although the poverty rate for female householders increased during this same period (from 26.4 to 26.5 percent), the increase for married couples was relatively more dramatic (from 4.9 to 5.3 percent). In addition, about 40 percent of persons in poverty in 2002 either were employed full-time or part-time. Census data in 2002 show that, among the working-age poverty population, approximately 11.2 percent held full-time year-round jobs (Erickson 2003).

2. Wilson (1987) contends that the official poverty threshold severely underestimates the number of poor people in the United States. In addition, he suggests that most poor persons earn substantially less than the threshold figure. Refer to Quillan (1999) for residential trends in urban settings. Cutler, Glaeser, and Vigdor (1999) suggest that the period from 1890 to 1940 witnessed the birth of the ghetto. African American migration patterns coupled with negative White response meant an increase from one ghetto in 1890 (in Norfolk, VA) to 55 by 1940. The authors contend that segregation peaked in 1970, has declined since then, but continues to be common, especially in inner cities.

3. According to United Auto Workers reports (2003), the recession and the September 11, 2001, attack have had continued negative effects on employment. About 1.5 million private sectors jobs were lost, and 2.6 million persons were unemployed. Earnings for manufacturing positions were flat at about $14.84 per hour (adjusted for inflation). In addition, the unemployment rates for African Americans rose from 7.5 percent in December 2000 to 10.2 percent in December 2001. Rate increases also occurred for Hispanics (5.8 to 7.9 percent), teenagers (from 13.1 to 16.2 percent), and adults ages 20–24 (6.9 to 9.6 percent) during that same period. As of January 2002, the national unemployment rate was about 5.6 percent.

4. Aponte (1991), Jargowsky (1994, 1996), Kasarda (1989), Massey and Denton (1993), Tigges, Brown, and Green (1998), Wilson (1987, 1996), and Wilson and Wacquant (1989).

5. Jarrett (1994), Newman (1999), and Wilson (1987, 1996).

6. By the later 1970s, steel production was down to 16 percent.

7. Mohl and Betten (1986).

8. For example, in 1981, a technically enhanced Chrysler auto plant in Detroit replaced production workers with 128 robots, such that 98

percent of the 3,000 welds that held together a Chrysler K Car were performed by robots (Flanagan 1999).

9. Refer to Herz (1991) for some of the economic hardship and quality of life problems faced by displaced production employees.

10. The relationships between the steel and auto industries, city enterprise, and the daily experiences of residents are depicted in Michael Moore's expose on Flint, Michigan, *Roger & Me* (1989).

11. Grogan and Proscio (2000, p. 38).

12. Refer to Anderson (1990) and Wilson (1996) regarding the tenuous relationship between African American urban residents and Korean shopkeepers.

13. Massey and Denton (1993).

14. Anderson (1999), Drake and Cayton ([1945] 1962), Hannerz (1969), Jarrett (1994), MacLeod (1995), Newman (1999), Williams (1981), and Wilson (1996).

15. James Q. Wilson (1983).

16. Anderson (1999), Barnes (2002), Newman (1999), and Wilson (1996).

17. Anderson (1999).

18. MacLeod (1995).

19. Grannovetter (1973, 1993), Tigges, Brown, and Green (1998), and Massey and Denton (1993).

20. See *The Media in Black and White* (1997) by Dennis and Pease for an examination of media rational for selecting stories and news clips and the resulting negative focus on African Americans and the poor.

21. Flanagan (1999, p. 125).

22. U.S. Bureau of Census (2000).

23. Differences in poverty rates are also correlated with income differentials. The U.S. median household income in 2000 was $42,148. Differences by race/ethnicity in 2000 were: non-Hispanic Whites ($44,226), Hispanics ($33,447), and African Americans ($30,439). Although the latter two groups experienced larger relative percentage gains, they continue to significantly lag behind their White counterparts. Household status continues to influence income earning potential. In 2000 the median income for female-headed households was $28,116. The figure was $59,346 for married couples (2000 U.S. Census). And while divorce can raise the living standard for men, women and children typically face financial hardship due to the lack of or partial child support payments (Brown 1997; Peterson 1996; Waldman 1992; Weitzman 1985, 1996). However, research suggests that, even controlling for father's income, African American women are more likely to receive child support than their White counterparts (Graham and Beller 1996).

24. Kaplan's (1996) work refutes the prevailing notion that out of wedlock births are socially accepted among the poor, especially among African Americans. Her findings show that some teenagers who become pregnant experience stigma from family members, especially from their mothers. The author describes economic and emotional strain, as well as moral indignation of mothers and suggests that the stigma of teen pregnancy varies by race, class, and gender.

25. Ortiz (1991).

26. Billingsley (1992) and Pearce (1983).

27. In Feb. 2002, President George W. Bush announced plans to set aside $300 million to provide marriage classes to encourage welfare recipients to get married. However, the plan did not provide additional childcare funding to facilitate parents working or attending school. (*The Washington Post*, April 1, 2002).

28. Research suggests that the majority of fathers provide consistent child support payments. According to census data, 16.7 percent of U.S. children were living in poverty in 2002 (an increase from 16.3 in 2001), and an estimated 12 million children reside in households with incomes at or below the poverty threshold. And although children represented only one-fourth (25.5 percent) of the total U.S. population, they were disproportionately represented among people in poverty (35.1 percent). Also refer to Eggebeen and Lichter (1991) on the plight of America's poor children.

29. For example, data from the Urban Poverty and Family Life Survey of Chicago (1987) show that 78.4 percent of the almost 500 sample women who "agree" or "strongly agree" with the statement that it is better for a woman to be alone than involved with an unemployed man are single mothers.

30. Drake and Cayton's *Black Metropolis: A Study of Negro Life in a Northern City Vol. I and II* (New York: Harper and Row, 1962) provides a detailed examination of urban Chicago living prior to and approaching de-industrialization and desegregation. Their account provides a portrait of similar "rust-belt" cities.

31. Chin (2001) and Wilson (1996).

32. Miller (1973) and Johnson and Campbell (1981).

33. High drug-related crimes and gang activity resulted in the city having the highest per capita murder rate in the nation for two years during 1993–1996.

34. Also see Greer (1979) and Hurley (1995) for details regarding the economic and social transformation of Gary, Indiana.

35. U.S. Bureau of Census (1990, 2000). Additionally, in 2000, there were an estimated 85 males for every 100 females in Gary. This represented the lowest male-female ratio of any place with a population of 100,000 or more.

36. Taken from "Gary, IN Metro Area In Depth Report 2000" compiled by the Indiana Business Research Center at Indiana University's Kelly School of Business based on U.S. Bureau of Economic Analysis (Dec. 13, 2002).

37. This practice has also been adopted in some cities. For example, Gary residents, typically older adults, pay a minimal start-up fee to local landowners and are able to farm small plots and keep the produce. Although theft occurs, such projects make use of dormant land, enable residents to have fresh vegetables, and provide experiences reminiscent of southern farm life most left behind years ago.

38. This may account for the substantial increase in poverty rates for female-headed households in Merrillville and Portage and their comparable rates with Gary. Refer to Table 2.1. Also note op-ed pieces by Keller (1984), Schreiner (1983), and Solis (1985) for challenges faced by poor rural White and African American farmers and migrant workers. Additionally, according to 2000 census data, about 70.8 percent of Indiana residents live in urban areas.

39. For example, based on 2000 census figures, urban and rural poverty rates for all residents in the New England division were 9.7 and 6.4 percent; the rate in central cities was 16.5 percent. When the Northeast region is considered, urban, rural, and central city poverty rates are 12.1, 7.6, and 20.4 percent, respectively.

40. Mohl and Betten (1986).

41. Ibid.

42. Ibid., p. 93.

43. *Prejudice, Racism, and Discrimination*, edited by Gaertner and Dovidio (1986) details the following forms of racism: old-fashioned, new, and aversive as well as the sociopsychological implications of each.

44. Aldon Morris's (1984), *The Origins of the Civil Rights Movement: Black Communities Organizing for Change,* provides a detailed account of the Civil Rights Movement and discussion regarding its effectiveness and outcomes.

Chapter Two

1. "The Multicultural Economy 2003" published by the Selig Center for Economic Growth (2003); 1998 Nielson study as referenced on Black CyberSpace Online, Inc.; Clingman (2001).

2. Catlin (1993).

3. Actual address is 3596 Village Court.

4. Ibid.

5. Catlin (1993).

6. According to 2000 census data, about 4.7 percent (also the national average) of Gary workers aged 16 and over rely on public transportation. Figures for Indiana, Indianapolis, Merrillville, and Portage are 1.0, 2.4, 2.1, and 1.3, respectively. The Clinton-Gore administration sponsored the Access to Jobs initiative that allocated $1.14 million to Gary, Indianapolis, and Muncie, Indiana, to fund transit projects to help welfare recipients and other low-income workers get to and from work.

7. According to Catlin (1993), in 1987, the 1,302 firms in Gary were about 71 percent Black and had per capita sales of $656.59 (of those cities with Black populations 80,000–130,000). These sales were higher than all other comparable cities save, Jackson, MS.

8. Research by scholars such as Brown (1997), Ortiz (1991), and Pearce (1983) illustrate the disproportionate percentages of women, in general, and women of color, in particular, as well as children who are among the growing ranks of the poor.

9. Grogan and Proscio (2000) note some of the limitations of focusing on macro-level indices to gauge urban renewal success and provide suggestions for more realistic criteria.

10. Based on the dynamics of supply and demand, potential challenges associated with service quality and availability can arise based on the lack of competition in a given locale, especially if only one health care provider exists. Statistics taken from the Lake County Economic Development Department, Milan Grozdanich, Executive Director, Dec. 28, 2002.

11. Currency exchanges are said to have replaced banks in poor inner-city areas. They are described as "banks of the poor where one can cash checks, pay bills, or buy money orders for a fee" (Wilson 1996: 5). Findings by Caskey (1994) support this observation, in that check-cashing establishments tend to be located in impoverished and minority areas. The author also suggests that, when banks remain in urban centers, they tend to have higher service fees. Many residents turn to check-cashing facilities (that also charge service fees) to meet their banking needs. One of the most historically significant changes in Gary occurred during the transition of Gary National Bank. As downtown businesses left the area for Merrillville and other suburban sites, the institution's name was changed to Gainer Bank and its main headquarters was moved to Merrillville; it eventually closed its branches in Gary. Bank One currently resides in the old Gary National Bank building on 5th and Broadway, downtown Gary. Current banks in Gary have varying checking and savings programs, and most provide a checking account option with no monthly fee or minimum balance. Although interbank costs vary, I did not note intrabank differential service fees based on locale. Statistics taken from the Lake County Economic Development Department, Milan Grozdanich, Executive Director, Dec. 28, 2002.

12. Lake County Economic Development Department, Milan Grozdanich, Executive Director, Dec. 28, 2002.

13. Census 2000 Summary File 3 (SF 3): Sample Data: Profile of Selected Economic Characteristics.

14. Gary Indiana Chamber of Commerce figures (Dec. 28, 2002).

15. "Gary, IN Metro Area in Depth Report 2000" compiled by the Indiana Business Research Center at Indiana University's Kelly School of Business based on U.S. Bureau of Economic Analysis (Dec. 13, 2002).

16. 2002 report from the Lake County Indiana Economic Development Department.

17. Census 2000 Summary File 3 (SF 3): Language, School Enrollment, and Educational Attainment.

18. Refer to John Obgu (1978), *Minority Education and Caste* and (1991), "Low Performance as an Adaptation: The Case of Blacks in Stockton, California." in M.A. Gibson and J. U. Ogbu (eds.), *Minority Status and Schooling* (pp. 249–285) for earlier posited reasons for low educational performance among African Americans.

19. Quantitative tests on the subject appear in James Ainsworth-Darnell and Douglas B. Downey (1998), "Assessing the Oppositional Culture Explanation for Racial/Ethnic Differences in School Performance," *American Sociological Review* 63: 536–553 and findings on the importance of education to get ahead in life in the appendix of William Wilson's, *When Work Disappears* (1996).

20. Census 2000 Summary File 3 (SF 3): Sample Data: Profile of Selected Housing Characteristics.

21. Refer to research on the importance of home ownership among the nonpoor (Baritz 1989; Newman 1988, 1993; Rubin 1994) as well as similar attitudes and behavior found among residents in poor urban areas (Barnes and Jaret 2003).

22. An estimated $5 million was spent to renovate the center that included increasing seating capacity and adding new restrooms, escalators, and concession stands. The city hosted the Miss USA pageant in 2000 and 2002. According to a March 2, 2001, CNN report, Gary spent $2.8 million to host the two pageants in an effort to increase business investment in the area and sales tax revenue. The Miss USA pageant owner, Donald Trump, owns Trump Casino-Hotel in Gary.

23. The mission of the Empowerment Zone is, "to develop partnerships that will enhance the economic, social, education, and environmental conditions of those who live, work or do business in the Empowerment Zone area. Its five-fold set of goals include; 1) To create employment and entre-

preneurial opportunities for Zone residents through business attraction, expansion, and retention, 2) To provide Zone residents with the job skills training, professional development and job placement services necessary to obtain sustainable employment, 3) To assist Zone residents in securing access to social services needed to move toward employment and self-sufficiency, 4) To restore the Zone neighborhoods to desirable, diverse, and vital places to live, and 5) To ensure that Zone-based improvements help to provide a quality, natural environment." Based on combined efforts between Gary, Hammond, and East Chicago Indiana, the cities were selected as one of fifteen projects in Round II Empowerment Zones, funded by the U.S. Department of Housing and Urban Development (HUD). The cities can continue to take advantage of tax credits and other abatements to attract new businesses. Additionally, residents who live within the boundaries of the Enterprise Zone receive tax cuts that are applied to their state taxes. This endeavor, under the direction of the nonprofit organization, Gary Urban Enterprise Association, as well as Manufacturing Direct loans, Business Growth Gap financing, inventory and real estate tax abatements, investments credits, gross income tax exemptions, wage tax credits, and individual wage exemptions are other measures in place to spur economic development within the city.

24. Grand Truck, N.&W., E. J. &E., C.&O., B.&O., C.S.S. & S.B., and Conrail as recorded by the Gary Indiana Chamber of Commerce (2002).

25. Refer to Luxenburg and Klein (1984) for a U.S. analysis and Orubuloye, Caldwell, and Caldwell (1993) for a study of the topic from an international perspective.

26. 2001 Trump Casino-Hotel progress report. Readers should also refer to the annual evaluation reports generated by the Center for Urban Policy and the Environment at Indiana University-Purdue University (references provided).

27. Based on yearly averages taken from June 30, 1999, through Dec. 31, 2000 (2001 Trump Casino-Hotel progress report).

28. Majestic does not publish data on the number of employees that are Gary residents.

29. The organization must pay a $3.00 admission tax per patron per cruise. $1.4 million is allocated to the Division of Mental Health to support programs for problem gamblers.

30. Based on the economic development agreement between Majestic Star and Gary, the casino remits 3 percent of adjusted gross receipts to Gary monthly. In addition, it remits a 20 percent tax to the State of Indiana and a $3.00 admission tax per guest per cruise to the state.

31. 2001 Majestic Star Casino Community Impact Report.

32. Chacko, Palmer, Gorey, and Butler (1997), Mascarenhas (1990), and Rosecrance (1986).

33. Ravitz (1988) and Rich (1990).

34. Skolnick (1979).

35. Miller and Schwartz (1998).

36. McNeilly and Burke (2001) and Stitt, Giacopassi, and Vandiver (2000).

37. Gotham (2001), Logan and Molotch (1987), Perrucci (1994), Rubin (1994), and Squires (1994).

38. In addition to employment, the greatest percentages of allocations from Majestic Star were used to: pave streets ($5 million); improve the infrastructure ($3.1 million); pavilion development ($2.3 million); Genesis Center renovations ($4.4 million); and repair, replace, or purchase police cars, fire trucks, and other city vehicles ($3.3 million).

39. Numerous failed attempts at revitalization through tourism in Flint, Michigan, are presented in Michael Moore's *Roger & Me* (1989). Given the parallels between Flint and Gary, as cities historically dependent on manufacturing industries such as steel mills, Moore's observations are somewhat foreboding.

40. Robert Catlin's (1993) *Racial Politics and Urban Planning: Gary, Indiana 1980–1989.*

41. For example, the Oct. 19, 1997, *U.S. News* reports that, of 219 U.S. cities evaluated, Gary has the worst living conditions for children. The findings were based on the Children's Environmental Index that proposes to consider indicators such as income, poverty, and crime and found that about 42 percent of Gary children live in poverty.

42. The documentary by Michael Moore, *Bowling for Columbine* (2002), examines issues of fear, urban and racial stereotypes, and gun control in the United States. According to the 1992 and 1997 Uniform Crime Reports, serious crime in Gary has fallen 16 percent since 1992.

Chapter Three

1. Quotation from Wilson (1996), p. 35.

2. Billingsley (1992), Chaisson (1998), Edin and Lein (1996), Hall and King (1982), Hondegneu-Sotelo (1995), and Stack (1974).

3. Ehrenreich (2002), Newman (1999), Wijnberg and Weinger (1998), and Wilson (1996).

4. Venkatesh (1997).

5. Auletta (1982), McLanahan and Garfinkel (1989), Mead (1992), and Murray (1984).

6. Catlin (1993), Greer (1979), and Hurley (1995).

7. Edin's (1991), "Surviving the Welfare System: How AFDC Recipients Make Ends Meet in Chicago."

8. Black Oak was selected, because it is a predominately White, somewhat self-contained, district in Gary that is experiencing poverty similar to that of the entire city. I wished to compare and contrast the availability and types of grocery stores and actual prices in Gary proper to those found in a predominately White nearby city/town with lower poverty and a predominately White locale *within* Gary with similar economic challenges.

9. This study includes all major stores in Gary and several smaller Gary stores, as well as suburban stores frequented by respondents. According to the 2002–2003 Northwest Indiana Yellow Book, there were 19 additional small grocery stores in Gary that were not included in this analysis (2 were identified as gas stations with food marts). Based on telephone queries on May 24, 2004, 10 were open, 5 were closed, and the status of 4 could not be determined (i.e., telephone line being "checked for trouble," no answer, or repeated busy signal).

10. Note the appendix for definitions of how prices were determined for unavailable items.

11. Transportation on buses in nearby East Chicago, Indiana, is free.

12. Jarrett (1996).

13. Although the majority of respondents tend to rely heavily on extended family for assistance, White respondents are more likely (60.0 percent) than African American (33.3 percent) and Hispanic (25.0 percent) respondents to seek aid from nonfamily members.

14. Catlin (1993), Squires (1994), and Wilson (1996).

15. Catlin (1993), Grogan and Proscio (2000), Logan and Molotch (1987), and Squires (1994).

16. Fefer (1993), Murphy (2002), and Uchitelle (1993).

17. Ehrenreich (2001) and Emert and Gellers (1995).

18. Grogan and Proscio (2000) and Squires (1994).

Chapter Four

1. Refer to Endnote 2 in Chapter 3 for related research on the subject. Anderson (1990) alludes to urban consumerism, when he discusses the tendency for young African American single mothers to dress their children in expensive, decorative attire. However, his discussion focuses on this practice

as a cultural marker and comparative expression for the young mothers rather than a direct examination on spending habits.

2. Some economists suggest that, in order for a community to prosper economically, money has to "turn over" there at least seven times. Without this "multiplier effect" in Gary and urban cities like it, residents help strengthen the tax base of surrounding areas and indirectly undermine their own.

3. 2000 family and individual poverty rates in the Tri-City neighborhood are 26.3 and 27.7 percent, respectively.

4. Other stores and businesses that were previously located in downtown Gary include; Sherndan (family clothier), Richman Brothers (men's apparel), Litton's Shoes, It's a Child's World (children's apparel), Goldblatt, Woolworth, Walgreen Drugstore, May Drugstore, Tittle's Grocery Store, A & P Grocery Store, and Dial Financial.

5. House of Brevardo (Afro-centric attire and artifacts), Sankofa Imports (Afro-centric artifacts), and Mini Me's (children's attire).

6. The downtown area is distinguished from the "midtown area" and consists of the region from 1st to 11th and Broadway. Fifty-third (53rd) Ave separates Gary from Merrillville.

7. According to a 1986 article in *The Times*, one-third of The Village stores are minority owned.

8. Goldblatt closed its downtown store in 1981 after filing bankruptcy and reopened in The Village Shopping Center in 1985 and remained there about 10 years before closing (Allen, David. 1985. "Goldblatt's New Gary Store to Employ 80 to 100 People." *Post Tribune* July 4. A3, and Allen, David. 1985. "Goldblatt Quietly Re-enters Gary Market." *Post Tribune* July 4. A6).

9. Banks, Judy. 1993. "Renovation Project Gives Village Center a New Face." *Post Tribune*. Sunday, Feb. 28: D14.

10. Refer to Perry, Mylinda. 1988. "Shopping Centers Rebound." *Post Tribune* and "Gary Announces Three New Store Openings." *Post Tribune*. July 8, 1986: A8 (staff reporter).

11. Strong, Audra. 1990. "Shoppers Urged to Spend in Gary." *Post Tribune*. Dec. 4: B3. Periodic newspaper appeals were made to encourage Gary residents to shop in the city. See also, Boswell, Al. 1991. "Gary Residents Need to Shop in Gary." *Gary INFO*. Dec. 12: 9.

12. A similar transition occurred at the Tri-City Shopping Center in Gary during the 1970s. And while the center has experienced a $3.2 renovation and attracted new stores, mostly discounters and small restaurants, it does not house a traditional anchor store or large retailer. Tri-City stores, such as Family Dollar and Walgreen, were identified as "Other" stores frequented by Gary respondents.

13. Twenty-one respondents noted specific amounts they spend on clothing monthly. Six respondents spent \$1–\$50, six respondents spent \$51–\$100, no one spent \$101–\$150, one respondent spent \$151–\$200, five respondents spent \$201–\$300, no one spent \$301–\$500, and three respondents spent \$501 or more monthly on clothing for themselves and their families. In addition to the average for the total group, I believe it is also important to estimate the group's spending average without the three outliers that are the two youngest respondents (discussed later in the chapter) and a larger-sized respondent who notes that she is often forced to pay higher prices for her clothing because of her size.

14. This figure is influenced by the several younger respondents from Gary who spend substantially more each month on clothes.

15. An argument can be made that Gary's economy is benefited by Gary residents who work at the mall. However, as these findings illustrate, much of their salaries are expected to be spent outside of Gary (i.e. do not turn over in the city) and hence would not greatly benefit Gary.

16. With the exception of the trendy and discount stores located in the Village Shopping Center.

17. African American and Hispanic respondents are more likely to shop at suburban locals that their White counterparts. They are also more likely to travel by public transportation to shop than are Whites.

18. The readers should note that various governmental and nonretail facilities are located in downtown Gary. They include a Courtesy Exchange checking cashing office, Nipsco (utilities), State Farm insurance, Gary Housing Authority (senior citizens building), Social Services (government aid), Gary Sanitation, a church-owned credit union (Tree of Life Church), Guaranteed Printing, Accent Beauty Salon, and L& M Travel & Tours.

Chapter Five

1. By and large, the narratives represent verbatim transcriptions. The use of several interview questions and corresponding probes have resulted in minimal false starts and seemingly more focused responses on the part of the three women. I have not corrected grammar, but attempted to provide punctuation true to the content and presentation of the statements by each respondent. In several instances, I include my probes (in brackets) to help clarify a respondent's comment. To make the interview more reader-friendly and to order her comments chronologically, several of Mary's comments were rearranged. However, I do not believe this alteration influenced the integrity of her comments.

2. Billingsley (1992).

3. Hochschild (1995) suggests that belief in the "American Dream" is common among the poor. Similarly, my research suggests strong achievement-orientation and belief in tenets of the "American Dream" among poor and near-poor urbanites (Barnes [2002]; Barnes and Jaret [2003]).

4. In Jarrett's (1994) study of poor, single-parent African American mothers, many respondents desired marriage, a home, and other more traditional markers of family life.

5. Fernandez-Kelly and Garcia (1989) and Hondegneu-Sotelo (1995).

6. Anderson (1990, 1999) and Wilson and Wacquant (1989).

7. Arvanites and Asher (1998), Billingsley (1992), Brownsberger (2000), Kleck (1985), Petersilia (1987), Sorenson, Hope, and Stemen (2003) and Winters (1995) on disparities in incarceration rates based on race and class.

8. Gallman (1991).

9. Anderson (1990, 1999), Billingsley (1992), Wilson and Wacquant (1989).

10. There is a large literature on the subject. Here I include some of the most commonly noted references. Billingsley (1992), Dilworth-Anderson (1992), Edin and Lein (1996), Fine, Schwebel, and James–Myers (1987), Hill (1997), Hogan, Hao and Parish (1990), Jarrett (1994), Jayakody, Chatters, and Taylor (1993), Stack (1974), and Staples (1999).

11. Hofferth (1984) and Marks and McLanahan (1993).

12. Benokraitis (2002), Burden (1986), and Edin and Lein (1996).

13. For the former assertion refer to Marks and McLanahan (1993) and for the latter, Parish, Hao, and Hogan (1991).

14. Hofferth (1984).

15. Hochschild (1989) and MacPhee, Fritz, and Miller-Heyl (1996).

16. Bonilla-Santiago (1992), Lopez (1999) and MacPhee, Fritz, and Miller-Heyl (1996).

17. Agbayani-Siewart (1994), Gardner, Robey, and Smith (1985), Sanchez-Korrol (1983), and Toro-Morn (2002).

18. Bonilla-Santiago (1992), Lopez (1999), and MacPhee, Fritz and Miller-Heyl (1996).

19. Sanchez-Korrol (1983).

20. Refer to Hill and Shackleford's (1999) research on the African American extended family in which they present typologies of extended families, reasons for formal and fictive adoption in African American families,

and economic challenges faced by extended family members, especially grandparents, who choose to rear children on limited incomes. Flaherty, Facteau, and Garver (1999) present qualitative findings on the centrality of grandmothers in multigenerational African American families.

21. Wilson (1996) provides a concise examination of these dynamics and challenges.

22. See Wilson's (1987, 1996) exploration of this theme.

23. Refer to the article on sexual attitudes and behavior for impoverished African American males by Benjamin Bowser (1994) in *Sexuality Across the Life Course* edited by Alice Rossi. Bowser provides a particularly thorough review of the limited literature on African American male sexuality.

24. Refer to *The Marx-Engels Reader* [1848] (1977), edited by Tucker and Billingsley (1992).

25. According to Franklin and Pillow (1999), many African American males believe in society's traditional male role as "Prince Charming" and expect to be both protectors and providers for their families. Conflict arises, especially for poor males, who have embraced this ideology, but who cannot behave accordingly due largely to structural forces that impede gainful employment. Their tensions can also manifest in the form of poor relationships with African American women and negative feelings of self-worth and self-efficacy.

26. Grogan and Proscio (2000).

27. For parallels between these families and middle-class dictates, refer to Anderson (1990, 1999), Baritz (1989), and works by Newman (1988, 1993, 1999) on the poor and middle class.

Chapter Six

1. Several respondents live in Valparaiso, so I consider it here as an additional suburban point of reference. In addition, the poverty rate of 24.4 percent in East Chicago, Indiana, is similar to Gary's. Although not the focus of this analysis, the reader should note additional demographic information about East Chicago, Indiana. According to 2000 census data the city has: an employment rate of 52.3 percent; median household and family incomes of $26,538 and $31,778, respectively; and family and individual poverty rates of 22.5 and 24.4 percent, respectively.

2. Oliver and Shapiro (1997).

3. Data show high school graduation rates for Gary, Merrillville, Portage, and Valparaiso are; 72.7, 86.5, 82.1, and 90.6 percent, respectively.

Percentage of residents with a bachelors degree or higher for Gary, Merrillville, Portage, and Valparaiso are; 10.1, 20.2, 10.1, and 34.5 percent, respectively.

4. Readers should note that East Chicago, Indiana, reflects similar economic conditions found in Gary. Note the following figures: percent households without an available vehicle or telephone service (25.1 and 8.0 percent) and percent of residents who have earned a high school diploma or bachelor's degree or higher (60.6 and 7.1 percent, respectively).

5. The current national minimum wage is $5.15 an hour ($0.25 in 1938 and increased to the current figure in 1997). Currently, the highest state-determined wage is $7.15 in Alaska. According to 2002 Economic Policy Institute results, a full-time minimum wage worker who is employed year-round earns $10,712, which is $3,417 less than the estimated $14,129 poverty threshold for a family of 3 (refer to Endnote 1 from Chapter 1 for actual census poverty thresholds). Proponents of a minimum wage increase contend that, with inflation, the 2001 minimum wage is 21 percent less than the minimum wage in 1979 and 27 percent less than at its highest point in 1968. Using the latter year as the benchmark, they contend that a wage most adjusted for inflation should be $7.08. The real value of the current minimum wage is expected to fall to $4.82 by 2004. Should it be increased to $6.65 by 2004, a full-time worker that year would make about $13,832 annually, which is about $1,300 less than the poverty level for a family of three. Persons also point to the benefits of an increase for welfare recipients, when the Oregon rate was raised to $6.50 in 1999—a larger percentage of past welfare recipients found work after the increase. In addition, 40 percent of minimum wage employees are the sole breadwinners in their families (Bernstein and Chapman 2002; Bernstein and Schmitt 1998; Thompson and Sheketoff 2001). Finally, U.S. Bureau of Labor statistics for 2000, suggest that over half of workers in more than 50 occupations are paid poverty-level wages (i.e., less than $8.47 an hour, which represents an hourly wage needed for a full-time worker to enable his/her family of four to live above the poverty level). Such jobs are concentrated in service, agricultural and sales occupations and positions that often involve providing care for children and the elderly.

6. Such respondents either received aid, such as AFDC or SSI in their families while growing up or as adults, but prior to these interviews.

7. The data show that these differences are due both to differential access to stores and, in several cases, higher spending patterns for the younger respondents from Gary.

8. Mean income for non-AFDC respondents is $27,187.82 (standard deviation of $22,649.65) and mean income of $8,055.57 ($9,120.44) for AFDC recipients. In terms of a summary profile, the seven female members of the latter group tend to be younger in age, have more children, travel fewer miles to shop for food, but a greater distance to shop for clothes, spend more

money for food *and* clothes, are more apt to use public transportation for shopping, buy generic foods, and receive family assistance, than their counterparts who do not receive AFDC.

9. Oliver and Shapiro (1997) define net worth as assets less debts. Net financial assets (NFA) exclude equity accrued in a home or vehicle from the calculation of the available household resources. Refer to pp. 58–59 in *Black Wealth / White Wealth* for further discussion on the two metrics. Their results show that married couples without and with children have about $8,334 and $1,003 in net financial assets, respectively; single heads of household and single-parent families with children have $700 and $0, respectively. When they consider "middle-class" families, White and African American married families have $11,500 and $0 NFA, White and African American two-earner couples have $8,612 and $0 NFA, White and African American two-earner couples 25–35 years old have $1,150 and $0 NFA, and White and African American white-collar couples have $8,680 and $0 NFA. The authors point to asset deprivation as the primary contributing factor in continued wealth differentials between African Americans and Whites. Given that their data show that African American families are more likely to save as their income increases compared to their White counterparts, this suggests other systemic factors serve to maintain continued wealth differences.

10. The authors show that, in 1984, for every dollar of average net financial assets owned by White middle-class households, their African American counterparts held only 20 cents.

11. The median value of owner-occupied units in East Chicago, Indiana, is $69,900.

12. 20.9 percent of houses in East Chicago have values less than $50,000.

13. Creative programs have been developed to increase the stock of low-cost urban housing. For example, "individual development accounts" require low and moderate income persons to place $50 or more monthly into a savings account designated specifically for future home ownership in targeted neighborhoods. Their savings are then matched by program sponsors on a 4:1 ratio (Emshoff, Courtenay-Quirk, Broomfield and Taylor-Greenway 2000). Other approaches include cohousing, lease-purchase homeownership, low-income housing trust funds, mutual housing associations, shared-equity financing, mortgage assistance pools, and limited-equity coops. Nationwide, there are about 224,000 limited-equity co-op units. In 1996, there were over 100 community land trusts in development or operation in the United States, accounting for over 4,000 housing units that improve the stock of low-cost housing (Harmon 1997; Kleniewski 1997; Nenno 1997; Van Vliet 1998). Sweat equity housing, such as the Atlanta-based "Habitat for Humanity" program, represents yet another approach to increase the number of low-income homes (Van

Vliet 1998). However, these types of programs are relatively few in number and do not adequately address the housing deficit or implications in terms of having funds to properly maintain a place of residence.

14. Fee, Jeff. 2002. "Helping Meet Basic Needs." *Indianapolis Star.* Sept. 29: L1.

15. Figure is calculated as 30 percent of the area median income of $57,479.

16. Additional NLIHC data show the number of hours a minimum wage employee must work weekly to afford an apartment in Indiana. They are: 55 hours (zero bedroom or efficiency), 68 hours (one bedroom), 85 hours (two bedrooms), 109 hours (three bedrooms), and 122 hours (four bedrooms). The 2002 Indiana fair-market rents are as follows: $369 for an efficiency, $455 for a one bedroom, $568 for a two bedroom, $728 for a three bedroom, and $816 for a four bedroom unit.

17. 2000 census data show 17.2 percent of East Chicago home owners spend 30 percent or more of their 1999 household income on mortgage. Median values for gross rent show that East Chicago residents pay $409 monthly and 35.1 percent of renters spend 30 percent or more of their household income on gross rent. Patterns for housing costs in East Chicago are somewhat similar to those in Gary, but do not tend to be as acute.

18. Wilson (1987).

19. Kane (2003) and Kunovich (2004) on the subject of group threat.

20. Refer to research by Bobo and Zubrinsky (1996), Charles (2000), Frey (1980), Harris (1999), and Kleinpenning and Hagendoor (1993).

21. 2000 U.S. Bureau of Census. This same source shows that there were an estimated 10 million single mothers in the United States in 2000 (the figure was 3 million in 1970). In 2000 about 26 percent of all families included a single mother (up from 12 percent in 1970). In this same year, an estimated 31 million households (3 in 10) were maintained by women with no husband present. According to Kamerman (2000), about 68 percent of married or cohabitating mothers are employed and 66 percent of their unmarried counterparts are employed.

22. Billingsley (1992), Burris (1991), Tienda, Donato, and Cordero-Guzman (1992), Pungello & Kurtz-Costes (1999), U.S. Department of Labor (1997), and U.S. House Ways and Means Committee (2000).

23. The goals of the Educare component of the Step Ahead program are to provide Indiana families with "access to affordable childcare that provides a safe, healthy environment staffed by qualified personnel who will meet each child's individual needs" (2003 Step Ahead Mission

Overview provided by the Indiana Family & Social Services Administration). Figures for 2003 show that $118,834 and $97,700 were leveraged at the state and local levels, respectively, for the Step Ahead program. In addition, some mothers receive childcare vouchers through Temporary Assistance for Needy Families (TANF). Of the 43,000 families and 90,000 children in Indiana who receive TANF, about 50 percent are White, 44 percent are African American, and 5 percent are Hispanic. Almost 60 percent of recipients are single, never married mothers. A typical TANF family consists of one parent and two children. Qualifying families must earn less than $288 monthly for a family of three. The average TANF family receives $235 monthly in cash aid.

24. Marcia Millman's (1991), *Warm Hearts and Cold Cash: The Intimate Dynamics of Family and Money.*

25. For example, White and African American households with one child have $31,000 and $3,610 in wealth, respectively (Oliver and Shapiro 1997). This tenfold difference informs our understanding of possible race-based economic and noneconomic costs.

26. Research is inconclusive in regard to appropriate metrics to determine what constitutes the "middle class." However, commonly used characteristics focus on occupation, income, education, and financial assets. In addition, other studies suggest a "middle class" ideology that transcends economic status (Bellah, Madsen, Sullivan, Swidler, and Tipton 1985; Newman 1988, 1993). Also refer to Katherine Newman's work on middle-class lifestyles and aspirations (1988, 1993). Research suggests that many middle-class families could only support their current lifestyles using their existing financial resources for about two months (Oliver and Shapiro 1997).

27. Wilson (1996).

28. Seventy-five percent of respondents lived in moderately poor neighborhoods, 20 percent lived in ghetto-poor neighborhoods, and less than 5 percent lived in low poverty neighborhoods.

29. Gans contends that the gap between the norms and aspirations among affluent people is narrower than those among the poor. Because impoverished persons tend to have fewer options and lack the economic resources to fulfill their aspirations, many retain "middle class" aspirations and values, but may develop behavioral norms that differ.

30. Refer to Billingsley (1992).

31. Refer to work by Lewis (1966), Mead (1992), Murray (1984), and Ogbu (1991, 1978) and implications of Moynihan (1967).

32. Anderson (1990, 1999) and Wilson (1996).

Conclusion

1. Ainsworth-Darnell and Downey (1998), Billingsley (1992), MacLeod (1995), Newman (1999), Pinderhughes (1997), and Waters (1999).

2. Anderson (1990), Fernandez-Kelly (1994), and Waters (1999).

3. This feature distinguishes validating experiences from assertions made by scholars such as Ogbu (1978) and parallel results, within the context of the sociology of education, found by Ainsworth-Darnell and Downey (1998).

4. Fernandez-Kelly (1994) and MacLeod (1995).

5. Newman (1999) and MacLeod (1995).

6. MacLeod (1995).

7. Anderson (1990), Glasgow (1981), Pinderhughes (1997), and Williams (1981).

8. Kasarda (1989), Massey and Denton (1993), and Wilson (1987, 1996).

9. A German term translated "to understand" and refers to the ability to thoroughly ascertain the meaning as intended by another person. According to Weber (1949), comprehensive social science requires the researcher to understand both the intentions and the specific context of a given situation. The process requires close interaction with respondents over long periods of time. Relative to urban sociology, this means lengthy periods in the field and close involvement with residents in urban spaces to understand their lived experiences.

10. Kirschenman and Neckerman (1991), Massey and Denton (1993), Oliver (1988), Patterson (1998), and Pinderhughes (1997) for details about negative conditions in poor urban areas.

11. Wilson (1996).

12. Grogan and Proscio (2000) suggest that urban improvements are initiated, when cities exhibit four characteristics: stable, proactive neighborhood grassroots organizations, private markets that stimulate employment and commerce, city deregulation, and comprehensive crime initiatives. Their renewal "blueprint" shows the importance of cross-racial, bipartisan political and economic alliances, prudent public/private investments, and innovative leadership.

13. Their manual would be an essential resource for creative urban rebuilding. It includes examples, success stories, sources and contact information for the success stories, and detailed diagrams and discussion of possible approaches for urban enrichment in an easy-to-read format. Other related sources for support and written material about economic revitalization include the National Congress for Community Economic Development

(NCCED) located at 2025 Eye St. NW, Washington, DC, 20006 (202-659-8411) and the $5.00 guide, "Working Neighborhoods: Taking Charge of Your Local Economy," developed by the Center for Neighborhood Technology, 2125 W. North Ave., Chicago, IL, 60647.

14. CDCUs must obtain their capital from the local community and must reinvest within specific community boundaries. CDLFs can attract capital from a broader base and also reinvest in many low-income areas.

15. Quite possibly the most broad-based set of suggestions most recently presented are by Wilson (1996) in his Universal Program, which features economic reform programs that target chronic unemployment and include judicious governmental involvement. He suggests needs-based policy reform that is, in essence, race-neutral and would potentially assist the poor and near poor in general. However, some of his suggestions are, in effect, indirectly race-based, because of the disproportionate percentages of racial/ethnic minorities among the poor and near poor. The program attempts to establish effective policies without alienating White constituents, who would reject initiatives believed to favor minorities. Its intent includes: to promote economic growth and sustained full employment, promote wage and price stability, establish favorable employment conditions, and unite man-power training programs with educational programs. The specific components include:

   a. better education in impoverished areas (includes more experienced teachers and addresses unequal allocation of funds for education),
   b. national performance standards in schools,
   c. nationwide preschool, child-support, and parental leave programs,
   d. shorter school-to-work transitions,
   e. city-suburban integration and cooperation,
   f. expansion of earned income tax credit,
   g. universal health care,
   h. privately subsidized car- and van-pools to transport inner city residents to jobs in suburbs, and
   i. government as the employer of last resort (possibly create jobs below minimum wage).

Wilson acknowledges that his solutions will not address the effects of long-term wage inequalities, but they would combat chronic joblessness that, in turn, would result in economic as well as intangible benefits. Similarly, Kasarda (1989) suggests increasing opportunities for urban residents to acquire better education to be competitive in new job markets, providing transportation to suburban jobs, increasing the stock of low-cost housing, and engendering self-help among the poor. Squires (1994) suggests co-ownership initiatives between employers and employees in urban settings to retain jobs and maintain critical industrial enterprise.

16. Research suggests that larger businesses often have additional buffers to minimize the risk, should their businesses fail. In some instances, the respective city helps bear the costs (Logan and Molotch 1987; Squires 1994).

17. For additional information of this specific example, contact Lawrence Avenue Development Corporation (Ladcor), Joel Bookman, 4745 N. Kedzie Ave., Chicago, IL 60625 (312-478-0202).

18. "The Village Celebrates Year of Expansion in 1986." *Post Tribune* 1986: 1, 4.

19. An example of the viability of this option is illustrated by the Tree of Life Church, which currently operates a credit union in downtown Gary, Indiana.

20. Detractors may consider church-casino alliances to be potentially counterproductive to the religious stance of the former institutions. Others may be skeptical of charitable choice options due to the perceived conservative bent of the current national administration and the belief that such support may infringe upon the religious independence of congregations. Research by Chaves (1999) suggests some churches, particularly African American congregations, are increasingly open to charitable choice support.

21. Catlin (1993).

22. Ehrenreich (2001) suggests that the working poor must also contend with redundant, demeaning jobs with insufficient pay, in addition to rules and regulations that violate their civil rights and rob them of their self-respect.

References

Agbayani-Siewart, Pauline. 1994. "Filipino American Culture and Family: Guidelines for Practitioners. Families in Society." *The Journal of Contemporary Human Services* 79(5): 429–38.

Ainsworth-Darnell, James W., and Douglas B. Downey. 1998. "Assessing the Oppositional Culture Explanation for Racial/Ethnic Differences in School Performance." *American Sociological Review* 63: 536–553.

Alex-Assesoh, Y. M. 1993. "Assessing the Effects of Family and Neighborhood Contexts on Political Orientations and Behavior." Ph.D. Diss., Ohio State University.

——— 1995."Myths About Race and the Underclass: Concentrated Poverty and 'Underclass' Behaviors." *Urban Affairs Review* 31(1): 3–19.

Allen, David. 1985. "Goldblatt Quiety Re-enters Gary Market." *Gary Post Tribune* July 4: A6.

———. 1985. "Goldblatt's New Gary Store to Employ 80 to 100 People." *Gary Post-Tribune*, July 4: A3.

Anderson, Elijah.1990. *Streetwise: Race, Class, and Change in an Urban Community*. Chicago: The University of Chicago Press.

———. 1999. "Code of the Streets." In Charles A. Gallagher (ed.), *Rethinking the Color Line: Readings in Race and Ethnicity*. New York: McGraw-Hill. 347–357.

Aponte, Robert. 1991. "Urban Hispanic Poverty: Disaggregations and Explanations." *Social Problems* 38(4): 516–528.

Arvanites, T. M., and M. A. Asher. 1998. "State and Country Incarceration Rates: The Direct and Indirect Effects of Race and Inequality." *American Journal of Economics and Sociology* 57(2): 207–221.

Auletta, Ken. 1982. *The Underclass*. New York: Random House.

Banks, Judy. 1993. "Renovation Project Gives Village Center a New Face." *Gary Post Tribune* (Sunday) Feb. 28: D14.

Baritz, Loren. 1989. *The Good Life*. New York: Alfred Knopf.

Barnes, Sandra. 2002. "Achievement or Ascription Ideology? An Analysis of Attitudes about Future Success for Residents in Poor Urban Neighborhoods." *Sociological Focus* 35(2): 207–225.

Barnes, Sandra, and Charles Jaret. 2003."The 'American Dream' in Poor Urban Neighborhoods: An Analysis of Home Ownership Attitudes and Behavior and Saving." *Sociological Focus* 36(3): 219–239.

Bellah, Robert, Richard Madsen, William Sullivan, Ann Swidler, and Steven Tipton. 1985. *Habits of the Heart.* New York: Harper and Row.

Benokraitis, Nijole (ed.). 2002. *Contemporary Ethnic Families in the US.* Upper Saddle River, NJ: Prentice Hall.

Berner, Robert, and Stephanie Anderson Forest. 2002. "WAL-MART is Eating Everybody's Lunch." *Business Week* Issue 3778 (April 15): 43–46.

Bernstein, Jared, and Jeff Chapman. 2002. "Time to Repair the Wage: Floor-Raising the Minimum wage to $6.65 Will Prevent Further Erosion of its Value." *Economic Policy Institute* (May 22).

Bernstein, Jared, and John Schmitt. 1998. "Making Work Pay—The Impact of the 1996–97 Minimum Wage Increase." *Economic Policy Institute* (March 19).

Bickford, A., and D. Massey. 1991. "Segregation in the 2nd Ghetto—Racial and Ethnic Segregation in American Public-Housing." *Social Forces* 69(4): 1011–1036.

Billingsley, Andrew. 1992. *Climbing Jacob's Ladder: The Enduring Legacy of African-American Families.* New York: A Touchstone Book.

Black CyberSpace Online, Inc. 2004. "African American Marketplace." Retrieved May 10, 2004 (http://www.blackcyberspace.com).

Blumer, Herbert. 1958. "Race Prejudice as a Sense of Group Position." *Pacific Sociological Review* 1:3–7.

Bobo, Lawrence, and Camille Zubrinsky. 1996. "Attitudes Toward Residential Integration: Perceived Status Differences, Mere In-Group Preference, or Racial Prejudice." *Social Forces* 74(3): 883–909.

Bonilla-Santiago, G. 1992. *Breaking Ground and Barriers: Hispanic Women Developing Effective Leadership.* San Diego, CA: Marin Publications.

Boswell, Al. 1991. "Gary Residents Need to Shop in Gary." *Gary INFO.* Dec. 12: 9.

Bowser, Benjamin. 1994. "African-American Male Sexuality Through the Early Life Course." In Alice S. Rossi, (ed.), *Sexuality Across the Life Course.* Chicago: The University of Chicago Press.127–150.

Brown, Irene. 1997. "Explaining the Black-White Gap in Labor Force Participation Among Women Heading Households." *American Sociological Review* 62: 236–252.

Brownsberger, W. N. 2000. "Race Matters: Disproportionality of Incarceration for Drug Dealing in Massachusetts." *Journal of Drug Issues* 30(2): 345–374.

Burden, D. S. 1986. "Single Parents and the Work Setting: The Impact of Multiple Jobs and Homelife Responsibilities." *Family Relations* 35: 37–43.

Burris, B. H. 1991. "Employed Mothers: The Impact of Class and Marital Status on the Prioritizing of Family and Work." *Social Science Quarterly* 72:50–66.

Caskey, John. 1994. *Fringe Banking: Check-cashing Outlets, Pawnshops, and the Poor.* New York: Russell Sage Foundation.

Catlin, Robert A. 1993. *Racial Politics and Urban Planning: Gary, Indiana 1980–1989.* Lexington, Kentucky: The University Press of Kentucky.

Chacko, James, Megan Palmer, Keven Gorey, and Nadina Butler. 1997. "Social Work with Problem Gamblers: A Key Informant Survey of Service Needs." *The Social Worker* 65(3): 37–45.

Chaisson, Reba L. 1998. "The Forgotten Many: A Study of Poor Urban Whites." *Journal of Sociology and Social Welfare* 25: 42–68.

Charles, Camille Zubrinsky. 2000. "Neighborhood Racial-Composition Preferences: Evidence from a Multiethnic Metropolis." *Social Problems* 47(3): 379–407.

Chaves, Mark. 1999. "Religious Congregations and Welfare Reform: Who Will Take Advantage of 'Charitable Choice'?" *American Sociological Review* 64: 836–846.

Chin, Elizabeth. 2001. *Purchasing Power: Black Kids and American Consumer Culture.* Minneapolis: University of Minnesota Press.

Clingman, James. 2001. *Blackonomics: The Way to Psychological and Economic Freedom for African Americans.* Los Angeles, CA: Milligan Books.

Craven, Paul, and Barry Wellman. 1973. "The Network City." *Sociological Inquiry* 43: 57–88.

Cummings, Scott. 1998. *Left Behind in Rosedale: Race Relations and the Collapse of Community Institutions.* Boulder, Colo.: Westview Press.

Cutler, David M., Edward L. Glaeser, and Jacob L. Vigdor. 1999. "The Rise and Decline of the American Ghetto." *Journal of Political Economy* 107(3): 455–465.

Dennis, Everette E., and Edward C. Pease (eds.). 1997. *The Media in Black and White.* New Brunswick, NJ: Transaction Publishers.

Dilworth-Anderson, P. 1992. "Extended Kin Networks in Black Families." *Generations* 16: 29–32.

Drake, St. Clair, and Horace R. Cayton. [1945] 1962. *Black Metropolis: A Study of Negro Life in a Northern City Vol. I and II.* New York: Harper and Row.

DuBois, W. E. B. [1899] 1996. *The Philadelphia Negro.* Philadelphia: University of Pennsylvania Press.

Duneier, Mitchell. 1992. *Slim's Table: Race, Respectability, and Masculinity.* Chicago: University of Chicago Press.

Edin, Kathryn.1991. "Surviving the Welfare System: How AFDC Recipients Make Ends Meet in Chicago." *Social Problems* 38(4): 462–474.

Edin, Kathryn, and Laura Lein. 1996. "Work, Welfare, and Single Mothers' Economic Survival Strategies." *American Sociological Review* 61: 253–266.

Eggebeen, David J., and Daniel T. Lichter. 1991. "Race, Family Structure and Changing Poverty Among American Children." *American Sociological Review* 56(6): 801–817.

Ehrenreich, Barbara. 2001. *Nickel and Dimed: On (Not) Getting By in America*. New York: Henry Holt and Co.

Emert, Carol, and Stan Gellers. 1995."Virginia Town Gives WAL-MART Thumbs Down on Plan for Unit." *DNR* Sept. 22, 25(183): 3.

Emshoff, James, Cari Courtenay-Quirk, Kim Broomfield, and Martha Taylor-Greenway. 2000. "Innovative Housing Policies: Increasing Owner-Occupied Housing in Low-Income Neighborhoods." Presented at annual meeting of the Urban Affairs Association, May 5, Los Angeles, CA.

Erickson, Anne. 2003. "New Census Data Shows Increase in Poverty: Children, Minorities, Married Couples Hard Hit." *Legal Services Journal* (October): 1–2.

Fee, Jeff. 2002. "Helping Meet Basic Needs." *Indianapolis Star* Sept. 29: L1.

Fefer, Mark D. 1993. "Pepsi Challenge. A Million Jobs." *Fortune* 128(14), Nov. 29:12.

Fernandez-Kelly, M. Patricia.1994. "Towanda's Triumph: Social and Cultural Capital in the Transition to Adulthood in the Urban Ghetto." *International Journal of Urban and Regional Research* 18(1): 88–111.

Fernandez-Kelly, M. Patricia, and Anna M. Garcia. 1989. "Hispanic Women and Homework: Women in the Informal Economy of Miami and Los Angeles." In E. Boris and C. Daniels (eds). *Homemaker: Historical and Contemporary Perspectives on Paid Labor at Home*. Urbana: University of Illinois Press. 165–179.

Fine, Mark, Andrew I. Schwebel, & Linda James-Myers. 1987. "Family Stability in Black Families: Values Underlying Three Different Perspectives." *Journal of Comparative Family Studies* 18(1): 1–23.

Fischer, Mary, and Douglas Massey. 2000. "Residential Segregation and Ethnic Enterprise in U.S. Metropolitan Areas." *Social Problems* 47(3): 408–424.

Flaherty, Sr. Mary Jean, Lorna Facteau, and Patricia Garver. 1999. "Grandmother Functions in Multigenerational Families: An Exploratory Study of Black Adolescent Mothers and Their Infants." In Robert Staples, (ed.), *The Black Family: Essays and Studies*. Belmont, CA: Wadsworth Publishing. 223–231.

Flanagan, William. 1999. *Urban Sociology: Images and Structure* (3rd ed.). Boston: Allyn and Bacon.

Fossett, M. A., O. Galle, and W. Kelly. 1986. "Racial Occupational Inequality, 1940–1980—National and Regional Trends." *American Sociological Review* 51(3): 421–429.

Franklin, Clyde W., and Walter Pillow. 1999. "Single and Married: The Black Male's Acceptance of the Prince Charming Ideal." In Robert Staples, (ed.), *The Black Family: Essays and Studies*. Belmont, CA: Wadsworth Publishing. 87–93.

Frey, William H. 1980. "Black In-Migration, White Flight, and the Changing Economic Base of the Central City." *American Journal of Sociology* 85(6): 1396–1417.

Gaertner, John, and Samuel Dovidio. 1986. *Prejudice, Racism, and Discrimination*. Orlando, FL: Academic Press.

Gallman, Vanessa. 1991. "A Form of Moonlighting." In Paul A. Winters (ed.), *Crime and Criminals: Opposing Viewpoints*. San Diego, CA: Greenhaven Press. 48.

Gans, Herbert. 1968. *People and Plans: Essays on Urban Problems and Solutions*. New York: Basic Books.

———. 1994. "Positive Functions of the Undeserving Poor: Uses of the Underclass in America." *Politics and Society* 22(3): 269–283.

Gardner, R., W. Robey, and C. Smith. 1985. "Asian Americans: Growth, Change, and Diversity." *Population Bulletin* 40(4):1–43.

Gary American. "Has Europe Come to America?" Oct. 12, 1945: 4.

Gary Post-Tribune. 1978. "Words to Alter Old Store, Names New Store Head." June 3: B5.

Gary Post-Tribune. 1986. "Gary Announces Three New Store Openings." July 8: A8.

Giddens, Anthony. 1984. *The Constitution of Society: Outlining of the Theory of Structuration*. Cambridge, England: Polity.

Glasgow, Douglas G. 1981. *The Black Underclass: Poverty, Unemployment, and Entrapment of Ghetto Youth*. New York: Vintage Books.

Goldstein, Amy. 2002. "Tying Marriage Vows to Welfare Reform." *Washington Post* (April 1): A01.

Gotham, Kevin. 2001. "Redevelopment for Whom and for What Purpose? A Research Agenda for Urban Renewal in the Twenty-First Century." *Research in Urban Sociology* 6:429–452.

Graham, John, and Andrea Beller. 1996. "Child Support in Black and White: Racial Differentials in the Award and Receipt of Child Support During the 1980s." *Social Science Quarterly* 77(3): 528–542.

Granovetter, Mark. 1973. "The Strength of Weak Ties." *American Journal of Sociology* 78(6): 1360–1380.

———. 1993. "The Strength of Weak Ties: A Network Theory Revisited." *Sociology Theory*. Stony Brook: State University of New York Press.

Greer, Edward. 1979. *Black Steel: Black Politics and Corporate Power in Gary, Indiana*. New York: Monthly Review Press.

Grogan, Paul, and Tony Proscio. 2000. *Comeback Cities: A Blueprint for Urban Neighborhood Revival*. Boulder, Colo.: Westview Press.

Hall, Ethel H., and Gloria C. King. 1982. "Working with the Strengths of Black Families." *Child Welfare*, Vol. LXI: 536–544.

Hannerz, Ulf. 1969. *Soulside: Inquiries into Ghetto Culture and Community*. New York: Columbia University Press.

Harmon, John. 1997. "Communal Living Moves South." *Atlanta Journal-Constitution* March 23: D8.

Harrington, Michael. 1984. *The New American Poverty*. New York: Penguin Books.

Harris, David. 1999. "'Property Values Drop When Blacks Move in, Because . . .': Racial and Socioeconomic Determinants of Neighborhood Desirability." *American Sociological Review* 64:461–479.

Herz, Diane. 1991. "Worker Displacement Still Common in the Late 1980s." *Monthly Labor Review* (May) 115: 3–9.

Hess, David. 2002. Gary, Public Library. The Gary Room Reference (Oct. 9).

Hill, Robert. 1997. *The Strengths of African American Families: Twenty-five Years Later*. Washington, D.C.: R & B Publishers.

Hill, Robert B., and Lawrence Shackleford. 1999. "The Black Extended Family Revisited." In Robert Staples, (ed.), *The Black Family: Essays and Studies*. Belmont, CA: Wadsworth Publishing. 194–200.

Hochschild, Arlie. 1989. *The Second Shift*. New York: Viking.

Hochschild, Jennifer. 1995. *Facing up to the American Dream: Race, Class, and the Soul of the Nation*. Princeton, NJ: Princeton University Press.

Hofferth, Sandra. 1984. "Kin Networks, Race and Family Structure." *Journal of Marriage and the Family* 49: 791–806.

Hoffman, Lois Wladis. 2000. "Maternal Employment: Effects of Social Context." In Ronald D. Taylor and Margaret C. Wang (eds.), *Resilience Across Contexts: Family, Work, Culture, and Community*. Mahwah, NJ: Lawrence Erlbaum Associates Publishers.

Hogan, Dennis P., Ling-Xin Hao, and William L. Parish. 1990. "Race, Kin Networks, and Assistance to Mother-Headed Families." *Social Forces* 68(3): 797–812.

Hondegneu-Sotelo, Pierrette. 1995. "Beyond 'The Longer They Stay' (and Say They Will Stay): Women and Mexican Immigrant Settlement." *Qualitative Sociology* 18: 21–43.

Hurley, Andrew. 1995. *Environmental Inequalities: Class, Race, and Industrial Pollution in Gary, Indiana, 1945–1980*. Chapel Hill: The University of North Carolina Press.

Indiana Business Research Center. 2002. "Gary, IN Metro Area in Depth Report 2000." Gary, IN: Indiana University's Kelly School of Business (Dec. 13) (www.ibrc.indiana.edu).

Indiana Family & Social Services Administration: Office of Community Planning. 2003. "Step Ahead Overview." Indianapolis, IN. 1–8 (http://www.in.gov/fssa/children/stepahead/process.htm).

Jargowsky, Paul A. 1994. *Poverty and Place: Ghettos, Barrios, and the American City*. New York: Russell Sage Foundation.

———. 1996. "Take the Money and Run: Economic Segregation in U.S. Metropolitan Areas." *American Sociological Review* 61: 984–998.

Jarrett, Robin L. 1996. 1994. "Living Poor: Family Life Among Single Parent, African-American Women." *Social Problems* 41(1): 30–49.

———. "Welfare Stigma among Low-Income, African American Single Mothers." *Family Relations* 45(4): 368–374.

Jarrett, Robin, and Linda Burton. 1999. "Dynamic Dimensions of Family Structure in Low-Income African American Families: Emergent Themes in Qualitative Research." *Journal of Comparative Family Studies* 30(2): 177–187.

Jayakody, Rukmalie, Linda M. Chatters, Robert Joseph Taylor. 1993. "Family Support to Single and Married African American Mothers: The Provision of Financial, Emotional, and Child Care Assistance." *Journal of Marriage and the Family* 55: 261–276.

Johnson, Daniel, and Rex Campbell. 1981. *Black Migration in America: A Social Demographic History.* Durham, N.C.: Duke University Press.

Kamerman, Sheila. 2000. "Early Childhood Education and Care: An Overview of Developments in the OECD Countries." *International Journal of Educational Research* 33: 7–29.

Kane, R. J. 2003. "Social Control in the Metropolis: A Community-Level Examination of the Minority Group-Threat Hypothesis." *Justice Quarterly* 20(2): 265–295.

Kaplan, Elaine Bell. 1996. "Black Teenage Mothers and Their Mothers: The Impact of Adolescent Childbearing on Daughters' Relations With Mothers." *Social Problems* 43(4): 427–443.

Kasarda, John D. 1989. "Urban Industrial Transition and the Underclass." *The Annals of the American Academy of Political and Social Science* 501: 26–47.

Keller, Bill. 1984. "Experts Describe 'Third World' Health Conditions of Farm Workers in US." *New York Times* May 24: 15.

King, M. C. 1992. "Occupational Segregation by Race and Sex, 1940–1988." *Monthly Labor Review* April: 30–36.

Kirschenman, Joleen, and Kathryn Neckerman. 1991. "We'd Love to Hire Them, But . . .": The Meaning of Race for Employers. *Social Problems* 38(4): 433–447.

Klebanow, Diana, Franklin Jonas, and Ira Leonard. 1977. *Urban Legacy: The Story of America's Cities.* New York: Mentor Press.

Kleck, Gary. 1985. "Life Support for Ailing Hypotheses: Summarizing the Evidence on Racial Discrimination in Sentencing." *Law and Human Behavior* 9:21–32.

Kleinpenning, Gerard, and Louk Hagendoor. 1993. "Forms of Racism and the Cumulative Dimension of Ethnic Attitudes." *Social Psychology Quarterly* 56(1): 21–36.

Kleniewski, Nancy. 1997. *Cities, Change, and Conflict.* Belmont, CA: Wadsworth Publishing Company.

Kretzmann, John P., and John L. McKnight. 1993. *Building Communities from the Inside Out: A Path Toward Finding and Mobilizing A Community's Assets.* Chicago: ACTA Publications.

Kunovich, R. M. 2004. "Social Structural Position and Prejudice: An Exploration of Cross-National Differences in Regression Slopes." *Social Science Research* 33(1): 20–44.

Lemann, Nicholas. 1991. "The Origins of the Underclass." *The Atlantic Monthly* 215:31–55.

Lewis, Oscar. 1966. "The Culture of Poverty." *Scientific American* (October) 115: 19–25.

Liebow, Elliot. 1967. *Tally's Corner: A Study of Negro Streetcorner Men.* Boston: Little, Brown.

Logan, John R., and Harvey L. Molotch. 1987. *Urban Fortunes: The Political Economy of Place.* Berkeley: University of California Press.

Lopez, Rebecca A. 1999. "*Las Comadres* as a Social Support System." *Affilia* 14: 24–41.

Luxenburg, Joan, and Lloyd Klein. 1984. "CB Radio Prostitution: Technology and the Displacement of Deviance." *Journal of Offender Counseling, Services & Rehabilitation* 9(1–2): 71–87.

MacLeod, Jay.1995. *Ain't No Makin' It.* Boulder, Colo.: Westview Press.

MacPhee, D., J. Fritz, and J. Miller-Heyl. 1996. "Ethnic Variations in Personal Social Networks and Parenting." *Children Development* 67(6): 3,278–3,295.

Majestic Star Casino. 2001. *2001 Community Impact Report.* 1–13.

Marks, Nadine F., and Sara S. McLanahan. 1993. "Gender, Family Structure, and Social Support Among Parents." *Journal of Marriage and the Family* 55: 481–493.

Marx, Karl. [1848]1977. *The Marx-Engels Reader.* Robert C. Tucker (ed.). New York: Norton.

Mascarenhas, Oswald. 1990. "An Empirical Methodology for the Ethical Assessment of Marketing Phenomena Such as Casino Gambling." *Journal of the Academy of Marketing Science* 18(3): 209–220.

Maslow, Abraham. 1954. *Motivation and Personality.* New York: Harper.

Massey, Douglas, and Nancy Denton. 1988. "Suburbanization and Segregation in United States Metropolitan Areas." *American Journal of Sociology* 94(3): 592–626.

Massey, Douglas S., and Nancy A. Denton. 1993. *American Apartheid: Segregation and the Making of the Underclass.* Boston, Mass.: Harvard University Press.

Massey, Douglas, and Mary Fischer. 2000. "How Segregation Concentrates Poverty." *Ethnic & Racial Studies* 23(4): 670–691.

McLanahan, Sara, and Irwin Garfinkel. 1989. "Single Mothers, the Underclass, and Social Policy." *The Annals of the American Academy of Political and Social Science* 501:92–104.

McNeilly, Dennis, and William Burke. 2001. "Gambling as a Social Activity of Older Adults." *International Journal of Aging and Human Development* 52(1): 19–28.

Mead, Lawrence. 1992. *The New Politics of Poverty: The Nonworking Poor in America.* New York: Basic Books.

Miller, William, and Martin Schwartz. 1998. "Casino Gambling and Street Crime." *The Annals of the American Academy of Political and Social Science* 556: 124–137.

Miller, Zane. 1973. *The Urbanization of Modern America: A Brief History*. New York: Harcourt Brace Jovanovich.

Millman, Marcia. 1991. *Warm Hearts and Cold Cash: The Intimate Dynamics of Family and Money*. New York: Free Press.

Mincy, Ronald B. 1989. "Paradoxes in Black Economic Progress: Incomes, Families, and the Underclass." *Journal of Negro Education* 58(3): 255–269.

Mohl, Raymond, and Neil Betten. 1986. *Steel City: Urban and Ethnic Patterns in Gary, Indiana, 1906–1950*. New York: Holmes and Meier.

Moore, Michael. 1989. *Roger & Me*. Hollywood, CA: Warner Studios.

Morris, Aldon D. 1984. *The Origins of the Civil Rights Movement: Black Communities Organizing for Change*. New York: The Free Press.

Moynihan, Daniel Patrick. 1967. "The Negro Family: The Case for National Action." In Lee Rainwater and William L. Yancey (eds.), *The Moynihan Report and the Politics of Controversy*. Cambridge, Mass.: The M.I.T. Press.

Murphy, Cait. 2002. "Fortune 500." *Fortune* 145(8), April 15: 94–99.

Murray, Charles. 1984. *Losing Ground: American Social Policy, 1950–1980*. New York: Basic Books.

Myrdal, Gunnar. 1962. *An American Dilemma: The Negro Problem and Modern Democracy*. New York: Harper & Row Publishers.

Nenno, Mary. 1997. "Changes and Challenges in Affordable Housing and Urban Development." In Willem Van Vliet (ed.), *Affordable Housing and Urban Redevelopment in the United States*. Thousand Oaks, CA: Sage Publications. 1–21.

Newman, Katherine S. 1988. *Falling from Grace: Downward Mobility in the Age of Affluence*. Berkeley: University of California Press.

———. 1993. *Declining Fortunes: The Withering of the American Dream*. New York: BasicBooks.

———. 1999. *No Shame in My Game: The Working Poor in the Inner City*. New York: Alfred A. Knopf and The Russell Sage Foundation.

Ogbu, John U. 1978. *Minority Education and Caste*. New York: Academic Press.

———. 1991. "Low Performance as an Adaptation: The Case of Blacks in Stockton, California." in M.A. Gibson and J. U. Ogbu (eds.), *Minority Status and Schooling*. New York: Grand Publishing. 249–285.

Oliver, Melvin. 1988. "The Urban Black Community as Network: Toward a Social Network Perspective." *The Sociological Quarterly* 29(4): 623–645.

Oliver, Melvin, and Thomas Shapiro. 1997. *Black Wealth / White Wealth: A New Perspective on Racial Inequality*. New York: Routledge.

Omi, Michael, and Howard Winant. 1994. *Racial Formation in the United States: From the 1960s to the 1990s*. New York: Routledge.

Ortiz, Vilma. 1991. "Women of Color: A Demographic Overview." In Maxine Zinn and Bonnie Dill (eds.), *Women of Color in US Society*. Philadelphia: Temple University Press. 13–32.

Orubuloye, I. O., Pat Caldwell, and John C. Caldwell. 1993. "The Role of High-Risk Occupations in the Spread of AIDS: Truck Drivers and Itinerant Market Women in Nigeria." *International Family Planning Perspectives* 19(2): 43–48.

Parish, William, Lingxin Hao, and Dennis P. Hogan. 1991. "Family Support Networks, Welfare, and Work among Young Mothers." *Journal of Marriage and the Family* 53: 203–215.

Patterson, Orlando. 1997. *The Ordeal of Integration: Progress and Resentment in America's "Racial" Crisis*. Washington, D.C.: Civitas/Counterpoint.

———. 1998. "Opening Up Workplace Networks to Afro-Americans." *The Bookings Review*. Spring: 17–23.

Pattillo-McCoy, Mary. 1999. *Black Picket Fences: Privilege and Peril among the Black Middle Class*. Chicago: University of Chicago Press.

Pearce, Diana M. 1983. "The Feminization of Ghetto Poverty." *Society* (Nov.–Dec.) 72: 70–74.

Perry, Mylinda. 1988. "Shopping Centers Rebound." *Gary Post-Tribune*, May 5: B7.

Perrucci, Robert. 1994. "Embedded Corporatism: Auto Transplants, the Local State and Community Politics in the Midwest Corridor." *The Sociological Quarterly* 35(3): 487–505.

Petersilia, Joan. 1987. *The Influence of Criminal Justice Research*. Santa Monica, CA: Rand Corporation.

Peterson, Richard. 1996. "A Re-Evaluation of the Economic Consequences of Divorce." *American Sociological Review* 61(3):528–536.

Pinderhughes, Howard. 1997. *Race in the Hood: Conflict and Violence among Urban Youth*. Minneapolis: University of Minnesota Press.

Piven, Frances Fox. 1998. "Welfare and Work." *Social Justice* 25 (1): 67–81.

———. 2001. "Globalization, American Politics, and Welfare Policy." *Annals of the American Academy of Political and Social Science* 577: 26–37.

Price, Lisa. 1997. "A Tale of Two Midwestern Cities." *U.S. News* Oct. 19: 1–3.

Pungello, Elizabeth, and Beth Kurtz-Costes. 1999. "Why and How Working Women Choose Child Care: A Review with a Focus on Infancy." *Developmental Review* 19:31–96.

Quillian, Lincoln. 1999. "Migration Patterns and the Growth of High-Poverty Neighborhoods, 1970–1990." *American Journal of Sociology* 105(1): 1–37.

Ravitz, Mel. 1988. "Community Development: Salvation or Suicide?" *Social Policy* Fall: 18–21.

Rich, Wilbur. 1990. "The Politics of Casino Gambling: Detroit Style." *Urban Affairs Quarterly* 26(2): 274–298.

Roedinger, David R., 1991. *The Wages of Whiteness: Race and the Making of the American Working Class*. London: Verso.

Rosecrance, John. 1986. "Why Regular Gamblers Don't Quit: A Sociological Perspective." *Sociological Perspectives* 29(3): 357–378.

Rubin, Herbert. 1994. "There Aren't Going to Be Any Bakeries Here if There is No Money to Afford Jellyrolls: The Organic Theory of Community Based Development." *Social Problems* 41(3): 401–424.

Rubin, Lillian Breslow. 1976. *Worlds of Pain: Life in the Working-Class Family*. New York: Basic Books, Inc.

———. 1994. *Families on the Fault Line: America's Working Class Speaks About the Family, The Economy, Race, and Ethnicity*. New York: HarperCollins Publishers.

Sanchez-Korrol, V. 1983. *From Colonia to Community: The History of Puerto Ricans in New York City 1917–1948*. Westport, Conn.: Greenwood Press.

Schiller, B. 1976. *The Economics of Poverty and Discrimination*. Englewood Cliffs, N.J.: Prentice-Hall.

Schreiner, Tim. 1983. "Poverty Plagues Farmers, Study Says." *USA Today* Dec. 22: 3A.

Second Year Evaluation of Riverboat Licensee for Gary, Indiana: Trump Indiana, Inc. 1998. Center for Urban Policy and the Environment—School of Public and Environmental Affairs. Indianapolis, IN: Indiana University-Purdue University October: 1–7 (http://www. spea.iupui.edu/cupe/cupe/htm).

Selig Center for Economic Growth. 2004. "The Multicultural Economy 2003." Athens: University of Georgia.

Sherraden, Michael. 1991. *Assets and the Poor: A New American Welfare Policy*. New York: Sharpe.

Skolnick, Jerome. 1979. "The Dilemmas of Regulating Casino Gambling." *Journal of Social Issues* 35(3): 129–143.

Solis, Dianna. 1985. "From Farm to Farm, Migrant Workers Struggle to Survive." *Wall Street Journal* May 15:1, 26.

Sorensen, J., R. Hope, and D. Stemen. 2003. "Racial Disproportionality in State Prison Admissions: Can Regional Variation be Explained by Differential Arrest Rates?" *Journal of Criminal Justice* 31(1): 73–84.

Squires, Gregory D. 1994. *Capital and Communities in Black and White*. Albany: State University of New York Press.

Stack, Carol. 1974. *All Our Kin. Strategies for Survival in a Black Community*. New York: Harper and Row.

Staples, Robert. 1999. *The Black Family: Essays and Studies*. Belmont, CA: Wadsworth Publishing Co.

Stitt, B. Grant, David Giacopassi, and Margaret Vandiver. 2000. "A Minor Concern? Underage Casino Gambling and the Law." *The Social Science Journal* 37(3): 361–373.

Strong, Audra. 1990. "Shoppers Urged to Spend in Gary." *Gary Post-Tribune* Dec. 4: B3.

The Times. 1986. "Gary Announces Three New Store Openings." July 8: A8.

Third Year Evaluation of Riverboat Licensee for Gary, Indiana: Trump Indiana, Inc. 2000. Center for Urban Policy and the Environment—

School of Public and Environmental Affairs. Indianapolis, IN: Indiana University-Purdue University June: 1–7 (http://www.spea.iupui.edu/cupe/cupe/htm).

Thompson, Jeff, and Charles Sheketoff. 2001. "Getting the Raise They Deserve: The Success of Oregon's Minimum Wage and the Need for Reform." *Oregon Center for Public Policy* (March 12).

Tienda, Marta. 1989. " Puerto Ricans and the Underclass Debate." *The Annals of the American Academy of Political and Social Science* 501: 105–122.

Tienda, Marta, Katherine Donato, and Hector Cordero-Guzman. 1992. "Schooling, Color, and Labor Force Activity of Women." *Social Forces* 71: 365–395.

Tienda, Marta, and Haya Stier. 1996. "Generating Labor Market Inequality: Employment Opportunities and the Accumulation of Disadvantage." *Social Problems* 43(2):147–165.

Tigges, Leann M., Irene Brown, and Gary P. Green. 1998. "Social Isolation of the Urban Poor: Race, Class, and Neighborhood Effects on Social Resources." *The Sociological Quarterly* 39(1): 53–77.

Toro-Morn, Maura. 2002. "Puerto Rican Migrants: Juggling Family and Work Roles." In Nijole Benokraitis (ed.), *Contemporary Ethnic Families in the US*. Upper Saddle River, NJ: Prentice Hall. 232–239.

Trump Casino-Hotel. 2001. *2001 Progress Report*. 1–20.

Tucker, Robert (ed.). [1848](1977). *The Marx-Engel Reader*. New York: Norton.

Uchitelle, Louis. 1993. "'Good' Jobs in Hard Times." *New York Times*, Oct. 3: 143(49673): Section 3:1.

United Auto Workers. 2003. "Income and Poverty in 2001." Jan/Feb.

Urban Poverty and Family Life Survey. 1987. Chicago, Il: University of Chicago. William Julius Wilson [principal investigator]. Inter-university Consortium for Political and Social Research [distributor].

U.S. Bureau of the Census. 1970. *General Social and Economic Characteristics: Census of Population Part 16 Indiana Section 2*. Washington, D.C.: U.S. Government Printing Office.

———. 1980. *General Social and Economic Characteristics: Census of Population Part 16 Indiana Section 2*. Washington, D.C.: U.S. Government Printing Office.

———. 1990. *General Population and Housing Characteristics Summary Tape File 1 (STF 1)*. Washington, D.C.: U.S. Government Printing Office (http://www.census.gov).

———. 1990. *Income and Proverty Status Summary Tape File 3 (STF 3)*. Washington, D.C.: U.S. Government Printing Office (http://www.census.gov).

———. 1990. *Income and Poverty Status*. Washington, D.C.: U.S. Government Printing Office.

———. 1996. *Poverty in the United States: 1996*. Current Population Reports, P60–198.Washington, D.C.: U.S. Government Printing Office.

————. 1997. *Income and Poverty* 42(1). Washington, D.C.: U.S. Government Printing Office (http://www.census.gov).

————. 1997. *Income and Poverty 1997.* Washington, D.C.: U.S. Government Printing Office.

————. 2000. *Profile of General Demographic Characteristics, Race and Hispanic or Latino Summary File 1 (SF 1).* Washington, D.C.: U.S. Government Printing Office (http://www.census.gov).

————. 2000. *Profile of Selected Economic Characteristics: Summary File 3 (SF 3).* Washington, D.C.: U.S. Government Printing Office (http://www.census.gov).

U.S. Bureau of Labor Statistics. 1965. *Employment and Earnings,* 42(1), Washington, D.C.: U.S. Government Printing Office.

————. 1995. *Employment and Earnings* 42(1): Washington, D.C.: U.S. Government Printing Office.

————. 1997. *Employment and Earnings* 42(1): Washington, D.C.: U.S. Government Printing Office.

————. 1996. U.S. Bureau of Labor Statistics. 2000. *Employment and Earnings* 42 (1): Washington, D.C.: U.S. Government Printing Office.

U.S. Department of Labor. 1997. *Current Population Survey.* Washington, D.C.: U.S. Bureau of Labor Statistics.

U.S. House Ways and Means Committee Green Book. 2000. *Child Care.* Almanac of Policy Issues. Washington, D.C.: U.S. Government Printing Office:1–1539.

Van Vliet, Willem. 1998. *The Encyclopedia of Housing.* London: Sage Publications.

Venkatesh, Sudhir Alladi. 1994. "Getting Ahead: Social Mobility Among the Urban Poor." *Sociological Perspectives* 37(2): 157–182.

————. 1997. "The Three-Tier Model: How Helping Occurs in Urban, Poor Communities." *Social Service Review* Dec: 574–606.

Vertrees and Gengler. 1953. *Gary Post-Tribune* October 4:A7.

Waldinger, Roger. 1997. "Black/Immigrant Competition Re-Assessed: New Evidence from Los Angeles." *Sociological Perspectives* 40: 365–396.

Waldman, Steven. 1992. "Deadbeat Dads." *Newsweek* May 4: 46–52.

Waters, Mary C. 1999. "Ethnic and Racial Identities of Second-Generation Black Immigrants in New York City." In Charles A. Gallagher (ed.), *Rethinking the Color Line: Readings in Race and Ethnicity.* New York: McGraw-Hill. 421–436.

Weber, Max. 1949. *The Methodology of the Social Services* (edited and translated by Edward Shils and Henry Finch). Glencoe, IL: Free Press.

Weitzman, Lenore. 1985. *The Divorce Revolution: The Unexpected Social and Economic Consequences for Women and Children in America.* New York: Free Press.

————. 1996. "The Economic Consequences of Divorce are Still Unequal." *American Sociological Review* 61(3): 537–548.

Wellman, Barry, and Barry Leighton. 1979. "Networks, Neighborhoods, and Communities: Approaches to the Study of the Community Question." *Urban Affairs Quarterly* 14(3): 363–390.

West, Cornel. 1993. *Race Matters.* Boston: Beacon Press.

Wijnberg, Marion H., and Susan Weinger. 1998. "When Dreams Wither and Resources Fail: The Social-Support Systems of Poor Single Mothers." *Families in Society: The Journal of Contemporary Human Services* 79: 212–219.

Williams, Melvin D. 1981. *On the Street Where I Lived.* New York: Holt, Rinehart, and Winston.

Williams, Vernon. 1978. "'Buy Gary' Urged to Boost Economic Viability." *Gary Post Tribune* (Sept. 24): B1.

Wilson, James Q. 1983. *Crime and Public Policy.* San Francisco, CA: ICS Press.

Wilson, William Julius. 1980. *The Declining Significance of Race: Blacks and Changing American Institutions* (2nd edition.). Chicago: University of Chicago Press.

———. 1987. *The Truly Disadvantaged: The Inner City, the Underclass, and Public Policy.* Chicago: University of Chicago Press.

———. 1996. *When Work Disappears: The World of the New Urban Poor.* New York: Alfred A. Knopf.

———. 2000. "Rising Inequality and the Case for Coalition Politics." *Annals of the American Academy of Political and Social Sciences* 568:78–99.

Wilson, William, and L. J. D. Wacquant. 1989. "The Cost of Racial and Class Exclusion in the Inner City." *The Annals of the American Academy of Political and Social Science* 501: 8–25.

Winters, Paul A. (ed.).1995. *Crime and Criminals: Opposing Viewpoints.* San Diego, CA: Greenhaven Press.

Index

adoption, 207, 208

AFDC. *See* Aid to Families with Dependent Children (AFDC)

African Americans, 19; assets of, 173; and business out-migration, 117; business ownership by, 36; and car ownership, 167; and clothing/household items shopping, 105–6; and consumerism, 95–96; control over youth of, 16; and crime, 28; customer service for, 83, 84, 85; discrimination against, 4, 26; educational achievement by, 42; and extended family, 155–56; in Gary, 21, 22, 23, 25–26, 35, 39, 40; and grocery stores, 68, 75, 76, 77, 92; and industry, 18, 25–26; in Merrillville, 39, 40; migration to Gary by, 21, 25–26; migration to North by, 18; and political accountability, 211–12; and politics, 35, 202; in Portage, 39, 40; and poverty, 17, 18, 19, 20; and public assistance, 172; resilience of, 5; as single mothers, 179, 188; and social isolation, 194; social status of, 28; spending power of, 33–34; as threat to Whites, 25, 26, 27; and unemployment,

22; wealth of, 34; and work, 25–26; and working class conflict, 29. *See also* race

agency: in concentrated poverty neighborhoods, 12, 13; and exchange *vs.* use value, 32–33; Gans on, 187; and grocery store problems, 91; and middle class expectations, 197; of ordinary *vs.* elite, 31–32; and personal finances, 115; and poverty, 1, 4–7; and shopping patterns, 68, 111–12. *See also* choice; strategies; values

Aid to Families with Dependent Children (AFDC), 169–70, 172–73, 183

AJ Wright, 118

aspiration, leveled, 96. *See also* sociopsychological dimensions; values

assets, 173, 187. *See also* homeownership; income

banking, 41, 205–6

Berner, Robert, 93

Betten, Neil, 25–26, 28

Billingsley, Andrew, 112, 154; *Climbing Jacob's Ladder*, 5

Black Oak, 40; grocery stores in, 70, 71, 72, 77, 80–81, 92, 93; and transportation, 81, 82; Whites in, 22